BRIEF ABSTRACTS

of

Norfolk County Wills

1710-1753

BY

CHARLES FLEMING MCINTOSH, B. L.

PUBLISHED BY

THE COLONIAL DAMES OF AMERICA
IN THE STATE OF VIRGINIA

1922

Please direct all correspondence and orders to:

www.southernhistoricalpress.com
or
SOUTHERN HISTORICAL PRESS, Inc.
PO BOX 1267
375 West Broad Street
Greenville, SC   29601
southernhistoricalpress@gmail.com

Originally published: Richmond, VA 1922
ISBN #0-89308-324-0
All rights Reserved.
Printed in the United States of America

PREFACE

In the Abstract of Lower Norfolk County and Norfolk County Wills 1637-1710 (Volume I), it was stated: "It is the intention of the Abstractor to continue this work from 1710 to 1800."

The delay in the appearance of the present volume was occasioned by the early entry of Mr. McIntosh into the Air Service, United States Army, in the Great War. He served as First Lieutenant and later as Captain, First Air Park (Mobile), A. E. F., until the close of the war.

The preface to Volume I serves as a proper introduction to the present volume. It is recommended that it be read in using Volume II.

Volume I embraces the following books and years:

1637-1646 "Minute Book 1637-1646 Norfolk County" (Indexed and commonly called Book A).

1646-1651 Book B.
1651-1656 Book C.
1656-1666 Book D.
1666-1675 Book E.
1675-1686 Book 4.
1686-1695 Book 5.
1695-1703 Book 6.
1703-1706 Book 7.
1706-1708 No Spread or Original Wills.
1708-1710 Book 8.

The present volume (Volume II) embraces the following books and years:

1710-1717 Book 9.
1717-1719 Book 10.
1719-1722 Book "Orders—Appraisements—Wills."
1721-1723 Book Fragments, unlettered, unnumbered and unbound.
1721-1730 Original Wills.

1721-1725 Book F (Contains No Wills).
1725-1730 Book G (Contains No Wills).
1730-1734 Book 11.
1734-1739 Book 12.
1742-1749 Book H.
1740-1753 Book I.

The condition of the original books in the Norfolk County Clerk's Office can readily be realized by the frequent repetition of the word "torn."

Book I. is in very bad condition and it is greatly to be regretted that little attempt to restore the books has been made, and that they are not kept in a fireproof building.

The wills contained in this volume were donated to the Colonial Dames of America, in the State of Virginia, by Mr. McIntosh.

KATE CABELL COX,
President Colonial Dames of America,
in the State of Virginia.

KEY

Dotted lines indicate matter intentionally left out by the Abstractor.

Italics indicate uncertainty of spelling.

The testator's name in heavy type is taken from the spelling of the name as given in the body of the will and not from the signature.

When the will has been torn, decayed or is illegible it is so stated in parenthesis.

The List of Wills so far as is possible is made up from the spelling of the testator's name in the signature, and is not taken from the body of the will.

Where the exact mark of the testator or witness cannot be set in type, a plus (+) is used.

Brief Abstracts

of

Norfolk County Wills

1710 - 1753

BENJAMIN HARGROVE . . .

Book 9 p. 5.

dated 15 March 1704/5.

proved 16 March 1710/11.

 . . . to my Sister Ann Mosby one breading Sow . . .

 . . . unto my kindsman Charles Griffing one brass Kettle
  . . .

 . . . my plantation with all the Lands belonging to it I give
 to my Daughter Sarah Hargrove . . .

 . . . my Daughter Sarah Hargrove my whole Executrix
  . . .

 . . . frends Alexander *Lis*borne and Edward Weston to be
 assistant to my Daughter to see my will performed . . .

witnesses: Edward Weston, Allix. *Lis*borne.

   Robert Thompson.

     Benjamine Hargrave & Seale.

WILLIAM KELLEY, of Western Branch of Norfolk County
in Virginia, Planter . . .

Book 9 p. 8.

dated 22 Jan. 1710/11.

proved 15 Mch. 1710/11.

 . . . to my Loveing brother Richard Wright my Plantation

where I now Live on . . . and all Every part and percell if my Said Land Lying and being in the branch and County afores^d . . .

. . . to my Loveing brother Edward Grant of the afores^d Branch and County to Say two head of Kattle . . .

. . . to my Kindsman John Powell Son of Thomas Powell of ye Said County and Branch to Say one Stear . . .

. . . to my Kinsman John Collings to Say one gunn and one Sword . . .

. . . to Elizabeth Collins a percell of Tobacco . . .

. . . to my brother John Bruce to Say all my hoggs . . .

. . . Kinsman Thomas Powell . . . onely Executor . . . .

witnesses: Walter b——yle.

Roger Briant.

Jno Willis.

William Kelly & Seale

THOMAS WILLOUGHBY, of Norfolk County of the Southern Branch of the Elizabeth River . . .

Book 9 p. 9.

dated 8 Jan. 1710.

proved 16 March 1710/11.

. . . unto my Son Thomas Willoughby a necke of Land called broad Mash Runing from a place called turtle gutt and from thence to an Oake it being a Corner Tree it being in the head of broad Mash . . .

. . . to my Son John Willoughby my Mannor plantation itt being the remainder part of ye Said Tract of Land . . .

. . . Unto my Son William Willoughby a percell of Land Lying and being in the head of westerne branch of Elizabeth River beginning at a gum standing at the run Side by Freemans Line and running up ye Said Run for Lengtht and from ye Said gum west by north 60 p^o for breadth . . . .

. . . to my Son Jno Willoughby my still . . . a brass Kettle and a gun and Sword . . . a puter Callender . . . .

. . . to my Six Daughters . . . to them Every one of them a Ewe . . .

. . . to Thomas and William to run on for them till they arive to the age of Eighteen . . .

. . . I make John Harbutt and faithful Cherry overseers over my Son Jn° to Se that he Dos not bassell away the Estate till he come of age to governe it him Selfe . . .

witnesses: John Harbut.

    Nicholas hill, his mark

    John Eastwood, his mark

          his marke

      Thomas Willoughby and Seale.

THOMAS NORCUTT . . .

Book 9 p. 10.

dated 26 Feb. 1710/11.

proved 16 March 1710/11.

. . . unto my Son James Norcutt and my Son John Norcutt all my Land that I am now possest with To be Equally Divided between them and the manner plantation that I now Live upon I Doe give unto my Son James Norcutt with the rest of the Land Equally to be Divided next to the plantation . . . one set of Coopers tooles . . .

. . . unto my Daughter Katherine Norcutt one feather Bed . . . .

. . . unto my Daughter Mary Deans wone feather Bed & warming pan . . .

. . . unto my Son Wm Norcutt wone piece of Land yᵗ Lyeth on the Back Side of his owne Land called by the name *ayoure*.

. . . unto my three Sons Wm. James and John Norcutt . . .

. . . unto my Daughter Anne Browne wone yearling heifer . . .

. . . unto my Daughter Elizabeth Deans wone yeirling heifer . . .

. . . my two Sons James and Jn° Norcutt my sole Executrix . . .

witnesses: ffrancis Harlowin.

    Wm. Blach, marke.

    Mary Carrney, marke.

      Thomas Norcutt & Seale.

        marke.

EDWARD WAKEFIELD, of Elizabeth River parrish in Norfolk County . . .

Book 9 p. 11.

dated 26 Jan. 1710.

proved 16 March 1710/11 by Ellnathan Tart and John Ward.

. . . to my brother John Wakefield all my Lands and plantation: that I now Live on to him the Said John Wakefield . . .

. . . unto my brother Joseph Wakefield one Cow . . . when he Shall come to age . . .

. . . my Said brother Jnᵒ Wakefield to be my whole and Sole Executʳ . . .

witnesses: John Ward, mark.

Mathew Spivey.

Elnathan Tart.

Edward Wakefield and Seale.

RICHARD CARNEY Sen'r . . .

Book 9 p. 12.

dated 3 Jan. 1710/11.

proved 16 March 1710/11.

. . . unto my Eldest Son Wm. Carney wone browne Cow . . .

. . . unto my Daughter in Law Ann Carney the Choice of her mothers Coats . . .

. . . unto my Son Richard Carney wone gunn . . .

. . . unto my four Sons Richard, Jnᵒ Thomas and Barnabee all my Land . . .

. . . unto my maide Martha Tomas wone of my wifes wareing Coats . . .

. . . my Two Eldest Suns Wm. and Richard to be my whole and Sole Executʳˢ . . .

witnesses: ffrancis Harlowin.

Wᵐ weston, marke.

William Critchitt.

Richᵈ Carney.

his marke.

GEORGE MASON, of Norfolk County . . .

Book 9 p. 12.

dated 15 Jan. 1710.

proved 16 Mch. 1710, by Maj^r Sam^{11} Boush, Capt George Newton & Mr Max^o Boush.

. . . unto my Loveing wife Phillis Mason my negrow girle named Jenny thirty pounds of good passabell Spannish moneys and her Side Saddle . . .

. . . unto my Son Thomas Mason my negrow man named Dick . . . my Sword Gunn & pistell . . . the Lot of Land I now Dwell on . . . Desiring they may be kept in good repair untill he shall attaine to the age of Twenty one . . .

. . . unto my Son George Mason my Negrow boy named Geinehouse and five pounds good pasable Spannish moneys to buy him Sword Gun and pistoles.

. . . my Plantation which formerly went by the Name of Marrinor Joanes to be Equally Divided between my Two sons Thomas and George Mason my s^d Son Thomas Mason to have his first Choice . . .

. . . unto my Said Son George Mason my Lott of Land adjoyning to the Lott I now live on . . .

. . . unto my Daughter Abigale my negrow Girle Called Betty . . .

. . . unto my Daughter ffrances my negrow man named prince . . . when She attaine to the age of sixteen . . .

. . . my Loveing wife Phillis Mason to be my Executrix . . .

. . . my Loveing Kinsman Capt. George Newton Mr Lemuell Newton and Mr Wm Craford to be Overseers . . .

witnesses: Sa Boush.

M. Boush.

Natha. Newton.

George Newton.

George Mason & Seale.

HENRY WIRICK, of the Southern Branch of Elizabeth River in the County of Norfolk . . .

Book 9 p. 25.

dated 28 Dec. 1710.

proved 20 "Aprile" 1711, by Thomas Nash, W^m. Barrington & Benjamin Beck.

. . . unto my Daughter Mary Barttee the plantation I now Live on . . . Dureing my Daughters maryes naturall Life and after her Decease to fall to my grandson Robert Bartee and to the first male heir Lawfully begotten of his body and In case he Dies without heire then to fall to the next surviveing heire and Soe from heir to heir for Ever without any Saile or Division on the Said Land.

. . . unto my Daughter Patient Odean and to my Son in Law Wm Odean Dureing here naturall Life my Plantation I bought of Jn° bright and after there Decease to fall to my Daughter patient Odean and to the first Male heire Lawfully begotten of her body and Incase She Dies without heire then to fall to the next Surviveing heire and Soe from heire to heire for Ever without any Saile or Division of the Said Land.

. . . Unto all my Grand Children Twenty Shillings . . .

. . . unto my Grand Daughter Patient Odean one negrow boy when she Comes to the age of Sixteen . . .

. . . unto my Daughter Mary Bartee my hand mill . . .

. . . the rest of my Estate . . . unto my Son in Law Wm Odean and my Daughter Mary Bartee . . . my Children Wm Odean and Patian his wife and Mary Bartee MAY maintaine their mother During naturall Life . . .

. . . as for the Dowmanizeing of this my Last will and Testament . . . appoint my Son in Law Wm Odean and Patian his wife and my Daughter Mary Barttee . . . Sole Executor and Executrix . . .

witness Dennis Maccory.

       Benjamine Beck.

       Wm Barington, mark.

       Thomas Nash, Senr.

               Henry Wirrick & Seale.

JOHN SMITH . . .

Book 9 p. 29.

dated 21 Oct. 1710.

proved 20 Apr. 1711.

.   .   . unto my Son Jnᵒ Smith all that part of my Land begining at the old field and Joyning up on henry Bowles and Wm Ellis and Soe to the mill Run and all *Sut*ward from the Said Run to the head of my Land.

.   .   . unto my Son Lemuell Smith to them and heirs or assigns for Ever, Onely my will is that my Loveing wife Shall have free privileige of the whole Dwelent During her natureall Life provided she Doe not marry with one that is Cross to my Sons and will not Lett them have priviledge, also my will is that my Son Lemⁱⁱ have priviledge in the old field and part of the Orchard which are in my Son Johns part.

.   .   . unto my Loveing wife Mary Smith my mill Dureing her naturall Life and after to my Two Sons Jnᵒ & Lemuell
.   .   .

.   .   . Unto my Son Thoˢ Smith all my Coopers and Carpinter Tooles   .   .   . at age of Twenty one   .   .   .

.   .   . Goods are not to be D. D. to them till they Come to the age of Twenty one   .   .   .

.   .   . wife Mary Smith   .   .   . Sole Executrix   .   .   .

witnesses: ELeazer Tarte Senʳ.

Thomas Smith Senʳ, his marke.

Wᵐ. Ellis, his marke.

Thomas Ward.

Jnᵒ Smith & Seale.

ROBERT BARTTEE, of the County of Norfolk   .   .   .

Book 9 41.

dated 19 May 1710.

proved 18 May 1711.

.   .   . for my Land I Give and bequeath to my three Sons (viz) Adrigan Robert and Samⁱⁱ Bartee to be Equally Divided between them   .   .   . Butt my Eldest Son to have the manner plantation after his mothers Decease

. . . butt if any my Said Sons Die without Issue then his portion of Land to fall to y⁰ next heirs the Surviving brothers . . .

. . . wife Mary Bartee . . . Sole Executrix . . .

witnesses : John Edwards.

Dennis Maccoy.

William Etheridge.

Robert Bartee & Seale.

his marke.

WILLIAM OWENS, Sen'r . . .

Book 9 p. 45.

dated 10 Dec. 1710.

proved 18 May 1711.

. . . unto my Son Wᵐ. owens one percell or tract of Land adjoyning to Richard and Jnᵒ Taylor and Soe running into the woods adjoyning on the Eastward Side on a place Called the Cow penns and along the old Road goeing to to the westerne branch as far as the first branch where and on yᵉ Southwest Side joyning on a new road as goes to the westerne branch as far as the first branch where there has been timber bridge and Soe up the northward Side of the Main runn as farr as the place Called the Live Oake Glade and Soe from thence to the Crucked Chincopine before mentioned.

. . . unto my Son Jnᵒ Owens my plantation I now live on with . . . adjoyning to the ould Road goeing to the westerne branch as far as the Crucked Chincopine and Soe Joyning upon Edward Lewelling his Land onely my *true* and Loveing wife Mary Owens to have her Life in the manner plantation without any Interruption.

. . . unto my Son Edward Owens all my Land on the Southwest Side of the new road goeing to the westerne branch and Soe joyning on John Taylor and George Ballingtines Lands according as the *Corses* of that Land runs.

. . . unto my Son Thomas Owens that parc. or percell of my Land which is Called by the name of the westerne branch Ridges and Soe Joyning on Edward Hues and Richard Lewelling and Edward Lewelling . . . Cutt no timber . . . until he comes to age . . . alsoe will that my four Sons Wm. John Edward and

Thomas personally Enjoy there Lands in Every part or percell accordingly as I have given it to them and there heirs Lawfully begotten of there bodyes for Ever and in Case Either of my Sons Dies without Issue that part or parcell of Land Shall be Equally Divided amongst the other three brothers and Soe I Intaile it from age to age that It may not be Sold Except it be from one brother to another.

. . . unto my Daughter Ann Oweings . . . pewter
. . .
. . . unto my Daughter Mary Owens . . . pewter to be Delivered to them at there mariage Day.
. . . unto my Daughter Elizabeth owens . . . pewter
. . .
. . . my Two Eldest Daughters Ann and Mary . . .
. . . my three brothers in Law Edward Daviss Richard Lewelling and Richard Taylor . . . Sole Executors
. . .

witnesses: Jnᵒ Taylor, his marke.

     Richᵈ Bunting Senʳ, his marke.

     Thoᵐ Nash, Senʳ.

               William Owens, Seal.

                  his marke.

HENRY BOWS . . . (nun cup sturs)

Book 9 p. 47.

The Deposition of Jnᵒ Petters aged about fourty & one years or thereabouts . . . Saith that Sum Small time before the Decease of Mr. Henry Bows I did here him Say that if he Died before he was married that Robert Stewart Should have all his Estate . . .

                  John Peters.

The Deposition of Josias Whitehouss aged about thirty years or thereaboutts . . . (Same) . . .

                  Josias Whitehouss.

The Deposition of Jnᵒ Wakefield aged about thirty and nine . . . (Same) . . .

                  John Wakefield.

The Deposition of Dorithy Wakefield aged about forty and three . . . (Same) . . .

                  Dorithy Wakefield.

Att a Court held for Norfolk County the 18th Day of May 1711.
the within Depositions . . . whene presented to the
Court by Robert Stewart which *was* proved in Nansemund
County Court and attested by *W*. Ragsdale Deputy Clerk
and . . . recorded . . .

Test   Tho⋅ Butt,

D. C. C.

HENRY BUTT, Sen'r, of the County of Norfolk . . .

Book 9 p. 47.

dated 28 Oct. 1710.

proved 18 May 1711.

. . . unto my Eldest Son Standhope Butt the Land he now
Lives upon to the Cypruss branch beginning at the head of
y⋅ branch and Soe Running East to the Land of Roger
Housden . . . with a provissor he my Said Son Doth
not Molest his brother, Sollomon Butt of the Manner plantation, which if he Doth he Shall forfeit all the Land that
I have given and bequeathed unto him and to returne to
my Son Sollomon Butt.

. . . unto my Son Henry Butt that Tract of Land knowne
and Called Cutt the name of the wallnutt neck and Soe
running from the walnutt neck to a branch Called the
Long beacon Ridge branch which Devides my Land &
from the Land of my brother Richard Butt and Soe runing
up the Said branch to branch that is called the Hummacker
branch and from the Hummacker branch Due South to
the Cypress Swamp which Said Land . . .

. . . unto my Son Sollomon Butt the plantation I now Live
upon being the remaining part of the Land Left me by
my father . . .

. . . unto my Son Henry Butt all that tract of Land Commonly known and Called by the name of Timber Neck
and granted to me by Pattent Dated the fourth of August
1675 which said Land . . .

. . . unto my Son Sollomon Butt the north Side of y⋅ Cypruss
branch bounding upon my Standhope Butts Land . . .
Likwise . . . that tract of Land Commonly knowne
and Called by the name of Ireland . . .

. . . unto my Son Henry Butt my Long Gunn and new Short
Gunn Carbine pistells and holsters a Reapur . . .

. . . unto my Son Sollomon Butt my next Longest Gunn and Musquitt & Clubb; & one Reaper . . .

. . . unto my Grand Daughters that is to Say Sarah Elizabeth Katherine & Jane the Daughters of my Daughter Jane which maried William Ship each of them a Ewe a peice . . .

. . . unto my Loveing wife Alice Butt my Two Negrows . . .

. . . my Two Sons Henry & Sollomon Butt Executors . . .

witnesses: Tho˙ Butt.

        William Butt.

        Ann Butt.

                      Henry Butt & Seal.

THOMAS MASON, of Eliabeth River parrish in the County of Norfolk Gentleman . . .

Book 9 p. 60.

dated 9 Jan. 1710/11.

proved 15 June 1711 by Cor˭ Thomas Willoughby and Doctor Wᵐ Miller.

. . . unto my Son Lemuell Mason all my Lands and plantation . . . onely my will and Devise is that my well beloved wife Elizabeth Mason Shall have yᵉ Maner plantation that I now Live on Dureing her naturall Life and the Benefitts of one halfe of the Orchard . . . the other halfe of the Orchard on my manner plantation unto my Son Lem˭ Mason with the plantation I formerly Lived to Injoy as Soon as he mary or at Leaswise when he Comes to the age of twenty one years.

. . . unto my Loveing wife Elizabeth Mason Twenty pounds

. . . Leave fifty pounds in good Spannish money to be raised and paid out of my Estate for the Keeping and Education of my Son Lem˭ Mason at the Gramer Scoole at Williams Brough and he to Continue there as Long as will maintaine him if please god he Lives.

. . . Negrow . . . Simon and Bess may be Equally Divided among my Children . . .

. . . unto my Son Lemuell Mason my grate Silver flagin my Silver hilted Sword and Best pare of pistolls and my Best Gunn . . .

. . . my four Children Lem" Ann Mary and Margarett Mason one negrow . . . when they Come of age or when any or either of them Shall marry.

. . . my . . . wife Elizabeth Mason . . . Sole Executrix . . .

. . . appoint my Loving brother Capt. George Mason and my Cosen George Newton overSeers . . . unto . . . each of them . . . fifteen shillings . . . to buy them a morning ring.

witnesses: James Tennent.

Thomas Willoughby.

William Miller.

Thomas Mason & Seale.

GOWIN CUTHERELL, of Eastermus Side of Southern branch in the County of Norfolk planter . . .

Book 9 p. 62.

dated 25 Nov. 1710.

proved 15 June 1711, by Gabwell Holmes and Edmund Creekmore.

. . . unto my beloved wife Katherine Cuthell all yᵉ Land Contained in the Two Deeds bought of my Two brothers in Law: Danell and Andrew mᵗᵗ fashon onely fifty acres being bounded as followeth and the Said Land I Give to my Said wife Dureing her naturall Life.

. . .unto my Eldest Son Thomas Tuthell one Shilling Sterling being in full of his pattremony.

. . . unto my Son John fifty ackers of Land being Called by the name of Duck Creek Neck . . .

. . . unto my Son Lem" Cuthell the Land that is above given to my beloved wife after her Decease . . .

. . . unto my Son Solomon Tuthell fifty acres of Land which Land is as above mentioned out of my wifes Deeds being bought of my brothers in Law . . . beginning at a pine marked this Day by Edmund CreeKmore and my Son John & cutting E. S. E. to a markt Sweet Gumm at the head of a branch.

. . . unto my three Sons William Joseph and Daniell *Tuthnall* all the remainder when my Sons Johns fifty acres is taken out) of Land Contained in Deed Seall from John

West to me being one hundred and Seventy acres . . .
they of age . . .

. . . four Sons Samuell William Joseph and Daniell . . .
as they Come of age . . .

. . . my Son Nathanell Cuthell when he Comes of age.

. . . to my Daughter Ann west one heifer . . .

. . . wife Katterin Juthell . . . Sole Executrix . . .

witnesses: Gab. Holmes

Edmund Creekmur.

Elizᵃ Creekmore.
her mark.

Gowin Jutherll
writt for Goeing Cutherel.

FRANCIS TULLY, Emperour of Princess Anne County in
the Colleney of Virginia Gent: . . .

Book 9 p. 71.

dated 26 May 1698.

proved 20 July 1711, by Capt. George Newton.

. . . unto my Loveing Son Francis Emperour my whole and
Sole Estate . . . at yᵉ age of Seventeen . . . butt
if my Said Son Francis Emperour Should Die and Decease
before he Comes to yᵉ age of Seventeen . . . then
. . . all my whole Estate in the barbados to the Children of Henry Ramsden begotten on yᵉ body of Elizabeth
Oiftine . . .

. . . If my Said Son Francis Emerouʳ Should Dye . . .
before . . . Seventeen . . . all my whole Estate
in veirginia to yᵉ Children to Tully Emperouʳ Equally
. . .

. . . my three trusty and well beloved friends the honourable
Corˡˡ Richd. Elliott, majʳ Danˡˡ Hooper and Joseph Hough
Gentˡ of yᵉ Island of yᵉ berbados . . . Sole Exoʳˢ . . .

witnesses: Francis Heulitt.

Sampʳ Power.

George Newton.

ffrancis Tully Emperour. Seale.

JOHN CREEKMORE, in the County of Norfolk . . .

Book 9 p. 80.

dated 4 Jan. 1708/9.

proved 17 Aug. 1711, by Emanuell Burgis.

. . . unto my Samuell Creekmur the plantation whereon I now Liveth which was formerly my fathers . . . Likewise I give my Son Sam^{ll} a Sword that he ye Said Sam^{ll} wares and my owne bible and a practice of piety Likewise . . . fifty acres of land . . . on the other Side of the n^o west river Joyning the Line of Edward Creekmur and Jno. Mesays Line where he now Liveth and to have as much in breath as in Length.

. . . unto my Daughter Jane one hundred and thirty acres of Land bounded along the northwest river unto the Line of Edward Creekmur and Soe for breadth to the fifty acres of Land of Sam^{ll} Creekmur . . . and a warming pan . . .

. . . And for the rest of my Land Lying on the South Side of the northwest Side of the river . . . unto my Son Jno Creekmur and George Creekmur and James Creekmur . . . unto my Son John Creekmur Junr fifty acres of Land Lying between Richard Hodgis and Henry Culpepper called by name of horse point and my Gun and Sword and his bible.

. . . my *pore* mans family book . . .

. . . unto my Daughter Sarah Creekmur my mare . . . Chest that I bought of Mr. Thomas Hodgis . . .

. . . unto my Daughter ffrancis Creekmur my mare . . . the looking Glass that was her Grand Mothers . . . at my wife Decease or at the Day of my wifes Marriage . . . wife Dorothy Creekmore my whole Executrix . . .

. . . if either of my Said Children Should Die John George and James . . .

. . . my brother Edmund Creekmore . . .

witnesses: Joseph Hodgis.

Thomas Randle, his marke.

Emanuel Burgis.

John Creekmur & Seale.

JAMES THELABALL . . .

Book 9 p. 124.

dated 24 Dec. 1707.

proved 18 Jan. 1711, by Samuel Wilder and Richard Bray.

. . . unto my Sonne Francis Thelaball the plantation whereon I now Live . . one Gold Seal ring which was my
Father's . . .
one Virginia Rugg . . . bolster marked on the Ticking F. T. . . .
. . . my Two Sons Francis and Lemuell . . .
. . . my wife Ann Thelaball . . .
. . . unto my Son Lemuell Thelaball my Plantation *at wolfes*
Neck . . . bolster which was my fathers . . .
one Gold hoop Ring . . . one pare of money scales
. . . one Small Table of Turners work . . .
. . . unto my Daughter Dinah Thelaball one Negrow
. . .
. . . unto my Daughter Elizabeth Thelaball one Negrow
till She comes to y° age of Sixteen . . .
. . . unto my daughter Ann Thelaball one negrow . . .
till She come to y° age of Sixteen.
. . . wife Ann Thelaball and my Son francis Thelaball my
full & whole Exec⁷ˢ . . .

witnesses: Samuell Wilder, his marke.

Edward Bray.

Lemuell Roberts, his marke.

James Thelaball & Seale.

WARREN GODFREY Sen'r . . .

Book 9 p. 168.

dated 19 Feb. 1711/12.

proved 18 Apr. 1712.

. . . to my Son Warran Godfrey a percell of Land begining
at a pine Standing at a head of a Little Neck branch
next to *warren* and from thence Runing N. N. East near
is the head of reidy branch and from thence Joyning upon
Daniell Godfrey his Line . . . unto my Son Warren

and to the Male heirs of his body . . . for want of Such heire to Come to my Son Petter Godfrey . . .

. . . to my Son Petter Godfrey all my plantation I now Live on Except what is already Given to him and the heirs of his body . . . for want of Such heirs to Come to my Son Mathew Godfrey . . . and for want of Such heirs to Come to frances and Sarah my Two Daughters . . .

. . . unto my grand Son Jonathan Godfrey all the Land all the Land that I have in the woods Joyning to where his father Did Live and to his heirs . . . if noe such heirs then to come to my Grandson Arthur Godfrey And to the heirs of his body . . . if noe Such heirs then to come to my Son Mathew Godfrey . . . my wife Shall have the use of the plantation till Jonathan comes to age . . .

. . . to my Son Petter Godfrey the third of my Lott of Land in town that third part where the house Stood . . . to my Son Daniell Godfrey one third part . . . the middle . . . to my Son Mathew the other third . . .

. . . to all my Children Elizabeth Murfee Daniell ffrancis & Sarah & Katherine and Matthew and Jane one Shilling . . . there portions . . .

. . . wife . . . Sole Executrix . . .

witnesses: Matthew Godfrey.

William Godfrey.

Matthew Godfrey, Jun.

Waren Godfrey & Seale.

THOMAS COTTLE, of Norfolk County in the western branch of Elizabeth River . . .

Book 9 p. 182.

dated 24 Jan'y ——.

proved 16 May 1712—, by Ralph & Edward Outlaw.

. . . unto my Eldest Son Thomas Cottle one hunded acres of Land on the South Side of my Line . . .

. . . unto my youngest Son Robert Cottle one hundred acres of Land on the northern Side that is the remaining part of

my land . . . my land be Equally Devided, between
These my Two Sons that is Length ways begining at the
Creek Soe running up to the head in the Swamp . . .
that my Sone Thomas Cottle Doe plant one hundred wint-
ter apple Trees one my Son Roberts part on the part called
Middle Neck on the uper part of it and that my Son
Thomas Manure the aple trees on y⁹ Said Land till his
brother Comes of age and that he plant the aple trees
twenty five foot Distance . . .

. . . unto my Loveing wife Mary Cottle all and Singular
the rest of the Cattles . . .

. . . unto my daughter Amy Cottle one three Gallon pot
. . .

. . . unto my daughter Mary Cottle Two Deep Dishes
. . .

witnesses: John Tucker.
> Tho⁰ Bustin, his marke.

> > Thomas Cottle & Seale.

Memorandum:
dated 24 Mch. 1711/12.

witnesses: Ralph Outlaw.
> Edwᵈ Outlaw.
> Jacob Talbutt.

> > Thomas Cottle & Seale.

THOMAS WILLOUGHBY, of Norfolk County in Virginia,
Gentleman . . .

Book 9 183.

dated 4 Feb. 1711.

proved 16 May 1712, presented by Mrs. Margarett Willoughby
> & proved by Henry Thomas, John Lambert Senʳ, & John
> Lambert Junʳ

. . . my Dwelling plantation with all its rights Members and
Appurtances to my Son Thomas Willoughby . . .

. . . Negrow boy Jake to my Daughter Margarett porter
. . .

. . . Negrow boy Isaac to my Daughter Elizabeth Willoughby

. . .
. . .   Negrow by Tom to my Daughter Sarrah Willoughby

. . .
. . .   Negrow Girle Pegg to my Daughter Mary Willoughby

. . .
. . .   furniture . . . Stands in the porch Chamber to
. . . wife Margarett Willoughby . . .

. . .   my Sword Belt Sadle Bridle Holsters Pistells and that
new Gunn I always Called mine & that which I Generally
caled my Little black Gunn to my Son Thomas Willoughby.

. . .
. . .   to my Son in law Mr John Porter my New Gunn

. . .
. . . my Daughter Elizabeth . . . when She Comes to
Sixteen . . .

. . . wife . . . and . . . Son . . . Sole Executors . . .

witnesses : ———— : Cocke.
        Henry Thomas.
        John Lambert Senr.
        John Lambert Junr.

                    Tho : Willoughby & Seal.

JOHN WAKEFIELD, of Norfolk County . . .

Book 9 p. 183.

dated 9 Apr. 1712.

proved 20 June 1712, by Sam^ll Shepherd & John Ward.

. . .   to my brother Joseph Wakefield all my Land and plantation I now Live on . . . if my wife be not with
Child ; butt if She be then . . . to the Child . . .
butt if it should Dye to my brother Joseph Wakefield

. . .
. . .   to my Loveing wife Sarah Wakefield all my Stock
. . . Desire her to bring up my brother Joseph till he
be fitt to be putt to trade . . .

. . . wife Whole and Sole Executrix . . .

witness : Sam^ll Shepherd.
        Thomas Ward, his marke.
        John Ward, his mark.

                            his
                    John Wakefield.
                        marke.

THOMAS WESSLEY, of Norfolk County in the western branch of Elizabeth River . . .

Book 9 p. 195.

dated 24 Apr. 1705.

proved 15 Aug. 1712, by Robert Spring & John Lavina.

. . . unto my Eldest Son Thomas Wessley one fire Lock fowling peace . . .

. . . unto my Son John Wessley one fire Locke Musquitt . . .

. . . unto my Daughter Mary Cherry one Ewe . . .

. . . unto my Daughter Anne Wessley one Ewe . . .

. . . unto my Daughter Maudlin Wessley one Ewe . . .

. . . unto my Loveing wife Mary Wessley all and Singular my personal and reall Estate . . . wife my Sole Executrix . . .

witnesses: William Powell.
Robert Spring.
John Lavina.

Thomas Wesley. Seale.

ELIZABETH COLLINGS, Widdow of Norfolk County . . .

Book 9 p. 199.

dated 13 June 1712.

proved 19 Sep. 1712.

. . . unto my Two Sone Namely John and Edward Collings after they have Received there part of there fathers Estate wone Shilling a peace in full of all there part of my Estate to Cutt them of of all ye Rest for Ever.

. . . unto my Daughter Mary Collings my Gold ring and Sattin Riben Girdle . . . when She comes to the age of Sixteen . . .

. . . my brother Edward Grant Should have the bringing up of my Daughter . . . who I doe appoint to be my Whole and Sole Executor . . .

witnesses: Thos Wright.
James Lambert.
ffrancis Thornton.

her
Eliz^a Collings and Seale.
marke.

JAMES WILSON, of the County of Norfolk in Virginia . . .

Book 9 p. 220.

dated 12 Nov. 1712.

proved 19 Dec. 1712, presented by Mrs. Elizabeth Wilson and
Willis Wilson Exo^{rs} & proved by Thomas Walk and Maximillian Boush.

. . . unto my Son John Wilson two hundred Acres of land
which land I bought of John fulford . . . all my
Land and houses being and Lying one the westmost Side
of wroad at the bridge at the head of the Southerne
branch . . .

. . . to my Son Willis Wilson all the land and the new Store
Standing on the Eastmost Side of the wroade by the bridge
. . .

. . . to my Said Son Willis Wilson my plantation whereon
I now live being about four hundred acres . . . allow-
ing my Dear and Loveing wife Elizabeth Wilson to have
the use of the Said plantation and Stock During her Naturall Life . . .

. . . till he recover his Negros of Capt. Robert Bolling or a
Determination of the Suite . . .

. . . unto my Grandson James Wilson Sun of my Son
Thomas Wilson Dec'd. the plantation whereon my Negrow
Sambo Lives one begineing one the South Side of Lambes
plantation at the Swamp Called the Sypruss Swamp and
runing into the woods upone a northerly Course one hundred and fifty poles and thence a north East Course to my
westermost Line . . . and in Default of Such heire
. . . to my Loving Son Solomon Wilson . . .

. . . unto my Grandson Willis Wilson Sun of my Decd Sun
Sam^{ll} Wilson four hundred acres of Land Known by the
name of poplar neck begining at the Northerly Line of
James Wilson and runing Such a Course that Shall Include
the Land whereon the poplars groed and thence to the
Cypress Swamp . . . into his possession at the age of
twenty one . . . in Default . . . to my Loveing
Son Solloman Wilson . . .

. . . my Grandson Willis Wilson Son of my Decd. Sun
Sam^{ll} . . . at the age of twenty one . . .

. . . unto my Son Solloman Wilson the plantation I bought
of Henry Bright being two hundred acres be it more or
be it Less . . . I give him my Said Son my land
Called the western Ridges . . .

. . . unto my Son James Wilson one hundred acres of Land Lying and being over the Gumm Swamp in the back woods . . .

. . . unto my Son Jn⁰ Wilson one hundred acres of Land Lying and being over the Gumm Swamp in the back woods . . .

. . . all the rest of my Land not already bequeathed unto my Son Willis Wilson . . .

. . . to Capt. George Newton one hundred acres of Land Called the Cowpens . . .

. . . to my Son Solloman . . . at the age of Twenty one . . .

. . . my personall Estate not before given . . . be Equally Didided between my Sons Willis John and Sollo-- mon and my Daughters affiah and Mary my Loveing wife Elizabeth to have the use of it During her Natural Life.

. . . to my Daughter Elizabeth the wife of Mr. Henry Svigany of Phillidelphins five pounds . . .

. . . to my Son Lem^{ll} Wilson five Shillings in full of his portion he haveing a Sufficient part already.

. . . to my Son James Wilson my pistolls and Sword . . .

. . . my . . . wife Elizabeth Wilson and my . . . Son Willis Wilson my whole and Sole Executrix and Exec^r . . .

witnesses : *M*. Boush.
Wᵐ Armistead.
Thomas Walke.
ffrances fflourn*o*y.
Nich⁰ Cur*le*.

James Wilson & Seale.

. . . unto my Grandson Solomon Wilson Sun if my Sunn James Wilson two hundred acres of Land being the Land I purchased of Joell Martaine Known by yᵉ Name of the Co*new* Neck . . .

witnesses : Nich⁰ Cur*le*.
Wᵐ Armistead.
M. Boush.
Thomas Walke.
ffrances fflournitaey.

James Wilson & Seale.

Codicell . . . proved 19 Dec. 1712, by Thomas Walke and Maximillian Boush.

JOHN FFULCHER . . . Norfolk County in Virginia
Book 9 p. 223.

dated 29 Oct. 1712.

proved (On or between 19 Dec. 1712 & 16 Jan. following).

. . . unto Thomas Langley Senr all my wearing apparoll
. . .

. . . unto Capt Horatio Woodhouse one hundred acres of
March between the wash and the Inlett . . .

. . . unto Mr. Thomas Walk my Negro man Tobe . . .

. . . unto my Godson Lewis Conn^r a Silver Tankard & a
Dozen of Silver Spoons marked J. F.—

. . . I give and ordaine all the remainer part of my Negroes
men and women and Children there freedom and I Clear
them from all bondage whatsoever after the day of my
Death I give these Negroes that I now Sett ffree all there
labour and what they Can Make to maintaine themselves
with all as long as won of them shall Live, I give and
ordaine all that part of my land at the hithermost fence
now Stands from the new ground branch to the Marsh
by San *burds* and from the Marsh into the river all that as
it called the grate pasture from the fence by b*rouns* to
Robert woody and purdy to and for all my free Negroes
men women and Children to live upon as long as they Shall
live or any of there Increase and not to be turn^d of nor
to be Disturbed butt there to live if they will or I give
them all Liberty and freedom to goe where they will and
noe body Shall hinder them . . .

. . . I Give John Bony my best maire and that peace of
Marsh from the Little Creak to Mr. Stanfords Line . .
. . .

. . . unto Easter walstone my bible . . .

. . . give Mary Critchett Two Cows . . .

. . . all my land A this Side the grate pasture with my
house where I now live I give unto Mr Lewis Conn^r
. . . all my land and Marshes in Princes Anne County
not already given to him . . .

. . . Mr Lewis Conn^r my whole & Sole Executor . . .
provided he performs my will if he Does not then I ordaine
Capt. woodhouse and Mr Thomas Walk hole Exec^rs to
perform my will . . .

witnesses: John Crithet.
Jacob Talbott.
Isaac Talbott.   John Fulcher & Seale.

JOS. MOSLEY. . . .

Book 9 p. 235.

dated 10 Nov. 1712.

proved 20 Mch. 1712, by Arthur Blake and Amos Moseley— 10
——mber 1713 by Benjamen Moseley.

. . . all my lands and Tenements that I Shall be possessed
with all at the time of my Decease be Soule by my aforesaid Executrix to the best purchaser for the payment of
all my just Debts.

. . . unto my Loveing wife blandina Moseley and my Daughter ffrances Mosely all the remainder of my Estate . . .
to be Justly & Equally Devided between them.

. . . my foresd Loveing wife Blandina Moseley to be Executrix . . .

witnesses: Arthur Blake.

Benja Moseley.

Amos. Moseley.

Joseph Moseley & Seale.

THOMAS WOODEN, of the County of Norfolk Planter . . .

Book 9f. 235.

dated 8 Dec. 1712.

proved 20 Mch. 1712.

. . . to my wife Margrett Wooden one hundred and one
acres of Land thirty acres of which was mortgaged to me
by William Wallis for Ninety nine years and the other
Sewenty one I bought of the Said Wallis as by the Pattent
and Deed will more largely appear . . .

. . . unto my Son Richard Wooden the plantation which I
bought of Thomas Price being Seventy acres of Land as
by bill of Sale . . .

. . . to my Daughter Anne Hempsen Twelve pence full
of her portion . . .

. . . to ann Willams one Lining wheel and one woolen wheel.

. . . to Jnº Grant one brown heifer . . . if he should
Die with out heirs . . . to amos Grant . . .

. . . wife Margarett and Son Richard Wooden to be my
Joynt Exec^{rs} . . .

witnesses: Thomas *Bosem*ore, his marke—

Joseph Jolliffe.

Sam^{ll} Shepherd.

> Thomas Wooden & Seal.
>
> his marke.

RICHARD POWELL, of Norf. County . . .

Book 9 p. 247.

dated 16 apr. 1713.

proved, 15 May 1713; by Jonnos Holladay & Jn° Starford.

. . . unto my Son Richard Powell all my lands . . .

. . . my Mother to have my Son Richard and to bring him up
till he attains the age of Seventeen . . .

. . . all the rest . . . to be Equally Divided between my
Dear and lawful wife and my children . . .

. . . my frend*s* Lim^{ll} Powell . . . Sole Executors.

witnesses: Jonnas Holladay.

Jn° *Star*ford, his marke.

Elizebeth Starford, her marke.

> Richard Powell. his marke.

RICHARD FFURLONG . . .

Book 9 p. 248.

dated, 5 Nov. 1712.

proved, 15 May 1713

. . . unto my Son W^m ffurlong the sume of thirty pounds
Sterling . . . when he shall attain the age of Twenty
one . . . my Desire is that^r Maj^r Sam^{ll} Boush do use
his best Indavieur to putt the same out at use into a good
Saive hand for the Benefit of my Said Son. . . .

. . . that Maj^r Sam^{ll} Boush do make a good and lawful
deed unto my Said Son William ffurlong of the land I
Bought of him . . .

. . . unto my Daughter Mary ffurlong my Molato Girle
. . . when she attaine to Full age . . .
. . . wife Anne ffurlong all the remainder . . .
. . . wife to be Executrix . . .
. . . acknowledged by Capt. Richard ffurlong . . . in

ye presence of us: William Miller.

Mary Miller.

Sa. Boush.

Richard ffurlong and Seale.

JOHN ROSS Sen'r, of the Southern branch of the Elizabeth River. . . .

Book 9 p. 268.

dated, 20 Oct. 1712.

proved, 21 Aug. 1713, by Thomas Etheridge and William ODeon.

. . . to my Son John Ross Junr my plantation I now live upon being the upper plantation only my loveing wife mary Ross to have her *third* for her Life time . . .

. . . unto my Son Alexander Ross my Lower plantation Joyning on the River & the Creek and a Division to be made by a line of marked Trees begining at a marked pine at the head of gutt and Runing so aCross my Said land to a Sawpitt or near the Same . . . bind my aforesaid Sons that if they have mind to Sell Either of there plantations to Sell to one another or Else to keep ye Same . . .

. . . wife Mary Ross one Cow . . .

. . . to my Son John Ross one heifer . . . one mus-Kett & Cuttless . . .

. . . to my Daughter Sarah Ross one heifer . . .

. . . to my Son Alexander Ross . . . one barrow one Long Gunn one Iron pissell . . . after he come to age and till Den my Son John To have the aforesaid

. . . accept my wife marry a Cross man to Debar my Sons to grind then my wife to Looses . . . her part

. . . to my Loveing frend Thomas Etheredge Cooper till he Comes to the age of one and twenty . . . to give

him Two years Larning\ to read & writte if he will be
Larned . . .

. . . wife . . . Sole Executrix . . .

. . . frinds Mr Wm Odean & Mr Thomas Etheridge to be
overseeres . . .

witnesses : Thomas Etheridge.
          William Odean.
          Dennis Maccoy.   John Ross Senr & Seale.
                                            his marke.

RICHARD BUNTING . . .

Book 9 p. 269.

dated 4 July 1705.

proved 21 Aug. 1713, by Robert Culpeper.

. . . unto my Son Wm. Buntin all the plantation which I now
live upon . . .

. . . unto my Son Richard Bunting fifty Acres of land
Lying at the head of a Creek in Newbys Neck Joyning
upon John Joyce . . .

. . . unto my Son John Bunting fifty Acres of Land where
my houses and Clear ground is in fishey Neck . . .

. . . unto my Son Thomas Bunting fifty Acres of Land
Joyning John's . . .

. . . unto my Son Henry Bunting fifty acres of Land out
of the Same pattent of fishing Neck . . . and In case
that Either of them . . . my Said Sons . . .
Decease without such heirs . . . that my Son Mathew
Shall have the fifty . . . of Land given the Deacesed
as aforesaid . . .

. . . It Shall and my be Lawful for any of my Sons to
Dispose and Sell there Land to Each other butt not to
any body else . . .

. . . wife Anne Bunting.

. . . my Loveing Brother Wm Wallice and my Loveing
wife Anne Bunting . . . Sole Executor & Executrix
. . .

witnesses : Eleazar Tarte:
          Robert Culpeper.
          James Smyth, his mark.
          Mary Smyth, her mark   the marke of
                                        Richard Bunting & Seale.

JOHN ALEXANDER, of the parish of Norfolk . . .

Book 9 p. 271.

dated 8 Apr. 1713.

proved 18 Sept. 1713, by Jacob Lindsay & Richard Watson.

. . . unto Owing Dockharty . . . my Land and all my personall estate . . .

. . . the s^d Dockharty and his wife to take honest care of my sister Alice towards the mentinance of her Dureing her life that She wants neither for lodging diet or Cloathes . . .

. . . unto my Sister Mary *to burrow* hoggs . . .

witnesses: Jacob Lindsay.

Rich. Watson, his mark.

Eliz. Watson, her mark.

John Alexander.
his mark Seale.

MARY CREATCH, of Elizabeth River parish in the County of Norfolk . . .

Book 9 p. 272.

dated 10 Aug. 1713.

proved 18 Sept. 1713, by Capt. Wm Langly & Elizabeth Oast.

. . . unto my Daughter Margaret Carney three puhern Dishes & one puter bason . . . one Chest that was my husbands . . .

. . . unto my daughter Dinah Creatch one feather bed . . . & bedstead belonging to it the ticking being made in Virginia of Cotten . . .

. . . unto my daughter Elizabeth Nichols one new Virginia cloath coat . . .

. . . unto my Grand daughter Nichol*es* one Small brass Kettle . . .

. . . unto my daughter Mary Veal one Silk *gore* hankerchief . . .

. . . unto my Son in Law Henry Nichol*es* one gun . . . .

. . . unto my Son John Creatch my hand milne but if my

Son John Creatch die before my Son William Creatch
then . . . to be wholly my Son William Creatches
. . .
. . . my Son John Creatch . . . Sole Executor . . .

witnesses: (none signed).

(Unsigned)   Seall.

EDWARD ETHERIDGE . . .
Book 9 p. 272.

dated ————————.

proved 16 *Oct.* 1713, by Wm Powell & Mary Whythall.

  . . . to Augustus Etheridge my Son this plantation which
  now I live upon containing one hundred acres . . .
  . . . my daughter Sarah *Ives* . . .
  . . . unto John Ives a pairing chissell . . .
  . . . unto my grand Son Edward Etheridge . . . **one**
  heifer . . .
  . . . to my grand Son Thomas Ives one heifer . . .
  . . . unto my daughter Mary Etheridge all the rest . . .
  Sole Executrix . . .

witnesses: Mary Whythall, his mark.
         Ignata Byard.
         William Powell.
         John Wythall, his mark.

December the 10^ht day 1714.

Edward Etheridge.
his mark.

WILLIAM BOND . . .
Book 9 p. 277.

dated 21 Oct. 1713.

proved 20 Nov. 1713, by Thomas Bond & Thomas Batters.

  . . . my estate Shall be equally devided between my Son
  William Bond and my Son John Bond only I *leave* my
  daughter Sarah Roe won English Twelve pence. I leve

my dafter Elloner Rose won English twelve pence my dafter Mary Hancocks children with one English twelve pence. William Executor   .   .   .

witnesses: Richard Bond, his mark.
　　　　　John Charles, his mark.
　　　　　Thomas Batters.

　　　　　　　　　　　　William Bond.   Seale.
　　　　　　　　　　　　his mark.

ALEXANDER FFOREMAN, of the County of Norfolk . . .

Book 9 p. 277.

dated 11 Oct. 1713, by Lem. Wilson & Gilbert Halliday.

proved 20 Nov. 1713. by Lemuell Wilson & Gilbert Halliday.

　.　.　. unto my Son William fforeman one Gun   .   .   . and Twelveth pence or Shilling in full of his portion of my real and perSonall Estate I haveing before given him by deed of conveyance what Land I ever designed for him.

　.　.　. unto my Grandson Alexander fforeman son of William fforeman my old Gun   .   .   .

　.　.　. unto my Grandson William fforeman son of William fforeman my son a part of the pilgrims ground lying Eastward from the place where my sd son William fforeman formerly began to cleare and rune along marked trees to a branch that parts the s^d Land and the Land of John Sycks and so to joyn the s^d Branch to be the lyne of the s^d Land being more or less   .   .   .

　.　.　. unto Israell Gramans my Son in Law twenty or thirty acres of Land beginning at the branch wher the above lyne of my Grandson William fforeman left of and so joyning upon the Millars lyne which said thirty acres be it more or liss   .   .   . as also I Give my daughter Elizabeth Grahams one Cow   .   .   .

　.　.　. unto my Grandson fforeman Smith the Son of Henry Smith a Neck of Land called Chincopen Neck.

　.　.　. unto my two Sons Benjamine and Joseph all the Land which I am now posessed with Except what I have given as is above to be equally devided between them by two Neutenall men   .   .   . but if my Son Benjamine or Joseph Should die before they arrive to the age of Twenty one years then the Survivor of them shall Inherite the whole   .   .   . if they Should both die without issue then the Land to fall to my Son William . . .

. . . to my daughter Mary Smith three Cupboard dishes
. . .

. . . to my Son Benjamine my Gun and Cuttlis when he
arrives to the age of Sixteen . . .

. . . unto my daughter Jane Tart wife of Elnathan Tart
one Shilling . . .

. . . unto my Loveing wife Mary fforeman one third part
during her Naturall life . . .

. . . unto my Sons Benjamine and Joseph & my daughter
Prudence all the remainder . . .

. . . unto my daughter Prudence one feather bed . . .
at the age of Sixteen . . .

. . . if they all should die without issue then to be devided
amongst the sisters of the blood of the said prudence
. . .

. . . wife my whole and sole Execer . . . .

witnesses: John Dickson Senr. his mark.

Lem. Wilson.

Gr. Holliday.

Alex^r fforeman & Seal.

JOHN CHAMBERLIN, of the County of Norfolk . . .

Book 9 p. 292.

dated 4 Aug. 1712.

proved 21 May 1714.

. . . unto my Son George Chamberlin my man^r plantation
. . . one gun & sword and belt upon this Condition
I obleidge my Son George Chamberlain to pay unto his
brothers John and Robert Chamberlin the value of forty
Shillings a peace when he Come to age . . .

. . . my Son John my Small gun . . .

. . . unto my Daughter Elizabeth Chamberlin one Shilling
. . .

. . . . wife Ann Chamberlin full holy and Solly Exe^{rs}.

witnesses: Wm Wilkins.

John Williams.

Wm Ives, his mark.

John Chamberlin & Seale.

ISREAL VOSS, of Norfolk County in Virginia . . .

Book 9 p. 296.

dated 14 Jan. 1713/14.

proved ——————— 1714, by Thomas Willoughby & John Lambert.

. . . to my Son John Voss one Crown I full of his Portion
. . .

. . . unto Israel Voss Jackson three Sheep in full of his Portion . . .

. . . unto my Daughter Ann Jackson one Crown in full of her Portion . . .

. . . unto my well beloved wife Mary Ross one hundred and thirty acres of Land more or less Dureing her Natuall life & after her Decease to William Vose & if he Should Die without Issue to Israel Voss & if he Should Die without Issue To Thomas Voss.

. . . my three Children William Voss, Israel Voss and Tho⁰ Voss . . .

. . . my three bots and Sailes . . .

. . . my three youngest Children . . . when they come of age . . .

witnesses: Thomas Willoughby.

Rene Hubard.

John Lambert, Junr.

Israel Voss & Seale.

———————

JOHN GRAHAM . . .

Book 9 p. 320.

dated 14 Apr. 1711.

proved 20 Aug. 1714.

. . . unto my Daughter Ellinnor Graham one feather bed
. . .

. . . unto my Son James Graham one Gunn . . .

. . . unto my Son John Graham one Gunn . . .

. . . unto my Son in Law Richard Corling one Gunn . . .

. . . unto my Grandson John Harlowin one . . . heiver
. . .

. . . unto . . . wife Elizabeth Graham the use of all the

rest of my whole Estate Reall & personall during her Life
& then to return to my Six Children . . .
. . . my Son in Law francis Harlowin & Humphrey Myers
Junr . . . Sole Executor . . .

witnesses : Michaell Ward.
         Hanah Ward. her mark.
         Ann Ward, her mark.

                   John Graham & Seale.

JOHN HODGIS . . .

Book 9 p. 330.

dated 27 May 1714.

proved 20 Aug. 1714.

. . . unto my Daughter Elizabeth Two Negroes . . .
when She Comes to the age of Eighteen . . .
. . . unto my Daughter Mary two Negroes . . . when
She Comes to the age of Eighteen . . .
. . . unto my Daughter Katherine Two Negroes . . .
when She Comes to the age of Eighteen . . .
. . . unto my Daughter Judith two Negroes . . . when
She Comes to the age of Eighteen . . .
. . . unto my beloved wife Elizabeth Hodgis the manner
plantation whereon I now Live to her Dureing her Naturall Life and the previlge of Driving and Keeping a Stock
on my Land above the head of the western branch this
River . . .
. . . unto my Son William five Cows . . . when he
Comes to the age of Twenty . . . a Carbine Gune
and a Small Squirrell Gunn . . .
. . . Mrs. ffrancis Hodgis my mother in Law . . . negroes now in her possession which I am heir at Law
: . .
. . . my five Children . . . pewter . . .
. . . the Education and bringing up of my Children . . .
unto . . . wife Elizabeth Hodgis . . .
. . . unto my Son William all my Land . . .
. . . wife Elizabeth Sole Executrix . . .

witnesses : *ffa. Ncwan.*
         Jno. Tucker.
         Lewis Conners.

                   John Hodgis & Seale.

JOHN COATS . . .

Book 9 p. 331.

dated 2 Apr. 1714.

proved 17 Sep. 1714, by Edward Wallis & John Bishop.

. . . wife Isabell Coats Executrix . . .

. . . unto my beloved wife all & Singular my Reall and personall Estate which I am now possest with . . . to be Clearly and freely hers . . . as She Shall See fit & Convenient to be Stow it upon according to her Discretion as my true & Lawfull wife and alsoe Executrix of my Estate which I now Leave Shall hereafter be pleased to order it.

. . . unto my Sonne John Coats and to my Daughter Mary Coats unto Each of them one Shilling . . .

witnesses: Edward Wallise, his marke.

James Tooley.

John Bishop.

John Coats & Seale.

THOMAS WILSON . . .

Book 9 p. 354.
dated, 27 July 1714.

proved, 15 Oct. 1714, by ffrancis Harlowin & John Johnson.

. . . unto my beloved brother Eleazer Tart all my hole Dividend of Land being two hundred & forty-six Acres Two guns . . . if my said brother Should Dye before he Comes of age I give it all to my Sister Prudence . . .

. . . unto my ffather in Law Eleazer Tart wone mare

. . . my Said ffather in Law Sole Executor.

witnesses: John Johnson,
his marke.

Edward Weston,
his marke.

ffrancis Harlowin,

Thomas Wilson & Seal
his marke

DANIEL PORTEEN, of Norfolk County . . .

Book 9 p. 355.

dated, 31 Oct. 1714.

proved, 19 Nov. 1714.

. . . first my Desire is that Soe much of my Lands which I haye in Norfolk and Princes Ann Countys be sold by my Said Exec^r as will be Sufficient to pay all my Debts and Funerall expenses . . .

. . . unto Mary ffurlong the Daughter of my Sister Ann ffurlong and her heirs one Lot of Land in Norfolk Town, being the Eastermost of my Six Lots all the Remainder of my Lands which Shall not be Sold by my Said Executor I give unto my Sonn Crodick Porten & . . .

. . . appoint my father in Law Maj^r Samuell Boush my Exec^r for the Disposing of my Lands and paying my Lawful Debts and Elizabeth my wife my Exec^r

. . . My Desire is that my Said wife Render unto the Court of westmoreland a true account of all my Estate . . .

witnesses: Mary Miller.

Margarit Thurston.

Ann King.

Dan^{ll} Porten & Seal.

MARY MASON, of Elizabeth River Parrish in the County of Norfolk . . .

Book 9 p. 355.

dated, "April ye 15*th* 1714"

proved, 19 Nov. 1714.

. . . to my Thomas Chichester Tenn pounds in Current money and won Large Silver Tan Kard of the newest fashion butt if my Son Thos Chichester Dyes without are beg otten then the Said Tan Kard to go to my Son John Chichester If he be a Live if not to the Eldest Sister that is a Live . . .

. . . to my Daughter Elizabeth Mason my Seal SKinn

Trunk . . . all the Rest of my Clothes Lining & Woolen to be Equally Divided betwixt my three Daughters . . . witnesses: William Mac K nary.

William Alett.

Mary Mason & Seal.

EDWARD OUTLAW . . .

Book 9 p. 360.

dated, 19 December 1713.

proved, 17 December 1714 & on Motions of Edward & Ralph
Outlaw admitted to Record.

. . . unto my well beloved wife Eli* Outlaw the use of all my whole Estate Lands and Liveing . . . During her Naturall Life and after her Decease . . . unto my Son Edward Outlaw one hundred and three Acres of Land . . .

. . . unto my Son Ralph Outlaw wone hundred & Two Acres of Land beginning at a markt persim on at the upper end of my orchard and Soe Running a long the Old Field to the persim on Trees more and from the last persim on to Run a line to make up the Com ple ment . . .

. . . unto my Daughter Sarah Bustin & my Son Ralph all my household Stuff . . .

. . . unto my Daughter Eliz abeth King wone negrow om an . . .

. . . my Two Sons Edward and Ralph . . . Sole Executors . . .

witnesses: John Freeman.
his mark.
Richard Woodin.
ffrancis Harlowin.

Edward Outlaw & Seal.

JAMES M A C MORRIN, Minister of Eliz abeth River Parish in Norfolk County . . .

Book 9 p. 361.

dated, 18 Oct. 1714.

proved, 17 Dec. 1714, by Thomas Scott & James Toomoth & on Motion of Capt. Wm Craford . . . recorded.

. . . appoint Capt. William Craford of Norfolk County and Mr. James Tennant of princis Anne County Minister to be my Sole Executors . . .

. . . my Said Exec^{rs} doe their utmost Indeaviour to Sell and Dispose of all my Estate of what Nature or Kind Soever it be of for bills of Exchange and to Remit the Same to Mr William Robinson Merchant old Jury London

. . . and what the Said Robison Shall Receive from my Executors to pay the Same unto Mr John Nabb and Eliz abeth his wife Living at Antrim in the North of Ireland . . .

witnesses: Tho: Scott.
James Toomoth.
Samp^m Power.

James McMoran & Seal

DANIELL GOREING . . .

Book 9 p. 382.

dated, 27 Dec. 1714.

proved, 19 March 1714/15, by William Langley Junr & Mr. Arthur Blake.

. . . my Son in Law Patrick fflan ag in my hole . . . Executor . .

. . . my Lands and Tenaments that I Shall be possesed with at the time of my Deciase be Sould by my aforesd Executor . . .

. . . to James Cordon the Son of Patric Cordon one Small Gunn . . .

witnesses: Arthur Blake.
Patrick Guy.
his mark.
William Langley.

Daniell Goreing & Seal.

ALEXANDER BALLINGTINE, of the Southern branch of the County of Norfolk . . .

Book 9 p. 389.

dated, 14 Jan. 1714/15.

proved, 20 May 1715.

. . . unto my Son George Ballin tine my house and plantation and all the woodland and ground belonging' to that
Devident.

. . . to my Son Alexander Ballingtine one hundred acres
of Land being the remaining part of that tract I bought
of my brother George and Known by the name of the
Wood & Pitt Ridge—

. . . unto my Son Wallis Ballentine one hundred acres of
Land being the remaining part of that tract I bought of
my brother George & Joyning with his brother Alexander and this is my will alsoe that I doe give these parcells
of Lands above mentioned to my three Sons george Alexander & Wallis and this is the true meaning of my will
that I doe give it to them & to there heirs for Ever
Lawfully begotten of their own body and neither of them
Shall make any Saile or Convey ance of Either of there
part or parts Except it is to one of there own brothers
and it Should please God that any of them Shall Dye without Such heirs his part to fall to my Son James Ballintine
and in Case that more than one should Die without
Such then his part to fall to my Son Henry Ballintine
and Soe it shall run from Generation to Generation—

. . . to my two Sons James and Henry Ballintine to Each
of them one young cow . . . when they shall come
to the age of one & Twenty—

. . . unto my Daughter Anne Ballintine one young Cow

. . . wife Margarett Ballintine my Sole Executrix . . .

witnesses: Richard Wallis.
   John Wallis.
   Edward Daviss.

         Alexander Ballintine.
            his marke.

SAMUELL ROBERTS Sen'r . . .

Book 9 p. 402.

dated 30 Mch. 1714.

proved 17 June 1715, by Anne Wilder & Charles Wood.

. . . unto my Son Sam^{ll} Roberts thirty pounds in money

. . . unto my Son Joseph Roberts a Negro woman . . .

. . . unto my Son Benjamine Roberts thirty pounds in
money . . .

. . . unto my Son Sam^{ll} Roberts all my' Lands in the Gunn
Grave Neck to Poplar branch belowe runing north to the
miles End according to the pattent of my Land.

. . . unto my Son Joseph Roberts the land which was formerly William Phillips begining for breadth at the north
branch of moles point and Soe Runing to the north branch
of the Hill neck then Runing Easterly to the miles End
according to my pattent.

. . . unto my Son Benjamine Roberts all the remaining
part of my Land not already given . . .

. . . unto my grand Daughter Elizabeth warding my Large
Trunk . . .

. . . unto my grand Son Lemuell warding thirty pounds in
money & In case he Shauld Dye in his none age then my
will is that his brother James Warding Shauld Enjoy &
. . . in case he Shauld Dye in his none age then to his
brother Samuell Warding.

. . . Sons Samuell & Joseph Roberts . . . Sole Exec^{rs}
. . .

witnesses: Henry Chapman.

Anne Wilder.

Charles Woods.
his mark.

Samuell Roberts & Seale.

JOHN PORTLOCK Sen'r . . .

Book 9 p. 434.

dated 15 June 1715.

proved 21 Oct. 1715, by Mr Thos Nash & Rebecka Martin . . .
on motion of Elizabeth Portlock . . . Recorded.

proved 16 Mch. 1715, by Wm Lowery.

. . . unto my Son John Portlock all & Every part & parcell
of that tract or Devident of Land I now Live upon . . .
onely my true & well Loveing wife Elizabeth Portlock
to have her Naturall Life upon the manner Plantation
without any Interruption.

. . . unto my Sons William & Paull Portlock all & Every
part & percell of that tract or Devident of Land which
took up & Patent myselfe to them Two Sons . . .

Equally to be Devided between them the Same being three hundred & five acres.

. . . all my books to be Equally Devided between my Seven Sons & my Two Daughters Lidia & Elizabeth . . .

. . . my four Sons (viz.) Charles Edward Petter & Lemuell . . .

. . . wife Elizabeth Portlock . . . Sole Exec^r . . .

witnesses: William Lowry.

Rebecka Martin.
her mark.

Thos Nash, Senr.

WILLIAM POWELL . . .

Book 9 p. 457.

dated 23 Oct. 1701.

proved 21 Jan. 1715, by Mary Cottle & Robert Spring.

. . . unto my Son William Powell Two hundred acres of Land that was Given me by my Grand father with all my *Seed* beside with E*ntreys* . . . Except 95 acres of Land that I Took up in a place Called the Short necks that I Give unto my Daughter Ellenner . . . and if Either of Them Dies without heirs then to Returne to the Survivor and if they both Die without Issue then to returne to Lemuell Powell my brother Johns Son and if he Dies without Issue then to the next heir at Law.

. . . all the rest of my Estate doe I give unto my well beloved wife Ann Powell and with all Doe make her my hole & Sole Executrix . . .

. . . my Children . . . there mothers widowhood . . .

witnesses: Robert Spring, his mark.

Aron Spring, his mark.

Mary Cottle, her mark.

William Powell & Seale.

WILLIAM DALE, of the westerne Branch of Elizabeth River Parish in Norfolk County in Virginia marriner . .

Book 9 p. 460.

dated 29 Oct. 1715.

proved 17 Feb. 1715.

. . . make my Loveing wife Dinah Dale . . . Sole Exec^r . . . in Case of her marrying &c: my will is that my brother in Law Thomas Herbert in ye Southerne branch in the Same County Marriner Should . . . be my oveseer & manager of this my will . . .

. . . to my Son Richard Dale the part of the Land that I Live on It being Divided by a Line of marked Trees the Swamp Land that belongs to it I Give Between him my Son Richard and my Son William Dale (the Said part of my plantation to my Son Richard Dale is to be the part where my Dwelling house Stands on . . .

. . . to my Son William Dale the other part of the plantation or tract of Land where I now Live on that is to Say the part at the other Side of the Line which Runs a Cross my Land which Said Line of trees I made a Cross for a Divission between These my Two Sons Richard and William that is between there parts of the Land . . . the Swamp to be Equall between them; and as before Richard to have . where my Dwelling house Stands that the part on the River side the Line) and my Son William to have the part on the other Side the Line of marked Trees which I made for the Said Divison between them my two Sons as aforesaid Richard & William the Said part of Land Joyning to my Son Richards part aforesaid to my Said Son William Dale . . .

. . . my will is that when my Son Richard Dale Shall attaine to the full age of one and Twenty years that if he my Said Son Richard Dale Shall & Doe well & Truely make and Give a *such* conveyance or deed as Shall or may by Law be good & firme of a Certaine tract of Land Lying on the other Side of the North west River Given to him by his Grandfather Dale to my Son William Dale . . . and putt him in Quiett possession . . . then my De- sire is that my Son William make the Same Title of the part of the plantation that I now Live on and have before given him) the Same I Say *I Say* I Desire that with the provisors before mentioned that he Give to my Son Richard (and then Richard will have all this Land where I Live on and William will have the Land on the other Side the northwest River as aforesaid.

. . . to my Son Richard . . . my Indian man Named Arthur . . .

. . . to my Son William . . . my Gould ring and my Small Kaine . . . when . . . twenty . . .

. . . to my Son Daniell Dale . . . a parcell of Land and priviledge which my father in Law Gave me for Sixty years . . .

. . . unto my three Children Petter Paule & Prudence my three Silver Spoons . . .

. . . my Executrix Shauld ffinish the Sloop that I am now abuilding . . .

. . . if my wife Doe mary . . . Son Richard Should be my Executor . . .

. . . if Either of my three Sons Richard William or Daniell Should Die before they come to age . . . to Petter . . . to my next Son Paule . . . To my Daughter Prudence I mean my Sone Petter & Paule . . .

witnesses: Robert Culpeper.
    Edward Lewelling.
    John Williams
         Wm Dale & Seale.

SAMUELL PAINE, Late of North Carolina . . .

Book 9 p. 462.

dated 17 Jan. 1715.

proved 17 Feb. 1715.

. . . to my Loving frind John McKenny Twenty Two barrells of Pitch now Lying in the hands of Capt John Hausted in Nansemund.

. . . at the northwest Landing . . .

. . . to John McKenny Son of John McKenny one young horse which I bought of William Russell . . .

. . . to Rachell Daughter of John McKenny one Large Pewter Bason to be Delivered by my Exec^r in North Carolina.

. . . to James and John Carson Six hundred & fourty acres of Land Lying in Bay County in North Carolina to be Equally Divided . . . to George Carroon Six hundred and fourty acres of Land . . . lying by Indian Island . . .

. . . to George Carroon all the remainder part of my Estate
. . . both Reall and personall . . .

. . . appoint James & John Carroon my Exec^{rs} . . . in
North Carolina and my frind John MacKenny my Exec^r
in Virginia . . .

witnesses: Thomas Critcher.
Kath^a Jones.
James Toomothy.

Sen Pane & Seale.
Sa^{ll} Pane.

JOHN HOLLOWELL, of the County of Norfolk in the Collony of Virginia . . .

Book 9 p. 498.

dated 15 "March" 1716.

proved 18 May 1716, by James Cumming & John Prescot.

. . . to my Loveing wife Mary Hollowell my Gray horse &
Side Sadle . . .

. . . to my Son Joseph Hollowell my Negro boy Sam
. . . at the age of Twenty . . . and in Case my
Son Joseph Should Die without Lawfull Issue . . .
to my Daughter Courtney Hollowell . . .

. . . unto my Daughter Mary Hollowell my Negro Girle
. . . at the age of Eighteen . . . Mary Die without Lawfull Issue . . . to my Daughter Sarah.

. . . wife Sole Exec^r . . .

witrnesses: Sol^o Wilson.
James Cumming.
John Prescot.

Jno Hollowell and Seale.

(Codicil).

. . . to my brother Luke my Druget Suite of Cloths & my
Blew Riding Coat.

witnesses: Sol^o Wilson.
James Cumming.
John Prescot.

John Hollowell & Seale.

DANIEL GODFREY, of Norfolk County in Virginia . . .
Book 9 p. 539.
dated 1 Feb. 1714/15.
proved 19 Oct. 1716, by Thomas & John Simons & John Barney.

. . . to my Daughter Abigall one Gold ring . . .

. . . to my Son Daniell Godfrey one pare of Silver Shoe buckles & one Musket . . .

. . . to my Son Warren Godfrey all my working Tools Coopers & Carpenters . . .

. . . what Land I possess in Norfolk Town to my Son Warren Godfrey & one Neck of Land called & Known by the name of brushy neck . . .

. . . to my brother Warren Godfrey one Coate one hatt . . .

. . . to my Loveing wife Leale Godfrey all the Remainder of my worldly Estate . . . for the maintainance of my Two Sons Daniell & Warren Godfrey untill they Shall attaine the age of Sixteen.

. . . my brother Petter Godfrey . . . Sole Exec.

witnesses : Thomas Simons.
        Jn⁰ Simons.
        Jn⁰ Barney.
        Jaˢ Toomoth.

                    Daniell Godfrey & Seale.

(Codicil).

dated 3 Feb. 1714.

witnesses : Thomas Simons.
        Jn⁰ Simons.
        Jn⁰ Barney.

                    Daniell Godfrey & Seale.

JOSIAS MAC KIE, of Norfolk County Minister . . .
Book 9 p. 540.
dated 7 Nov. 1716.
proved 16 Nov. 1716, by Thomas Butt Senʳ & Thomas Butt Junʳ

. . . unto Elizabeth Wishard and John Wishard Sonn & Daughter of James and Mary Wishard tenn pounds in money . . .

. . . unto William and Mary Johnson Children of Jacob Johnson Deceas^d and Margaritt Tenn pounds in money . . . the said Johnsons when they Come of age . . .

. . . unto the Severall Children now Liveing of my three Sisters Mary Margarett, & Rebecca, Daughters of Mr Patrick MacKie Some time of St Johnstone in the county of Donigall of the Kingdom of Ireland all the remaining part of my money which is in Ready Cash in virginia . . . transmitted home by my Exec^{rs} . . . in bills of Exchange . . . by them Direct to Such person or persons as they think Best in the City of London and from thence to Mr John Harvey of London Derry Merch^t and by him transmitted to the Children of the persons above Named; alsoe I Give to the Severall Children of the Said Mary, Margaret, & Rebecca fourteen pounds four Shillings & Eight pence Sterling Due from Mr William Squire & Petter Hall Merchants in Liver Poole alsoe all the money Due to me by a just account from Mr William Bowden Merchant in London . . .

. . . to John Sherly Senr one hundred & fifty acres of Land Lying & being in princess Ann County near the back Bay being the Remainder of a tract of Land Purchased of Capt ffrancis Morse . . .

. . . my more Schoolastic Books of the Learned Languages as Lattin Greek and Hebrew to be Equally Divided Between Mr Henry. Mr Mampton & Mr MacKness nonconforming Ministers at Poakomoake or thereabouts . . .

. . . will and Ordain that my Exec^{rs} well & truly observe the paper of Directions by me Left under my owne hand Relating to the Disposall of the remainder of my Books not before Disposed of as alsoe Concerning Lesser Legacys and Debts . . .

. . . unto John Sharley Senr all Such Sums . . . Indebted . . .

. . . unto Capt. Horatia Woodhouse two Mares out of my Stock at the Sea Side . . .

. . . unto Thomas Butt & Elizabeth Butt Children of Mr Richd Butt two mares . . .

. . . to Mary Cocke Daughter of Christopher Cocke one young mare . . .

. . . to Henry Butt Son of Mr. Richard Butt one young mare.

. . . unto Thomas Butt Son of Thomas Butt Dec^d two young mares . . . my Riding horse Bridle & Sadle alsoe one Silk Damask vest . . . mare I had from Mr Lewis Conner . . .

. . . unto Mr Richard Butt Senr my Greate Riding Coate with Twenty yards of Brown Lining that is in the Chest of Goods.

. . . unto Mrs Martha Thruston a piece of black flowered Damask being the Same She fformerly gave me.

. . . my English good Books . . .

. . . appoint my frinds Cor^ll Edward Moseley & Mrs Martha Thruston to be my Exec^rs in trust . . .

witnesses: Sarah Butt.

Natha^ll Butt.

Thos Butt.

Thos Butt, Junr.

Josias MacKie & Seale.

ROGER HODGIS, Late of Norfolk County and in the Collony of Virginia . . .

Book 9 p. 541.

dated 18 Aug. 1716.

proved 16 Nov. 1716, by Richard Hodgis & further

proved 21 Dec. 1716, by Wm Wilkins.

. . . wife Mary Hodgis . . . hole Exec^r . . .

. . . my Son William Hodgis my Dwelling plantation with one hundred acres of Land belonging to it . . . my Son Roger Hodgis one Gun & one hundred acres of Land . . . my Son Edward Hodgis one hundred acres of Land . . . Joyning to his brother Roger . . . my Son Caleb Hodgis fifty acres of Land Joyning to Roger & Edward his brother . . .

. . . my Daughter Mary one Cow . . . my Daughter Abigall one Cow . . . my Daughter Dinah one heifer . . . my Daughter Anne one heifer . . . when

they come to the age of fourteen . . . my Sons to be
at full age when they Come to the years of Sixteen
. . .

witnesses: Sa^{ll} Reausher.

Richard Hodgis.

William Wilkins Junr.

Rogger Hodges & Seale.

HENRY DEALL Senr of Elizabeth River in Norfolk County
Book 9 p. 569.

dated 21 Oct. 1716.

proved 18. Jan. 1716.

. . . ffrances Deal my wife to be my Sole Executrix . . .
. . . to my wife ffrances Deall the plantation She now
    Liveth upon onely the part of the plantation now Called
    Henrys the which part I have heretofore sold him, butt for
    my wife ffrances Deale . . . Soe Long as She Re-
    mains Widdow and the aforesaid Henry Deall Junr after
    my Decease to have and to hold that part of the plantation
    called Henrys . . . but if he Dies without heir then
    to return to my Son John Deall . . . that is the Plan-
    tation I Live upon, and the plantation I bought of Roger
    Hodges Butt if ye heirs Dye without Issue then . . .
    to my Daughter Dinah, and afterwards to my Son Thomas
    Harbert, and after my Son Adam Comes to ye Age of
    Eighteen years then for my Son Henry Deall to pay or
    Cause to be paid to my Son Adam Deal one thousand
    weight of Tobaco, butt if he Dies before he comes to
    the aforesaid age then . . . to be paid to my Sonn
    David according as their Trustees *thin getts* for there
    use in Schooling . . .
. . . to my Son John Deale and Richard Deale my Carpin-
    ters Tools . . .
. . . to my Son John Deale my trumpet muskit Gunn
. . . to my Daughter ffrances Deale one hundred acres of
    Land which is the remaining part of the Land Lying
    out heirs then to return to the Successive heirs & Soe
    from heir to heir.
. . . to my son Richard Deale the Land Lying at the head of
    Deep Creek bounded betwixt the Two runs . . . but

if he Dyes without heirs then to goe from heir to heir Sucksessively . . .

. . . to my Sone Thomas Deale the Trydall Ridge with one acres of Land adjoyning to it . . . butt if he Dies without heirs then to return to the Successive heirs or heir.

. . . to my Two Sones and Two Daughters David Deale Adam Deale Elizabeth Deale and Margaret Deal all the remaining part of the Land adjoyning to William Deall Lying up on the head of Deep Creek . . . butt if they Die without Issue then to goe ffrom heir to heir Successively.

. . . to my Grandson Henry Harbert all the remaining part of the Land belonging to me adjoyning up on William Clogstons & John Barrington to him and his heirs for Ever butt if he Dyes without heir then to Returne to the Successive heirs as formerly.

. . . to appoint Thomas Herbert after my wifes Decease or at her marriage to be Sole Trustee to See my Estate Equally Disposed according to my will . . .

witnesses : Samuell Moore.

  Edward Effluellin.

    his

  Samull Porter.

    marke.

        the mark of

          Henry Deale.

JOHN MANING Senr of the Southern branch of Elizabeth River Parrish in the County of Norfolk . . .

Book 9 p. 570.

dated 22 July 1715.

proved 18 Jan. 1716.

. . . my Loveing wife Sarah Maning and my Loveing Son Joseph Maning Exec^{rs} . . .

. . . to my Loveing Son John Maning the plantation whereon he now Liveth . . . with the woodland Ground thereunto appertaining the Same being bounded betwixt Two banks begining at the head of a gutt Soe runing from the Said up a Line of Marked Trees to the head Line Same being Compossission one hundred acres more or less.

. . . To my Loveing Son Joseph Maning after the Decease of Sarah my wife the plantation whereon I now Live . . . the Same being bounded (viz) begining and Runing from the head of the Gutt that my Son John Maning beginning *as* runing up the Said Line to the head Line and Soe bound Round by Line of Marked Trees to the begining: the head of the said Gutt Containing one hundred acres more or less . . .

upon the North west River . . . butt if She Dies with-. . . my Son Joseph Maning . . . his mother . . . my wife . . .

. . . to my Loveing Son William Maning the plantation whereon he now Lives . . . the Same being by Estimation Sixty acres more or less as it is bounded round by a Creek and a Line of marked Trees . . . he my Said Son William . . . Shall or may have a ffree outlett for his or there *Cre*tures without any Step Barr or hindrance.

. . . to my Loveing Son Thomas Manning a Certain tract & Dividen*d* of Lands of ffourty acres more or less bound round by a Creek and a Line of Marked trees . . . Joyning to my Son Williams Land . . .

. . . all my Children . . .

witnesses: John Manning Jun[r].

Joseph Hodgis.

John Willis.

John Maning & S——.

JOSEPH MEENS Sen[r] of the westerne branch in Elizabeth Parrish in Norfolk County Planter . . .

Book 9 p. 572.

dated 4 Apr. 1716.

proved 15 Feb. 1716, by Aron Roods & John Willis & upon motion of Sarah Meens the Exec[r]x. admitted to Record.

. . . to my Son John Meens my plantation and all my Lands it being the Lands on which I now Live on . . . and if my Son John Dye without Such heirs that then the Intale to be Clear and that the Lands Shall fall to my Son Joseph . . .

. . . wife Sarah Meens . . . Sole Executrix . . .
. . . my three Daughters Sarah Webb Mary Cristal and
Joana Givin one shilling a piece . . .

witnesses: Aaron Roods.

        William Walker.

        John Willis.

                    Joseph Meens Senr & Seale.

WILLIAM ETHERIDGE the Elder of the Southerne branch
of Elizabeth River Parish in the county of Norfolk in
virginia . . .

Book 9 p. 572.

dated 30 Oct. 1715.

proved 15 Feb. 1716, by Wm Portlock Paull Portlock and John
Phillips.   Motion of Exec^rx. admitted to record.

. . . my Loveing wife Anness Etheredge Exec^rx and my
Loveing frind Thomas Nash Senr Exec^r . . .
. . . unto my Son William Etheredge . . . one Shilling
. . . having given unto him before in the Life time by
Deed of Gift . . . his full part and portion of Land
. . . full of his filliall portion . . .
. . . unto my grandson Willis Etheredge Son of my Son
Charles Etheredge Seventy five acres of Land it being
the Same whare his Deceased father Charles Etheredge
Lived . . . to have and Enjoy the Same after the
Decease of his mother Ann widdow . . . when he
Comes to the age of Twenty one years.
. . . my grandson Charles Etheridge Son of Charles Etheridge Seventy five acres of Land . . . Leing between
his brother Willis his Land and my Son Amoss Etheredge
his Land . . . at the age of Twenty one . . .
butt if Either of my Said Grandsons will have aimed to
Dispose of There part . . . to Lett his brother have
the Same and noe other person or persons whatsoever
butt to be Entailed to the byer of the Two brothers . . .
. . . unto my Son Amoss Etheredge after the Decease of
Aness my wife one hundred acres of Land it being the
plantation with the woodland ground thereunto belonging

whereon I now Live according as it is Laid out by Lines
of marked Trees . . .

. . . unto my Son Thomas Etheredge Seventy five acres of
Land be it more or Less the Same being one Moiety or
halfe part of my Devident of Land of one hundred and
fifty acres of Land which I bought of Joseph Miller
Lying and being on a Creek Called by the name of Little
Creek . . . his part being that which he now Lives
on . . .

. . . unto my Son Adam Etheredge Seventy five acres of
Land as it is Laid out and bounded by a Line of marked
trees it being the other Moiety or halfe part of the hundred
and fifty acres of Land that I bought & purchased of
Joseph Miller Lying on the North Side of the Said Little
Creek . . . Joyning to my Son Thomas Etheredge
his Land on the North Side thereof which Said Land is
already by a Line of Marked trees from my Son Thomas
his Land . . . butt if Either my Two Sons Thomas
and Adam Etheredge them there heirs Should Chance to
Die without Issue Either male or female then the Surviving his or his heirs of the Said brothers . . . to
have and Injoy the other Land . . . but and if my
Two Sons Thomas and Adam Etheredge them & their
heirs Should hapen to Die without heirs then in Such Case
there Lands to fall & Decend to my Daughter Grace
Etheredge . . . butt and if my Daughter Grece Etheredge her heirs Should alsoe Die without heirs . . .
as well as the Two brothers then there Lands to fall and
Decend to my Son Amoss Etheredge and my Grand Sons
Willis and Charles Etheredge, butt and if it Should Soe
please god that my three Sons Thomas Amoss & Adam
and my Two grandsons willis and Charles Etheredge and
my Daughter Grace then & there heirs Should all Die
without heirs . . . then in Such Case there Lands
to fall & Decend as followeth Amoss Willis & Charles
Etheredge them there heirs these Lands to fall & Decend
unto my Grand Daughter Judith wife of Richard Wallis
. . . and my Sons Thomas and Adam Etheredge there
Lands to fall and Decend unto my Grand Daughter Dar-
cuss Nash . . .

. . . wife Annis Etheredge . . .

. . . the *use* plantation before named and after her Decease
to be Equally Devided betwixt my three Daughters Elizabeth Portlock Ann Nash & Grace Etheredge . . . butt

if my Daughter grace Die without heirs then her part to
be Divided between her Two sisters . . .

witnesses: John Portlock.

Wm Portlock.

James Mohune.

his
John Phillips
mark.

William Etheridge & Seale.

AGNESS HANLAND of Norfolk county widdow . . .

Book 9 p. 574.

dated 4 Sep. 1716.

proved 19 Apr. 1717, by John Barnes & Isaac Barington.

. . . unto my Son William Mille all my Lands which Doth
Any way belong to me as well out of possession as in
possession . . .
. . . unto my Son Hew Hanlan two Shilling & Sixpence
Sterling infull of all his portion.
. . . unto my Son in Law William Miller all the rest of my
Estate . . .
. . . Son in Law William Miler . . . Sole Executor
. . .

witnesses: Thos Corprew.

John Barns.
his   Her
Isaac Barington   Agness Hanlan & Seale
mark.   mark.

JOHN JOLLOFF . . .

Book 9 p. 575.

dated 28 Nov. 1716.

proved 19 Apr. 1717.

. . . to my Son Joseph Jolloff my Land being Two hundred
& Sixty Seven acres . . . being by Pattent Dated

the Twentieth Day of Aprill in the year one thousand Six hundred & Eighty Two   .   .   .

.   .   . to my Son Joseph and to John Bacon my Mill and all that Doth belong to her   .   .   .

.   .   . to my Son John my Long Gun   .   .   .

.   .   . to my Son Johns Daughter Mary one bed   .   .   .

.   .   . to my Son Thomas one Eight Gun   .   .   .

.   .   . to my Son Peter one Ben mettle pott   .   .   .

.   .   . to my Dafter Sarah one brass Skillit   .   .   .

.   .   . to my Dafter Mary one Large Dish   .   .   .

.   .   . my Son Joseph to be my Executor   .   .   .

witnesses: John Ives.

        Edward Wingitt
           his mark.

        Samuel Wingitt
           his mark.

                            John Jolloff & Seale.

HENRY LOE of the county of Norfolk in virg[a]   .   .   .

Book 9 p. 588.

dated 31 Dec. 1713.

proved 17 May 1717, by Thomas Scot & John Norcot.

.   .   . to my Eldest Son Henry Loe the Land that I had of Capt. W[m] Craford and part of my Tother Land bought of Thomas Scot begining at a Spannish Oake and ruuing Sout west to the hed Line to be Laid out by M[r] W[m] Rustin and Richard Ballintine & Thomas Scot as they Shall think ffitting   .   .   .

.   .   . to my Son Petter Loe the houss and the rest of the Land not Given to my Son Henry Loe that I now   .   .   .

.   .   . wife Sarey Loe my true ad Lawfull Exec[rs]   .   .   .

witnesses: Georg Boush
           his mark.

        John Norkitt
           his mark.

        Tho: Scott.   his
                          Henry Loe and Seale.
                          marke.

PATRICK CORDON now resident in the County of norfolk   .   .   .

Book 9 p. 590.

dated 14 May 1716.

proved 17 May 1717, by James Marley & John Barney.

   .   .   . my wife ffrances Cordun Shall   .   .   . injoy my
      after her Decease   .   .   . unto my Daughter Sarah Cor-
      dun   .   .   .
      my Son James Cordon and if in Case the Said James Cor-
      to the age of Sixteen and that Mr Martha Thruston and
      Mr Richard Cheshire To bind him out to Some trade
      .   .   .
   .   .   . my wife ffrances Cordun Shall   .   .   . injoy my
      D'welling house and the third of my Land and orchard
      Dureing her Naturall Life and after her Decease then to
      my Son James Cordon and if in Case the Said James Cor-
      dun Should Dye before he arrives at   .   .   . Twenty
      one years then to my Daughter Jane Cordun: if She Die
      then to the next Youngest and if the before mentioned
      Should Die then the Said Land to be Sould and To be
      Equally Devided amongst the rest ;   .   .   .
   .   .   . wife ffances Cordun and my ffrind Mr Richard Cheshire
      .   .   . Sole Exec^rx & Exec^rs   .   .   .

witnesses : the mark of
      James Marley.
      John Barney.   the mark of
      Anne Marley.   Patrick Cordon & Seale.

MATHEW GODFREY   .   .   .

Book 9 p. 591.

dated 13 Mch. 1715/6.

proved 17 May 1717.

   .   .   . to my Cusen Mathew Godfrey the son of my brother
      John Godfrey my Negro man Called Tom Butt my wife
      to have the use and work of the said Negro Dureing her
      Naturall Life   .   .   .
   .   .   . to my Cosen Joseph Perry all my Land in Corotuck
      Bay Called the Raged Ilands and alsoe my part of the
      Ceader Island   .   .   .

. . . to my Cusen Thomas Perry one Cow . . . on Seader Island . . .

. . . my Cattle that I shall have in Corrotuck . . . Devided among my Sister Jacksons Children . . .

. . . my Cusen William Godfrey and Anne Tatum and A*mee* hutchings Each of them Tenn Shillings a piece to make Each of them a ring . . .

. . . my Cusen Randle Thomas George and James Egerton Tenn Shillings a piece to Each of them To make them a ring . . .

. . . to my Cusen Arthur Godfrey the Son of my Cusen John Godfrey Deceased all that part of Land that I bought of the Sikes at yᵉ Great Bridge in the Southern branch of Elizabeth River all which part is to be noe more butt from the foot of the great Bridge on the Easterd Side of the Road or highway that goeth into the woods a Longst the Said Road or highway untill it Comes to the South End of Mʳ Willis Wilsons now Store house that was given him by his father Corⁿ James Wilson & from thence Easterly untill he Comes to a gutt or Creek in a Marsh and Soe a Longst the Said Gutt or Creek untill he Comes to the foot of the Said bridge where it first begins . . . and for want of Such heirs then to Come To the nearest male kindred of Blood to me the first giver . . . from Jeneration to Jeneration Successifty . . .

. . . to the Said Arthur Godfrey my negro . . . when he comes to age of Twenty one . . .

. . . my Great Sloop called the America . . . The Sloop that I have begun to build at the Quarter near the North river in Norfolk County . . .

. . . to my Cosen Matthew Godfrey the Son of my brother War—(torn)—all my part of that Land that I bought of Mʳ Even Jones that is near the nor—(torn)—in in Norfolk County . . . and to the meale heirs of his body . . . in case of of want of Such *hyrs* then to the next male heirs that Shall Bear the name of Godfrey that shall be nearest of kinn by Blood to me the first giver . . . to Come to Generation Successifly as Long as there is any Live that is of kinn by Blood and that shall Bear the name of Godfrey . . .

. . . alsoe give unto the Said Mathew Godfrey all that part of Land that I bought of the Sikes that is at the Great Bridge which Said Part is to begin at a Gutt or Creek by the Bridge Side that goeth to the norwest River and from thence Northerly a Long the road Side the it comes to the north End of a Storehouse that is building now by

Michall vestary and Stands near the Road that goeth from the Said Gutt or Creek Towards the Great Bridge and from the north End of the Said Storehouse Easterly to a marsh and Soe Sotherly alongst and through the marsh to the first begining Gutt or Creek . . . with the Same intailement as the above said Land near the north river is given unto him . . .

. . . to the Said Mathew Godfrey my Negro Toney . . . when he comes to age . . . alsoe . . . my Negro Girle Febby . . . butt if the Said Mathew Should Dye without heirs . . . to be Devided between Petter Reoldalphus and John Malbone and Malbone Simons . . .

. . . I further give to my Cosen Mathew Godfrey the Son of my Brother Warren Godfrey . . . fourty foot of Square Land in Norfolk Town which Said Land is to be out of that Land I bought of Joseph Church one that End towards Mr Powers his Land . . .

. . . to my Cusen Arthur Godfrey the house in Norfolk Town that I bought of Mr Joseph Church and all the Land that it Stands one and alsoe to have the Same bredth of Land as the house is in Length halfe way of the Said Land alongst the Street Easterly . . .

. . . to my Son in Law James Wilson thirty foot of Land out of that Lot that I bought of Joseph Church in Norfolk Town which Said thirty foot is to begin at the Easterd End of the said Land by the Street and to be thirty foot Square . . . and all the remaining part of the Said Land that is not already Given . . . to be Equally Devided Between my brother Warren and my brother John there male Children Liveing at my Death . . .

. . . Gold Rings . . . to the above sd. Arthur and Mathew Godfrey . . .

. . . Desire that what marsh and Sunken Ground that doeth belong to the Land at the bridge that is not given may be Equally Devided to the above said Arthur and Mathew Godfrey . . .

. . . Desire that what marsh and Sunken Ground that doeth belong to the Land at the bridge that is not given may be Equally Devided to the above said Arthur and Mathew Godfrey . . .

. . . to Elizabeth Murphee tenn Shillings . . .

. . . to Mr Josias Mackie Tenn pounds of good passable Silver money . . .

. . . to my Son in Law James Wilson fifty foot of Square Land out of that Land that I bought of the Sikes at the great Bridge the which Said fifty foot of Square Land is to begin at the Six foot of the South End of Mr Willis Wilson his now storehouse that was given him by his father . . . and Soe along the road that goeth towards the northwest River and Towards the house that the Smith Mr Norris Did work in and Soe fifty foot Easterly & fifty foot northerly and fifty foot westerly to the first beginning . . . & if want of such heirs then to come to the nearest of kin by Blood to me the first given . . . twenty Shillings in money to make him a ring . . .

. . . to my boy Thomas Wright thirty foot of Land that I have in Norfolk Town near the Church which Said Lott of Land the Said boys father Did formerly Give me the which Said thirty foot of Land is to begin at the northward End of the Said Land next the road or Street and Soe thirty foot alongst the road or Street that goes into the Town and from thence Easterly Clear through the said Lott of Land & Soe northerly and westerly along the Courses of the Said Land to the first begining . . . and further . . . Two thousand pounds of Good Tobacco . . . when he comes to age . . .

. . . to the Poor of Norfolk County one hundred acres of Land or thereaboutt that I have Joyning upon that Land the Did formerly belong to the *tipp*ins or Egertons and alsoe Joyning upon Gevins and Jacksons which Said Land was former bought of Mr Wm Porten by my brother John Godfrey & my Selfe & this Said hundred acres of Land being my Part I Doe freely give to the Poore of Norfolk County for Ever and Ever . . .

. . . unto Petter Malbone John Malbone Reodalphus Malbone and Malbone Simons and Arthur godfrey all my English goods or treading Stock that shall be in my Store at my Plantacon near the north river in norfolk County . . .

. . . to Mathew Malbone the Son of Petter Malbone all my Cattle all my Cattle that I may have in the north river woods . . . near the plantacon that is now Richard Stones . . .

. . . my Store at the Great Bridge . . .

. . . what Land I have at the Great bridge that is not given . . . to be Equally Devided between my brother Warren Meale Children and my brother Johns meale Children that Shall be Liveing at my Death . . .

. . . my Cusen Dina Godfrey the Dafter to my Cusen John Godfrey Deceased my Negro boy called Mingo . . .

. . . to my Cusen Warren Godfrey two Ews . . .

. . . wife Isabella Godfrey . . . my Executrix . . .

witnesses: John Corprew.

Robert Stewart.

Wm Roe.

Matthew Godfrey & Seale.

Proof: Jonathan Godfrey the heir at Law being Legally Sum-onesed and personally present in Court & on the motion of the said Exec^rx . . . admitted to record.

JOHN CARNEY of Norfolk County . . .

Book 9 p. 596.

dated 14 May 1717.

proved 21 June 1717.

. . . unto my Cousin William Carney one Gun: . . .

. . . unto my godson Hugh Gr——is two pewter plates

. .

. . . to Sarah Harris one Large Pewter Dish . . .

. . . unto my godson Hugh Tr——is two pewter plates

. .

. . . unto my Cousin Carney Wright . . . all my Land houses & Orchards in as full and ample manner as I have it my Selfe . . .

. . . wife Mary Carney . . . Sole Executor . . .

witnesses: Thos Wright.

John Harris.

Abigall Maning.

her

Elizabeth Harris

mark

his

John Carney & Seale.

mark

JOHN EDMUNDS . . .

Book 9 p. 597.

dated 26 Nov. 1705.

proved 21 June 1717, by James Berry.

motion of Sarah Edmunds is admitted to record.

. . . one halfe of my Land to my son Richard Edmons

. . . the other halfe of my Land unto my son Nathaniel Edmons . . . if Either of my Said Sons Depart this Life without Issue . . . then the Survivor Shall have all my Said Land . . .

. . . unto my Son John Edmunds halfe a Crown in full for his part of my Estate.

. . . wife Sarah Edmons . . . Sole Exec'x . . .

witnesses: John Portlock.

> her mark
> Ellenor Bigg.
> his mark
> James Berry.

John Edmonds & Seale.

SARAH HOLLOWELL wido of the aforesaid County of Norfolk . . .

Book 9 p. 609.

dated 19 July 1715.

proved 19 July 1717, by Thomas Scott.

. . . to my Loveing Son John Hollowell one hanging Glass shelfe . . .

. . . all the rest . . . To my Loveing Son Luke Hollowell . . .

. . . my Loveing Grandson William Rusill one mare . . . after he comes to the age of Twenty and one . . .

. . . to my Loveing Grand Children Joseph Mary and Elizabeth Russill one you a peace . . . after they come to age and to my Loveing Daughter Catern Russill all my warin Clothes . . .

. . . appoint . . . son afore Mentioned Luke Hollowell Exor . . .

witnesses: Tho. Scott.

Elizabeth Scott

> her
> Sarah Hollowell & Seale.
> Signe.

WILLIAM DAINS of Norfolk County . . .

Book 9 p. 628.

dated 11 Sept. 1714.

proved 20 Sept. 1717 by Lewis Conner & on motion of Mary
  Daines ordered to be recorded.

  21 Aug. 1719, by John Conner & Aron Oliver.

. . . to my Dear wife Mary Daines the plantacon I now
  Live on . . . Dureing her Naturall Life & after
  . . . the Same with all the rest of my Land to my
  Two Sons Henry Daines & ffrances Daines to be Equally
  Devided . . .

. . . to my Daughter Elizabeth Thomas one heifer . . .

. . . to my Two Sons Joseph & Richard Daines one pewter
  Dish Each . . .

. . . to my Son Thomas Dains all my wearing apperrell
  . . .

. . . to my Daughter Mary McWilliams one Ewe . . .

. . . to my Dear wife Mary Daines . . . Sole Exec'x
  . . .

witnesses : Lewis Conner.
          John Conner.
          Aron Oliver.

                          Will : Daines & Seale.

MICHALL WILDER of Norfolk County in Virg* . . .

Book 9 p. 666.

dated 13 Mch. 1716.

proved 21 Feb. 1717, by Ja* Toomoth & Jeremiah Wilder.

. . . to my Daughter Ann Marly my plantation . . .

. . . to my Daughters Ann Marly Sarah Wilder and Dinah
  Wilder Each of their proportionable part of Eighty three
  peces of pewter as Dishes basons plates Tankards flagons
  poringers Tumblers . . .

. . . to my son in Law James Marley my My Negro wench
  Called bess . . .

. . . my grand Daughter Abigall Godfrey . . . pewter
  . . .

. . . to my brother frances Wilder one Silver headed Cane
  . . .

. . . John & Edward Colly have Each of them one good
suite of Apparrell fitting for all partes of their body
. . .
. . . my daughter Dinah . . . Come to Age . . .
. . . my pistoles and holsters . . . my Sword & belt
. . . to my Son in Law James Marley . . .
. . . Son in Law James Marley and my Daughter Sarah
Wilder my Exec^r and Execrx . . .

witnesses: Jeremiah Wilder

Dinah Wilder.

Ja^s Toomoth.

Michall Wilder Seal.

THOMAS CRITCHER in Norfolk Towne . . . (nuncupative) . . .

Book 10 f. 3.

Recorded 22 Feb. 1717.

. . . his death did in the presence of wee the subscribers
. . .
. . . did give his wife Pheebe his bed hee layd upon . . .
. . . to his Eldest daughter Sarah the bed & furniture that
Stod in the Shop . . .
. . . to his Son John . . . bed . . .
. . . his youngest daughter Catherine . . .

Agnis Edwards.

Mary Edwards.

. . .

JOHN COOPER of Norfolk County in Virginia . . .

Book 10 f. 7.

dated 7 ———.

proved 18 Apr. 1718, by Wm Cooper Edwd Cooper & James
Toomoth.

. . . to my two Sons John and Solomon Cooper all my
Land in Gen^ll to be Equally Devided . . .
. . . ye plantation . . .

. . . to my Sonn Thomas Cooper one white mare . . .

. . . to my Son Abraham Cooper on hoss Colt . . .

. . . to my Daughter Amiah Cooper one black heifer . . .

. . . peter Godfrey my Son in Law . . . till they come to age . . .

. . . to my Daughter Abigall Godfrey one Large pewter Tankard . . .

. . . wife Naemy Cooper one feather bed . . .

. . . Estate of Thomas Crisp Dec^d . . .

. . . the two Daughters I have had by my sd. wife Naemy: one Ewe to Each . . .

. . . my four Sonns John Solomon Thomas and Abraham four Stears . . .

. . . my Son John and my Son Solomon . . . Sole Exect^{rs} . . .

witnesses: Wm. Cooper.
Wm. Cooper Ju^r.
Ew^d Cooper.
James Toomoth.

John Cooper and Seale.

ANDREW TAYLOR of Norfolk County . . .

Book 10 f. 10.

dated 13 Oct. 1716.

proved 16 May 1718.

. . . unto my grandsonn Wm Taylor ye plantation I now Live on being the one halfe of all my land . . . Like wise . . . ye Land which I Leased of Jno Tucker . . .

. . . unto my Grandson Thomas Taylor ye plantation Commonly Known by the Name of John Whitehalls being the other halfe of my Land . . .

. . . wife Ann Taylor . . .

. . . my two grand Children . . . if they boath Should Dye to ye next in age . . .

. . . my daughter Elizabeth and her Children . . .

. . . William Boulton and Sam¹ Porter Devide yᵉ Estate

. . . wife Ann Taylor . . . Sole Exetʳ . . .

witnesses: Robᵗ Spaing.

John Johnson.
mark.
ffrances Herlowin.

his
Andrew —(torn)—
m —(torn)—

WILLIAM LANGLY of Elizabeth River parish in yᵉ County of Norfolk Gentⁿ . . .

Book 10 f. 12.

dated 19 July 1715.

proved 16 May 1718, by Tho: Willoughby, James Thelaball, Golwin Oast Junʳ & John Langley.

. . . Son William Langley fifty Acres of Land joyning to yᵉ Land yᵗ he now Lives on it being *part* of a pattent of two hundred Acres of Land by pattent Taken up by my father it being yᵉ north End of yᵉ sd Land: run South for length to yᵉ main road and East for breadth along —(torn)—of yᵉ roade According to yᵉ bounds of yᵘ sd. Land . . .

. . . unto my Son Wllᵐ Langley . . . my Gunn marked W—(torn)—upon yᵉ barrall and my Great Chest and Chaire of black wallnutt . . .

. . . unto my son Nathan Langley a Aplantation wᵗʰ one hundred and fifty Acres of Land more or Less According to yᵉ bounds of yᵉ pattent Lying at yᵉ head of a branch of Tanners Creeke called yᵉ *Tucker* Town branch as by the pattent dooth Appeare . . . and fifty Eight Acres of land more wᶜʰ I Tooke up Joyning to it as by pattent doath Appeare in Swamp and Joyning to yᵉ Land of John Griffinn decad. yᵉ sd. two hundred and Eight Acres of land as by yᵉ pattents it will Appeare . . .

. . . unto my son James Langley . . . a peace of land lying up on yᵉ head of the Indian Creek of ye North west river containing two hundred Acres more or less Joyning to yᵉ land of Thomas Miller and on yᵉ East ward side of a grate *runn* called yᵉ beaver dam to begin at a pine tree by yᵉ dam a line tree of Millers Joyning to my land and soe

running up ye main runn of that old beaver dam to y^e
head of it and Soe Strait to out side line of my land and
Soe along ye sd. Line to ye corner tree y^t Joyne to Millers Land and *soe* along that line to ye bever dam aforesd to
a pine tree as may Appeare by Survey and by my deed
from Joeb Martin for ye sd. land being part of Six hundred Acres of Land as by ye deed may Appeare . . .

. . . unto my[i] Son Abraham Langley . . . two hundred Acres of land being part of Six hundred Acres
of land I bought of Joel Martin as may Appeare by y^e
deed ye sd. two hundred Acres of land to begin*us* by y^e
Swamp side upon that line that parts my cosen *Tim°*
Langleys Land and mine and Soe runing along that line
for length to ye head line and soe along ye head line for
breath of ye sd. two hundred Acres of land and soe by
a Strait corse down to a Swamp and soe to ye first beginning.

. . . unto my son Jacob Langley . . . all ye remainder of my land that I bought of Joell Martin containing
land that I have given to my son James Langley and
two Hundred Acres more or Less Lying between the
my Son Abraham Langleys land according to bounds as
may Appeare by ye deed and my Survey . . . negro
. . . Robin to him . . . when he comes to y^e
age of twenty one . . .

. . . unto my most Dutefull son Jeremiah Langley my
now dwelling plantation y^t I now live upon and all y^e
land belonging to it according to ye bounds of the pattent
containing five hundred acres more or less . . . to
my sd. son . . . one peace of land Adjoyning to y^e
sd aforesaid land given to him Containing one hundred
acres more or less according to ye bounds of ye pattent
Called by ye name of *horners* tree swamp y^u sd.
land I tooke up and pattented as may appeare by y^e
pattent ye sd. land . . . unto my sd. son . . . my
land and housing in Norfolk town . . . according to
ye bounds, thereof as may Appeare by ye deed and Survey
thereof . . . my great Coper still and worm & Tubb
thereunto belonging and my Great Pitch *Kettle* . . .

. . . to my daughter Marg^{tt} Johnson . . . negro girl
Cald by name bess . . . in full of her portion . . .

. . . unto Lem^l Thelabald who married wth my daughter
Joyce five pounds in money in full of her portion . . .

. . . unto George Ivy who married my daughter *Eliza-*
beth one Shilling in full of her portion . . .

. . . ye remainder of my Estate boath reale and personall

not here to fore given away . . . of what nature
or quality Soe Ever . . . to my aforesd. two sons
Jeremiah Langley & Jacob Langley . . . Share and
Share alike . . . these my two sons . . . sole
Exect^rs . . .

witnesses: Thomas Langley.
Ja mes Thellabali.
Thomas Willoughby.
Godwin Oast.
      his
James Guy.
      mark.
John *Denby*.

           Wm. Langley & Seal.

SAMUEL PORTER of the Southern branch in Norfolk
County . . .

Book 10 f. 14.

dated 7 July 1717.

proved 16 May 1718, by Richard Wallice & Richard Lluelen Senr.

. . . unto my Son Samuel Porter my plantation I now
live in wth orchard . . . and the wood land ground to
a branch runing out of *Cross* Creeke lying betweene my
lower plantation and uper plantation and Soe runing
aCross my land deviding it in ye middle . . .

. . . unto my Son William Porter my uper plantation w^th
ye woodland Ground above my Son Samuel Porters his
land Containing fifty acres . . .

. . . my Son Samuel Porter Shall pay unto my third Son
John Porter when he Shall Come to ye age of one and
Twenty the Sum of three pounds to be paid in tar . . .

. . . unto my Daughter Ann Porter one yearling heifer
. . .

. . . as for my three Elder daughters Elizabeth and Mary
and Amy they have had their portions at there mar-
idge . . .

. . . my wife . . .

witnesses: Richard Wallice.
Richard Lluelen.
Richard Lluelen Junr.

           Saml Porter & Seale.

THOMAS MERCER of the Southern branch of Eliz^a river in Norfolk County in Virgin^a . . .

Book 10 f. 17.

dated 16 Jan. 1718.

proved 16 May 1718, by William Wilkins.

. . . unto my Son Joseph Mercer one hundred & fifty acres of land be it more or less according to a deed of Guift I given him my Said Son Joseph & is recorded in the abovest County records . . .

. . . unto my Son Thomas Mercer one hundred and fifty acres of land be it more or less according to a deed of Guift I gave him . . . recorded in ye Records of the abovest County . . .

. . . unto my Son John Mercer one hundred and fifty acres of land be it more or less according to a deed of Guift Given by me to my Said Son . . . recorded in the abovest County Records . . .

. . . to my two Grand Sons Thomas Mercer & Joseph Mercer one hundred & fifty acres of Land to be Equally devided between them wch Said Land was givin before . . .

. . . unto my Grand Son Xopher Mercer Son to John Mercer one Gun . . .

. . . unto my Grandson William Mercer son to Joseph Mercer one Gun . . .

. . . to my Loving wife Catherine Mercer all the rest . . . during her Naturall life and tobe at her disposeing to whome Shee Shall give it or bequeath it as Shee Shall See fitt . .

. . . Son Joseph Mercer & my Son Thomas Mercer & my Son John Mercer . . . Sole Exec^{r}s . . .

witnesses: Wm Wilkins.

Joseph Mercer.

John Willis.

Thomas Mercer & Seale.

JAMES WILSON of Norfolk County Junr . . .

Book 10 f. 18.

dated 7 Apr. 1718.

proved 18 July 1718, by William Godfrey & on motion of Solo. Wilson . . . recorded.

19 Sept. 1718, by Jn° Hutchings.

. . . unto Richard Ball Senr four yards and halfe of Kersey and three yards and halfe of *rembzigs* . . .

. . . unto Robt Watson Senr four yards and a halfe of Kersey and three & halfe yards of *Zembrigs* . . .

. . . unto my Aunt Sarah Malbone fourty Shillings to buy her a mourning Suite . . .

. . . to my Uncle Lem^{ll} Wilson as much Druggett with Suittable triming as will him a suite of Clothes . . .

. . . unto my Uncle Willis Wilson my black Suite . . .

. . . unto John Hulitt of pocoty a full Discharge for all Debts . . .

. . . unto my uncle Emanuel Burgis a full Discharge . . .

. . . unto the widdo of Thomas Cuthrill Lately Dec^d four barrells of Corn . . .

. . . unto James Cumings to make him a ring . . .

. . . unto uncle Solomon Wilson all ye remaining part of my Estate . . . both real and personall . . .

. . . my deare mother and my Uncle Solomon Wilson . . . Sole Exec^rx and Exec^r . . .

witnesses : — Hutchings.

     William Godfrey.

     Hillliary Moseley.

                  James Wilson J*un*^r

                          Seal.

Wm. BLANCH of Norfolk County . . .

Book 10 f. 22.

dated 24 Feb. 1717/8.

proved 20 June 1718.

. . . to my two daughters Ann and *Mary* one hundred acres of land to be Equally Devided between them Ann to have her first Choyce & if Either of them dyes in there minority my Daughter *mary* to have there part) . . .

. . . to my well beloved Giles randolph and to my well beloved Sister Mary Randolph for ye great kindness . . . in my Sickness . . . Ten pounds . . .

. . . to my wife Dorathy & my three daughters Ann mary & Elizabeth . . . w^t Remains . . . .

. . . my beloved brother Giles Randolph & my Sister mary Randolph full and whole Executrix . . .

witnesses: Thoˢ Cherry.

         John Hulitt.

         Giles Randolph jun^r.

            mark.   his

                            Wm Blanch & seale.

                               mark.

LEMUEL POWELL of Norfolk County boate Right . . .

Book 10 f. 24.

dated 25 Dec. 1717.

proved 20 June 1718, by Wm Staford & Samp^n Powers & on motion of Martha Powell Recorded.

. . . unto Martha my well beloved wife a feather bed . . .

. . . unto my daughter Eliz^a a feather bead . . .

. . . unto my beloved Son John a feather bead . . .

. . . unto my daughter Susanah a feather bead. . . .

. . . unto my Son Lemuel a fine feather bedtick to be levied out of my Estate . . .

. . . unto my daughter Catherine a fine feather bed . . .

. . . the boys at the aige of Eighteen years of aige and the Girls at the aige of Sixteen . . .

. . . unto my Daughter Elizabeth an Iron pot and a spitt . . .

. . . wife my hole & Sole Exec^x . . .

. . . my Carpenters & Joyners toles . . .

witnesses: Samp^n Power.

         Thoˢ Bruce.

         William Staford.

                        Lemuel Powell & Seale.

JOHN CRETCHIT of Elizabeth River parish in the County of Norfolk . . .

Book 10 f. 43.

dated 4 Mch. 1717/8.

proved 19 Sept. 1718.

. . . give my negro to my Son John Cretchitt of twenty
        years . . .
. . . to my wife Sarah Cretchit my Riding horse . . .
. . . my wife and three daughters all the rest . . .
. . . wife Sarah Cretchitt . . . Sole Executrix . . .

witnesses : Lemuel Simmons.

   Dinah Hugh*es*.

   mark.

        John Cretchitt & Seale.

EDWARD DENBY, Senr Norfolk County . . .

Book 10 f. 43.

dated 29 Apr. 1718.

proved 15 Aug. 1718. by Richard Moseley.

. . . all my land to be Equally Divided betwixt my two
        Sons Edward Denby and Charles his youngest Brother
        my Son Edward to have the manor place with the houses
        . . .
. . . to loveing my wife my best bed and furniture . . .
. . . ye remainder of my Estate personall and reall to be
        Equally Devided between my two Sons John and W^m and
        my fower Daughters . . .

witnesses : Richard Moseley.

   Edward Denby, Junr

       Edward Denby & Seale.

RICHARD ROBERTS of the Western Branch of Norfolk
  County . . .

Book 10 f. 48.

dated 28 Xbr. 1718.

proved 20 Feb. 1718, by John Willis & Joseph Munds.

. . . all my land lying in the Southern Branch betweene
        John Joyce and Edward Joyce John to have his part of the
        Said lands on piney Ridge and Edward to have his part on
        the ridge where my Tarkell is on all wch my Said lands to
        be Equally devided betweene John Joyce and Edward
        Joyce . . .

. . . to my sd. Son in law John Joyce one bed . . . now
at Wm. Dayles in the Southern Branch . . .
. . . to Mary Davis my Daughter in law one Cow . . .
. . . to John Bruces Son Jonas three yards of Drugitt to
make him a Coate . . .
. . . to David Joyce my fine hat and Greate Coate . . .
. . . wife Rachell Roberts . . . Sole Execux . . .

witnesses: Joseph Willy.

Joseph Munds.

John Willis.

Richard Roberts & Seale.

JOHN SMITH of Norfolke County . . .

Book 10 f. 48.

dated 2 Sep. 1718.

proved 20 Mch. 1719.

. . . unto my beloved brother Richard Smith one Cow
. . .
. . . unto my beloved brother in Law James Sikes . . .
one Small parcell of land being in the aforesaid County
Joyning on Capt Lem¹ Wilsons land on the one Side and
my father Henry Smiths on yᵉ other Side the Said land
. . . brother in law James Sikes . . . Sole Exeʳ . . .

witnessses: William fforeman.

John ffife.

William Sikes.   his mark.
            his mark.   John Smith—*Seal.*

MOSES ETHEREDGE of Norfolk County . . .

Book 10 f. 48.

dated 23 Dec. 1717.

proved 20 Mch. 1718/9, by Sam¹¹ Moore & John Hodgis.

. . . Appoint Elenor Etheredge my Dearely beloved wife to
be my Sole Executrix . . .
. . . my dearly beloved wife Ellenor Etheredge all my Land

and posessons . . .   Solely to her Selfe and her Heirs
for Ever . . .

witnesses: Sam¹ Moore.

Joseph Batchellor.
his mark.

John Hodgis.
mark.

his mark
Moses Etheredge & Seale.

THOMAS RICHARDSON Senʳ of yᵉ County of Norfolk

. . .

Book 10 f. 48.

dated 10. Nov. 1716.

proved 20 Mch. *1718/9*, by John Willoughby Faithfull Cherry
and Henry Culpeper.

. . . Appoint my dearly beloved wife and Son Thomas Richardson . . .   Sole Exectʳs . . .

. . . unto my beloved Son Thomas Richardson my maner
plantacon which I now live one yᵉ pattent Containg fifty
acres & Likewise a pattent Containing Ninety-nine Acres
it being my uper pattent . . .

. . . to my beloved Son Moses Richardson my Other pattent
. . .   and if Either of my Sons remove from yᵉ aforesaid land he Shall not Sell it Except he Sell it to the Other
and my request is that my two Sons Thomas Richardson
and Moses Richardson Shall affter yᵉ death of my wife pay
unto my Son Aaron Richardson fifty Shillings A peace
Each . . .   and if Either of them my Said Sons aforementioned refuse to pay the aforesaid money Lett him return his land to yᵉ Aforesaid Aaron and yᵉ money Shall be
viod . . .

. . .

. . . as for yᵉ land wᶜʰ I have given to my two Sons Thomas
and Moses the dividing line wᶜʰ I made in my life time
Shall Stand between them . . .

. . . unto my five daughters Marey Frances Margarett Ruith and Sarah one Shilling a peace and to y⁰ heirs of my Daughter Elizabeth one Shilling . . .

witnesses: Faithfull Cherry.
Nich⁰ Hill, mark.
Jo⁰ Willoughby.
his
Henry Cullpeper.
mark.

Thomas Richardson & Seale.

WILLIAM BUNTING of the County of Norfolk . . .

Book 10 f. 49.

dated 22 Feb. 1718/9.

provel 20 Mch. 1718/9, by Wm. Walker & Frances Thornton.

. . . unto my Son Richard Bunting my two Gunns and Nine pounds in Cash . . . when he Shall Come to y⁰ age of one and twenty . . .

. . . unto my daughter Sarah Buntin one Iron large pott and four pounds Ten Shillings in Cash . . .

. . . unto my daughter Mary Bunting . . . four pounds Tenn Shillings in Cash . . . when they Come to Age . . .

. . . my Daughter Mary being my Youngest Child five Pounds . . .

. . . unto my brother Tho⁰ Bunting one Kersey Cote . . .

. . . to my brother Mathew Buntin one Coate & all my Shoemakers tooles . . .

. . . my three Chilldren . . .

. . . my Loveing Frends Wm. Wilkins and Richard Wallice to be my Exect⁰⁰ . . .

witnesses: Jn⁰ Willis.
Wᵐ Walker.
Frances Thornton.

Wm. Buntin & Seale.

JAMES LOWRY of Norfolk in Virg⁰ . . .

Book 10 f. 49.

dated 9 July 1716.

proved 20 Mch. 1718/9.

. . . to my Son William Lowrey one tract of land Called by the name of *fosters* field begining at a white Oake at y⁰ head of black wallnut necke thence along wardens line to Mathew Godfrey Junʳ Standing at y⁰ bottom of y⁰ Necke being a Corner tree between my Selfe and y⁰ Sd. Bramble*s* butt if he my Said Son die without a male Heire Lawfully begotten by his body then I give y⁰ Same to my Son James Lowry . . .

. . . to my Said Wm. Lowry . . . one book Called a Call to y⁰ Unconverted And a book Called Christ's Certain and Sudian Appeareance to Judgmᵗˢ . . .

. . . to my Son John Lowry my manner plantation begining at y⁰ head of a branch which divided y⁰ Land between my Selfe and Henry Bramble Thence a runing the Line of marked Trees and along the Sd. branch to fos-*testers* field . . . butt if he my Said Son dyes wᵗʰout heire yⁿ . . . to my Son Jacob Lowry . . .

. . . unto my Sons William and John my mill . . .

. . . to my daughter phillis Lowry one red Trunk . . . one pewter Tankard . . .

. . . to my daughter Mary Lowry one large red Trunk one Silver Spoone one Gold ring . . .

. . . to my daughter Margᵗᵗ Lowry one Silver Spoone one gold ring one red Trunk . . .

. . . to my Said Son John Lowry . . . at y⁰ Age of Sixteen or Eighteen at farthest at y⁰ Courtes Pleasure butt not to be removed from his mother till he Shall attaine to y⁰ age of twenty-one . . .

. . . to my daughter Jane one Shilling in full of her portion . . .

. . . to my Son Robᵗ Lowry one Shilling in full of his portion . . .

. . . to my Son Thomas Lowry one Shilling in full of his portion . . .

. . . to my Loveing' wife Judith Lowry all y⁰ Remainder of my part of my Estate . . .

. . . wife Judith Lowry . . . Sole Execʳx . . .

witnesses: James Toomoth.

Mary Toomoth.

John McCoy.

James Lowry & Seale.

HUGH HANLAND of the County of Norfolk . . .

Book 10 f. 51.

dated 12. Feb. 1718.

proved 17 Feb. 1718.

> . . . to my beloved frend Joseph Hodgis is whome I ap-
> point to be my whole and Sole exec^r . . . all and
> Singular my Lands wch I have in possession and out
> of possession . . .
> . . . to my Sister Elizabeth Miller one Shilling peace . . .

witnesses: Faithfull Cherry.

> Jn° Manning.
> Dinah Davis.
>
>   Hugh Hanland.

RICHARD WALLIS of Norfolk County . . .

Book 10 f. 64.

dated 4 Mch. 1719.

proved 15 May 1719.

> . . . unto my Son John Wallis all my land & housen w^th
> all priviledges as it belongs to me only Excepting for my
> true and Loveing wife that Shee Shall have her wido Shipp
> in the Maner plantation . . . halfe the Orchard when
> he Comes to Aige . . . my Gun y^t was my fathers
> . . .
> . . . unto my Daughter Judeth one largest pewter Dish
> . . .
> . . . to my daughter Elizabeth the Next large flatt dish and
> three plates . . . my Books to be devided between
> them . . .
> . . . to my three youngest Daughters Dianah Sarah & Mary
> to Each of them *five* Shillings . . .
> . . . my youngest Daughters Nursing . . .
> . . . my wife . . . Ex^rx and Do Impower my to Sell
> Light wood or timber on my part of the fishing point neck
> towards the payment of my Debts . . .

witness: Edwd Davis.

> Edward Davis jun^r
> John Davis.
>   his mark.
>
>   Richard Wallis & Seale.

MATTHEW SPIVEY of Norfolk County . . .

Book 10 f. 64.

dated 16 Feb. 1718.

proved 15 May 1719, Mrs. Hanah Holliday, Robert Bowers & John Bowers.

. . . unto my Said Executrixes the use of my Watter Mill wth the Rents of my lands and use of my male Catell and old baren Cows . . . Stock of hoggs in the hands of Edward Wood Edward Weston and William Ward in the government of North Carolina . . . the aforesd. Mill and lands unto my Said Executrixes &c towards the bringing up and Schooleing of my fower youngest Children and if please god that my mother Should Die . . . my Daughter Sarah Should live upon the Man^r Plantation . . . untill my Son Matthew Spivey Comes of full aige at which time . . . Said Maner plantation with the Water Mill thereon to the Said Mathew Spivey allways is provided . . . he . . . Shall make a firm bill of Sail . . . for a Certain tract of Land now in tenor of John Staford unto my young Son George Spivey . . . and if my Said Son Matthew faile . . . that then . . . my Son George Inherit . . .

. . . my land in North Carolina to my Said Son George . . .

. . . my present Loveing Mother . . .

. . . my Six Children (vizt) Sarah Judith Thomas Elizabeth Matthew and George Spivey . . .

. . . unto William Johnston one *Dueroyes* Coate trimd with black one holland Striped Jacket and one ditto britches . . .

. . . my Said Loveing Mother M^rs. Judith Nichols Joyntly together with my Tender Daughter Sarah Spivey . . . Sole Executrixes . . .

witnesses: Hanah Holliday.

Robert Bowers his
mark.

Thomas Mannings.
mark.

John Bowers.

Matth: Spivey & Seale.

JONAS HALLIDAY of Norfolk County . . .

Book 10 f. 65.

dated 4 Jan. 1713/4.

proved 18 Feby. 1718, by Capt. Matthew Spivey.

recorded 15 May 1718, on motion of Mrs. Hanah Holliday.

. . . my present . . . wife Hanah Holliday fower Negroes . . .

. . . unto my Cosen Anthony Halliday the Son of my Brother Joseph Halliday late deceased one Negro . . .

. . . unto my Cosen John Holliday one more of the Sons of my Said Brother Joseph Halliday one Negro . . .

. . . unto my Sister Charity Halliday⁰ wife of my Said Brother Joseph Holliday one plantation or tract of Land Known and Called by the name of Ell*its* together with one halfe of my water Mill thereto adjoining Dureing her Naturall life and after her decease to fall to my Cosen John Halliday . . .

. . . unto my present Loveing wife Hanah the Other halfe of my Said Watter Mill during . . . life and after to my Said Cosen John Halliday . . .

. . . unto my Said loveing wife Hanah Hanas Holliday my Watter Mills which I baught of Marmaduke Etheredge lying & being on one of the runs of deepe Creeke in the Southern Branch of this County . . . dureing her Naturall life and after . . . to my Brother Samuel Halliday . . .

. . . unto my Brother in law James Knott one Negro . . .

. . . unto my Brother in law William Murphee and to his wife Sarah yᵉ use of one Negro . . . dureing their Naturall lives and after . . . to his daughter Katherine . . .

. . . my Negro girle Named Sarah . . . free . . . as a Slave . . .

. . . rest of my Estate . . . to my present Loveing Tender & Virtuous wife . . . appointing her . . . Sole Executrix . . .

witnesses: Jas. Mcmorran.
John Hodgis.
John Bow*res*.
Matth Spivey.

Jonas Halliday & Seale.

JOSEPH CURLING, Senior . . . (Nuncupative) . . .

Book 10 f. 71.

Recorded 17 Apr. 1719.

> The Deposition of Wm. Taylor, Aged fourty years or thereabouts . . . Sworn Saith That . . . in May Last he was requested by Joseph Curling Senior to Sign as Evidence to his will in which Said will he gave to his Son Anthony Curling the plantation he then lived upon wth a hundred acres of land Adjoyning to it . . . and likewise to his Son Walter Curling his plantation whereon he formerly lived on with one hundred Acres of land Adjoyning to it . . . to his Son Joseph Curling he gave an Iron milling pott . . . to his daughter Ann one heifer . . . And the rest of his Estate he willd to his wife rebeca during her life and After . . . to be Equally Divided Amongst his Children . . .
>
> Wm. Taylor.

> The Deposition of Thomas Taylor aged thirty four years or thereabouts . . . Sworn Saith: the Same . . . and further that he had the will in Keeping by Joseph Curling's request and at the Instance of Walter Curling this Deponent was a going Down wth the sd. will to Deliver it to ye Court and on the way Mr. James Wilson and Walter Curling Overtooke me . . . wth Anthony Curling: and the Said James Wilson Ordered me to Deliver the will to the Said Walter Curling . . .
>
> Thomas Taylor.

WILLIAM MILLER of the County of Norfolk in Virginia . . .

Book 10 f. 76.

dated 3 Apr. 1719.

proved 17 July 1719, by Sol^o Wilson, John Smith & Henry Price.

> . . . to my Son Willis my plantation called hogg neck containing two hund^d acres of land And Seventy nine beginning at a Corner tree standing by the fence side so running North East along a line of Marked trees as far as the farther side of the Polly ground it being a line be

twixt John Smith and me then running such a course as
will make it Two hund^d Sixty acres . . . all the Stock
of hoggs belonging to the sd. plantation called hog neck
. . .
. . . one old Slender gun and sword . . . forty *Ells*
of Prince's linnen . . . thirty free square of land up
on the road it being a moiety of a parcell of land bought of
Mr. John Wilson upon the Island Commonly Known by
the name of Costin's Island which s^d land I give my beloved Son Willis . . .
. . . unto my Son William Miller one plantation with two
hun^d and fiften acres belonging to it which I bought of
Coll. James Wilson Joyning upon Arthur Godfrey and
Sol^o White . . .
likewise . . . thirty foot square land near the great
bridge upon the Island formerly known by the name of
Costin's Island joyning up on his brother Willis Miller
. . . Three joynt Chair frames one pair of Pistols and
holsters . . . when he comes to age of Eighteen
. . .
. . . unto my Son Solomon Miller one tract of land containing two hund^d & fifteen acres joyning up on Henry Price's
line and so along the great Cypress Swamp and binding
upon his brother William Millers Line . . . one gun
. . . fourteen pounds in Cash . . .
. . . forty Ells of Princes linnen . . . and thirty feet
Square of land near the Great bridge up on the Island
formerly Known by the name of Costen's Island joyning
up on his Brother Williams land . . . when he comes
to the age of Eighteen . . .
. . . unto my Son Lemuel Miller the plantation with the
land that I had of my Mother Stanly . . . one Cor-
bine gun . . . thirty feet Square of land near the
great bridge up on the Island commonly known by the
name of Costin's Island joyning up on his brother Sol^o Miller's land . . . when he comes to the age of
Eighteen . . .
. . . unto my Son Peledge Miller the Plantation whereon I
live with five hundred acres of land belonging to it
at the age of Eighteen . . . thirty feet Square of land
near the great bridge up on the Island Commonly Known
by the name of Costin's Island joyning upon his brother
Lemuel Miller . . .
. . . unto my daughter Prudence Miller a piece of land near
to the Great bridge joyning to William McNorin which I
bought of Richard Silvester

. . . unto my daughters Elizabeth Agnes & *Cozbi* two Cows
. . . all the remayning part of my land upon the Island
comminly known by the name of Costin's island not yet
given away to be equally divided . . .
. . . my beloved wife . . , Sole Exetrx . . .

witnesses: John Smith.
Sol° Wilson Junr.
Henry Price.
James Cummings.

William Miller.

THOMAS BOWLS . . .

Book 10 f. 77.

dated 4 Mch. 1718/9.

proved 17 July 1719.

. . . unto my Cousin Thos Smith one hund^d acres of land
Joyning on the Main branch on the South side of the s^d
branch joyning to Mary Smith and Wm Ellis . . .
. . . unto my Cousins John Smith and Lemuel Smith a parcel of Swamp land containing thirty acres more or less to
be equally divided between them and lying up on the same
Side of the s^d branch . . .
. . . unto Loveing Cousin Lemuel Powell son of John Powell
one hund^d acres of land Scituate lying and being in the
Southern branch of Elizabeth river joyning to Thos Tuckers land . . .
. . . unto my Loving Aunt Mary *Smith* a parcell of Staves
contgining three thousand pieces and lay upon the Swamp
land before given away . . .
. . . unto my Loving Cousin John Smith the plantation I
now live on . . . my great looking glass . . .
. . . unto my Loving Cousin Dorcas Battess a sute of Cur-
tains and Vallance . . .
. . . unto my Loving Cousins Ann, Dorcas, & Diana, which
is now in *Pamphio* all and Singular my Estate which is
given away . . .
. . . my Loving Cousin John Smith . . . Sole Exec^{t}r
. . .

witnesses: Samps. Powers.
Fra^n Sigiaves.
Wm. Sigiaves.

Thomas Bowlls.

CAPT. JOHN HALSTEAD'S Verball Will . . .

Book 10 f. 77.

dated "27 day of May 1719."

Recorded 17 July 1719. Proved by Tho⁵ Nash, Tho⁵ Whiddon.

Memorandum of a Verball Will made by Capt. John Halstead on his death bed the 27ᵗʰ day of May, 1719 in presence of Sundry witnesses whose names are underwritten.

. . . unto John Portlock his water Mill.

. . . unto John Mathias his part of the Sloop for one part belonged to him the said Mathias before.

. . . unto William Portlock the Plantation that the sᵈ Wᵐ Portlock lives on, also he gave Elizabeth Portlock one Negro . . .

. . . unto William Portlock the books relating to the Sherifs office with what Tobacco due to him.

Also he desired his brother to let the said Wᵐ Portlock have the Horse called Rainbow . . .

witnesses: Tho. Nash, Senʳ

Johsua Porter.

Thomas Whiddon.

Motion of Wm. Portlock is admitted to Record.

Notice: Book Marked: "Orders—Appraisements—Wills Feby. 19, 1719 Aug. 18, 1722, Norfolk County" will be abreviated: O. A. W. in this abstract.

MARY GODFREY of Norfolk County . . .

Book, O. A. W. p. 38.

dated 16 May 1719.

proved 18 — bᵉʳ 1719.

. . to my Son Mathew Godfrey one horse Called Robin

. . . to my Son William Godfrey one whip Saw which is now at my Son in Law Tatems and one pair of Money Scales

. . . to my Daughter Amy . . . two Heaters . . .

. . . to my Daughter Ann Tatem One Feather bed . . .

. . . to my Daughter Amy Huchens One feather bed . . .

. . . to my Son Mathew One house bell . . .

. . . to my Daughter Whitkhouse One Small feather bed
. . . Six leather Chairs . . .

. . . all my Children Mathew and William and Mary &
Daughter Ann and Amy . . .

. . . my two Sons Mathew and William Godfrey . . .
Sole Executors . . .

witnesses: Lem¹¹ Simmons.
            Cath⁰ Godfrey.

                                    Mary Godfrey & S.

ROBT. GAMMON . . .

Book O. A. W. p. 40.

dated 14 Jan. 1718.

proved 21 Aug. 1719.

. . . unto my Two Sons John & James Gamon all my Land
to be Equally Divided between yᵐ but my Son John to have
yᵉ Plantation I now live on and yᵗ half which when Divided Shal be adjoyning to it when the Division is made
So that My Son James Gamon may have my old plantⁿ &
yᵗ half yᵉ land adjoyning to it when the Division is made
the aforesaid land and Plantation . . .

. . . unto my Daughters Jane & Susanna Elizabeth & Abigail Lucretia . . . all yᵉ Remaining part off my Estate
to be Equally Divided . . .

. . . appoint my wife Jane Gamon & Joseph Sickes . . .
Sole Exˣ and Exʳ . . .

witnesses: Solo. Wilson.
            Jnº Nicholas.
            Jno. White.

                                    Robert Gamon & Seal.

JOHN SIKES off Nffolk County . . .

Book O. A. W. p. 41.

dated ——— ———.

proved 21 Aug. 1719.

. . . all my Lands to be Equally Divided between my three Sons John & Solomon and William Sikes . . . But in Case the Unborn Child which my wife Goes with Be a boy to have a Equall p^r of the beforemention'd Land . . .

. . . my Will is that my Son William Sikes have the plantation I now live on . . .

. . . I give my Son John Sikes my hand mill & and Iron Pestell . . .

. . . wife Sarah Sikes . . .

. . . to my beloved Son Solo^n Sikes . . . my Small Iron pot . . . my Gun . . .

. . . my three Daughters Sarah Ann and Grace Sikes . . . Cattle . . .

. . . my Loving Wife Sarah Sikes and my Son John Sikes . . . Sole Ex^{rs} . . .

witnesses: J. Fife.
        Joseph Sikes.

                            Jno Sikes & Seal.

SAMON ROGERS of the County of Norfolk . . .

Book O. A. W. p. 42.

dated 6 June 1719.

proved 21 Aug. 1719. by Mr. Sam Boush and Mss (Mr^s Thruston.

. . . unto my Son Samon Rogers my Molatta Girl Sary . . .

. . . unto my Son William Marshall Rogers my negro Girl Violett . . .

. . . appoint my loving Br^r Wm Rogers & my loving wife to be Ex^{rs} . . .

witnesses: Sa Boush Junr
        Marg^{tt} Thruston*nn*.

                            Samon Rogers.

JAMES CARNEY off Norffolk County . . .

Book O. A. W. p. 43.

    dated 1 Apr. 1719.

    proved 21 Aug. 1719.

. . . unto my Son James Carney my Plantation which fformerly my Brother Richard Carney Lived upon . . .

. . . unto my Son David Carney . . . the plantation which I now Live upon & one Cow . . .

. . . unto my abovesaid Son James and David all the Rest off my Land Equally Betwixt them . . .

. . . my youngest Son Philip Carney may be Educated with Reading and Writing at the Cost of my Eldest Sons . . .

. . . unto my Daughter Elizabeth Carney one Cow . . .

. . . unto my Wiffe Elizabeth Carney the Use of my Plantation which I now live upon with Necessary priviledges In the Wood land Grond & Swamp ffor the Plantation use During her liffe . . .

. . . the Rest off my Estate not beffore Given Should be Equally divided amongst my Wife and all my Children.

. . . If Either off my Two Sons namely James Carney Or David Carney Should Dye without Heir or Issue off their Body that my Youngest Son Philip Carney Should Enjoy their part of Land . . .

. . . I Give my Son David Carney liberty to Build and live In the Old ffield Called Richard Chambers Old field which is in the Plantation which I gave my wife during her liffe provided he will not Disturb his mother . . .

. . . Wife Elizabeth Carney and my Son James Carney . . . Sole Executrix & Executor . . .

witnesses: Tho: Wright.

Thomas Carney.

Barnabee Carney.

James Carney & Seal.

JOHN TUCKER off Norffolk County . . .

Book O. A. W. p. 44.

dated 11 Jan. 1718/19.

proved 18 Sep. 1719, by Thomas Hobgood & ffrances Harlowen & Ex^r herein mentioned.

. . . unto my Son John Tucker all my whole Dividend of Land . . . and If the Said Jn° Should Dye without Issue the Said Land to Return to my Son Thomas . . . and If the Said Thomas Should Dye without Issue the Said Land to Return to my Son Thomas . . . If the said Thomas Should Dye without Issue to be Equally Divided amongst my Daughters . . .

. . . my two Sons be at Age when they are Eighteen . . .

. . . unto my well beloved Mary Tucker two off the Best Pewter Dishes . . .

. . . unto my Daughter Mary two pewter basons . . .

. . . unto my Daughter Sarah two Pewter basons . . .

. . . my Wife Mary . . . Sole Executrix . . .

witnesses : Jnº Gibson.

ffrancis Harlowin.

Jnº Tucker & Seal.

JOHN DICKSON off Norfolk County blacksmith . . .

Book O. A. W. p. 46.

dated 19 May 1716.

proved 21 Aug. 1719, by Ewd. & Benjamin Miller . . .

. . . unto my loving Wife Mary Dickson the houses and Plantation whereon I now Dwell with all the Appurtences . . . During her Naturall life and after her Decease yᵉ houses and yᵉ part of the Plantation whereon I now live unto the Dividing Line which begins at Benjamin Millers Line at a Sower Wood and So Runs by marked trees to a pine a bears Rubing Tree yᵗ Bottom of my neck unto my Loving Daughter mary macnerren . . . But in Case my afore'sᵈ Daughter or her heirs Should Claim any Right Title or Interest by Inheritance unto the yᴵ Plantation which my ffather in Law Jnº Corprew gave me then . . . ye before mentioned Land shall be Equally devided between my two youngest Grandaughters of my Son John Dickson Decᵈ . . .

. . . unto my Grandaughter Elizabeth Dickson yᵗ Part of my Land and Plantation from yᵉ Deviding Line before mentioned into yᵉ other Line off that land which my ffather Jnº Corprew Gave me . . . but if it should happen that She Should Depart this Life without Such Issue . . . then to fall to yᵉ next Survivor and Issue . . .

. . . unto my Son in Law William Mcnerren that piece of Ground which I bought of Mr. Silvester at yᵉ bridge . . . which sᵈ Land he have in his possession at this Time . . .

. . . unto my Grand Son Gilbert Macnerren all my Smiths
Tools . . .

. . . unto my Daughter Mary Mac Nerren my Warming pan
. . .

. . . unto my Grand Daughter Mary Dickson one ffeather
Bed . . .

· . . unto my youngest Grand Daughter of my Son John
Dickson Dec^d being unbaptised one pewter Dish . . .

. . . wife my whole and Sole Ex^r . . .

witnesses: Thomas Corprew.

Benj. Miller.

Edward Miller.

Jno Dickson & Seal.

THOMAS ETHERIDGE Elder of Norfolk County . . .

Book O. A. W. p. 48.

dated 13 May 1719.

proved 17 July 1719.

. . . to my Son Robt Etheridge All ye Land that I am possessed with and my Plantation . . .

. . . my loving Wife Elenor Etheridge ffiffteen Shifts of
fine Linnen . . .

. . . wearing Clothes and Woolings . . . to my five
Sons that is to say my Son in Law Edward Etheridge to
have as good part in my Clothes and Wollen as Either of
my own Sons . . .

. . . my mill to my Son Robert Etheridge and my Son In
Law Edward Etheridge . . .

. . . appoint my two Sons Edward and Robert Etheridge
. . · Sole Exr^s . . .

witnesses :Dennis Maccoy.

Henry Etheridge.

Tho: Etheridge & S.

WILLIAM CRATCHETT . . .

Book O. A. W. p. 49.

dated 28 May 1719.

proved 15 Jan. 1719/20, by Wm. Denby.

19 *Jan.* 1719/20, by Jno. Denby.

. . . to my Loving Wife and Richard W. Silvester all my personable Estate . . . they being wholly and Solely Executor and Executrix . . .

witnesses: Wm. Denby

John Denby's mark.

his
William Cratchett & Seal
mark.

JOHN SOUTHERLAND of Norfolk County . . .

Book O. A. W. p. 87.

dated 21 Feb. 1719/20.

proved 20 May 1720.

. . . unto my Brothers David Southerland & Richard Southerland my Plantation at the head of the Southern Branch . . . binding upon Jn° Smith and Jn° White . . .

witnesses: David Carney.

Abraham Weston.

Richard Cording.

Jn° Southerland & S.

ROBERT HATTON of Norfolk County . . .

Book O. A. W. p. 87.

dated 26 Oct. 1719.

proved ———— 1720, by Eleanor Hatton Ex^x, James Grimes and Thomas Wright.

. . . unto my Son francis Hatton all my Land . . . and if it Should please God that he Dye without Heir my will is that my Son Robert Hatton Shall Enjoy ye land as afores^d . . .

. . . unto my Wife Elinor Hatton all my Realy money

. . . wife Elinor Hatton my . . . Sole Exe[x] . . .

witnesses: Thos. Wright.

James Grimes.

Carney Wright·

Robert Hatton & Seal.

RICH[d] BACON, Sen[r] . . .

Book O. A. W. p. 121 & p. 134.

dated 27 Nov. 1717.

proved 15 July 1720.

. . . to my Son John Bacon all my Land that I now live on

. . . to my daughter Sarah Bacon one feather bed . . .
one Tankard . . .

. . . to my two Grand Children *Judey* and Richard Bacon
Each of them a pewter dish . . .

. . . all the rest of my whole Estate to be Equally devided
between my beloved wife Mary and my Son John and
after my wife's Decease it all to be my Son Johns owne
Estate. Provided he tacketh Care of his mother . . .

. . . Son John . . . whole and full Exec[r] . . .

witnesses: Joseph Watford.

Sam[l] Windgate.

Joseph Joll*iff*.

Recorded twice.   Rich[d] Bacon & Seal.

DANIELL PHILLIPPS of Norfolk County in Virg[a] . . .

Book O. A. W. p. 121.

dated 1 Feb. 1718.

proved 15 July 1720, by Ann King & frances Dixon.

. . . to my Son John Phillips one plantacon Containing two
hundred Acres as by one bill of Sale for the Same Lying
in the hands of John Willis . . . and my will is that
Mr. *Sam*[l] Boush Jun[r] may dispose of the Same at his will

and pleasure for the use of my Said Sonn when he Shall attain to age . . . Mr. Samˡ Boush Shall have my sd. Sonn untill he Shall Attain to age.

. . . the Remaining part of my Estate to be Equally divided between my Sonn John and my Daughter Susannah
. . .

. . . my frend Mr. Samˡ Boush Junʳ . . . Sole Execʳ
. . .

. . . The plantacon above given Lying in North Carolina
. . .

witnesses: James Toomoth.

     Francis Dicon.

     Ann King.

              Danˡ Philips & Seal.

RICHᵈ SAYER of Norfolk County . . .

Book O. A. W. p. 122.

dated 30 Apr. 1716.

proved 15 July 1720, by Mr. Edward Thruston & Mr. Frances Tucker.

    12 July 1720. by Mr. Robᵗ Tucker.

. . . to my Loveing frends Mr. John Britt and Elenor his wife all my Lands in Norfolk County duereing there Naturall Lives . . .

. . . to my god daughter Rosiana Britt that plantation of mine Commonly Known by the Name of Iveys: and being that part Mr. John Britt now Dwells on being two hundred acres more or les . . .

. . . to Frances Britt Daughter of John and Elenor Britt one neck of my Land Commonly Called the forked Neck and bounding on the uper Side of *Draine* Neck and On my brother Charles Sayers line and Soe up to the Side of the Southern branch Road it being fifty Acres more or Less
. . .

. . . unto my Godson Arthur Sayer one hundred Acres of land of that part where the manner house Stands after the Decease of John Britt and Elenor his wife . . .

. . . unto my Brother Charles Sayer fourty Shillings to buy a ring in Memory of me . . .

. . . unto my Sister King— man: my Sister Smith Mr. John Morris, *Mrs.* Mary Ann Britt Mrˢ Elizᵃ Britt and John

Britt Jun[r] and to Each of them twenty Shi[ll] a peace to
buy them a Ring in Memory of me   .   .   .
.   .   .   unto M[r] John Britt and Elenor his wife   .   .   .   all the
Rest of my Estate of w[t] Kind Soever   .   .   .
.   .   .   App[t] Mr. John Morris and John Britt Jun[r] my   .   .   .
Sole Exec[rs]   .   .   .

witnesses : Edw[d] Thruston.

Frances Tucker.

Rob[t] Tucker.

Rich[d] Sayer & Seale.

JOHN BRUCE . . .

Book O. A. W. p. 124.

dated 5 Apr. 1720.

proved 19 Aug, 1720, by Joseph Munds & John Maning.

.   .   .   unto my Son John Bruce the plantacon where on he
now lives including all the land between Lambert's branch
and poplar branch Soe runing for length Right on Cross
my land as far as it Goes for breadth   .   .   .   and if my
Son John dyes with out heirs to fall to my Son Jonas and
my will is my Son John Shall in Noe Case Stop the Cartway from the Cartway down to my house.

.   .   .   unto my Son Abraham Bruce the plantacon whereon he
now lives on; begining at the mouth of the Creek Soe
runing to pullins branche Side Continueing the Course as
far as my land Goes   .   .   .   if my Son Abraham dyes
wth heire to my Son Benjamin   .   .   .

.   .   .   unto Loveing wife Mary Bruce the plantacon whereon
I now Live on Dureing her Natureall Life and after her
Decease to my Loveing Son James Bruce   .   .   .

.   .   .   my Son James live wth his mother and if they cannot
Agree for my Said Son to build any where on the
Mouth of Lamberts branch Soe making Use of any part
of the Land in that Necke   .   .   .

.   .   .   unto my Loveing Sons Jonas and William Bruce all my
Land wch is not yet Given away to be Ecequaly Divided
between them by two men that they Shal Chose   .   .   .
And if Either of my Sons dyes wth out heirs To fall to the
other the land beginning at the open side of poplar branch

Including all the land that Lyes above my Son John's
. . .

. . . unto my Loveing daughter Eliza Avis Twenty Shillings . . .

. . . unto m y loveing daughter Mary Cullpeper Three Sows wth pigg or them that hath piggs . . .

. . . unto my Loveing Daughter Sarah Bruce twenty-five Shillings . . .

. . . unto my Daughter Catherine my New pewter dish that Stands on the Cupboard . . .

. . . unto my Son James all my Coopers and Carpenters Tooles . . .

. . . wife Mary Bruce . . . Sole Exo^r

witnesses: Samp^n Powers.

Joseph Munds.

Jno Manning.

Jr.° Bruce & S.

SUSAN BRYAN . . .

Book O. A. W. p. 181.

dated 10 Apr. 1719.

proved 19 May 1721, by John Staford Junr & John Staford Senr

. . . unto my loveing Grand Daughter sarah Cretcher one New feather bedd . . . when She attains to ye age of Sixteen . . .

. . . unto my loveing grand Son Richd Powell all & Singular my Estate both wth in dores & with out dores . . .

. . . unto my four daughters Mary Sarah Susanah & Dorcus 12 pence . . .

. . . my loveing Grand son Richd Powell . . . Sole Exec^r . . .

. . .

witnesses: John Staford.

John Staford Junr.

Samp^n Powers.

his
Susan Bryan & seal.
mark.

JUDATH NICKOLLS . . .

Book O. A. W. p. 181.

dated 26 Oct. 1720.

proved 19 May 1721.

. . . unto yᵉ Children of my Son Mathew Spivey dec'd all my Cattle . . . as they shall Come to age According to Law . . .

. . . unto Tamer Spivey & Elizabeth Spivey my two Gold Rings . . .

. . . all my hoggs to be Equally devided between Sarah Spivey Judath Spivey Tamer Spivey Mathew Spivey and Elizabeth Spivey . . .

. . . warming pann which I give unto my Cusin John Bowers . . .

. . . profitts of my Negro man Sambo to my Exʳ towards yᵉ mentainance & schooling of Tamer Spivey, Elizabeth Spivey & Mathew Spivey and when yᵉ Sd. Mathew Spivey Shall Attaine to the age of twenty one . . . his . . .

. . . Appoint John Bowers . . . Sole Exʳ . . .

witnesses: Wm. Tarte, his mark.

Sarah Spivey.   her
                              Juduth Nickolls & Seal.
                              mark.

ROBERT BUTT, Sen'r of Norfolk County in Virgᵃ . . .

Book O. A. W. p. 182.

dated 16 Aug. 1719.

proved 18 Aug. 1721, by Isaac Barrington & Henry Price.

. . . to my Son in law John Pinkerton that married my daughter Ann Butt that percell of land which he and my daughter his wife now lives upon . . . during there Naturall lives and after there decease to Revert to my Grandson Robert Pinkerton . . . it being bounded as followeth (Vizt) by a branch that devides the woolf pitt neck and yᵉ plantation neck & Soe Runing along Mʳ Halstead's line . . .

. . . unto my daughter Sarah Butt that piece of land Commonly Known by yᵉ name of woolf pitt neck with yᵉ

Swamp and Branches belonging to it Joyning up on Mr. Halsteads line y^t devides his line & mine & two Cows
. . .
line y^t devides his line & mine & two Cows . . .
. . . unto my daughter Emy Butt all that part of Turkey Ridge & that part of forked Hickory & that belongeth to mee . . . with ye Swamp and Branches belonging to ye S^d pieces of Ridges of land & two Cows . . .
. . . to my daughter Margaret Butt that Ridge of land Commonly Known and Called by ye name of Grape Vine Ridge wth all ye broken ground belonging to it . . .
. . . unto my daughter Elizabeth one Stear . . .
. . . unto my daughter dinah Butt one feather bedd . . ..
. . . to my daughter Mary two Cows . . .
. . . to my daughter Edie Butt two Cows . . .
. . . unto my daughter Jane Butt two Cows . . .
. . . to my Son Wm Butt after my wifes decease all ye Remaining part of my land not before given away . . . all my Carpenters & Coopers tools and my gunn & my pistols & holsters . . . one large Iron pott y^t about tenn Gallons that belonged to his Grandmother . . .

witnesses: James Cumming.

        Isaac Barrenton.

        Henry Price.

                    Robert Butt.

The following nineteen wills were abstracted from a book found in a drawer. The volume contained about twenty-five pages and parts of these pages were torn. There were also court orders in this volume. The cover was half gone.

JOHN WHIDDON of Norfolk County in Virg^a . . .
    (Gift?).

Book G f. 168.

dated 13 Aug. 1729.

ack 15 Aug. 1729, by Capt. John Whiddon.

. . . I give and bequeath to my well beloved friend Chris^r Cawson full liberty of ye plantation whereon Mr Jones Cawson late of this County deced lived on wth any Interruption or hindrance by me or any other person by my ord^r during my life . . . when he shall attain to ye age of twenty one . . .

. . . to my Loveing friend Argall Cawson my negro man Benebus after ye decease of my wife . . .

. . . to my Loveing friend Jones Cawson my negro boy . . .

. . . to my Loveing friend Ann Cawson ye first Child y^t shall hereafter be borne of my negro wench Dinah . . .

. . . unto my well beloved friend Abigall Cawson ye second Child . . .

. . . unto my well beloved friend Kezia Cawson my Negro wench Dinah . . .

. . . to my loveing Friend Jennitt Cawson my negro . . .

. . . before mentioned legacyes . . .

witnesses: Thos Nash jun^r.

his
John Clark.
mark.

John Whiddon jun^r   John Whiddon & Seale.

PETER GODFREY of Norfolk County . . .

Will Book —— p. 4.

Dated 4 Feb. 1722.

Proved 18 May 1723 by all the witnesses.

. . . to Cozen Wm. Godfrey, all the Land I have at the great bridge wch said land fall to me by my Un —(torn) Mathew Godfreys will . . .

. . . to my well beloved Son Lem^l Godfrey all the rema —(torn- of my land . . .

. . . my daughter Leddy Godfrey . . .

. . . my Daughter in law Mary . . .

. . . my well beloved wife Elizabeth Godfrey . . . appoint . . . wife . . . whole—(torn)—

witnesses: Matthew Godfrey.

Dinah Godfrey.
her
Ann + Thellaball.
mark.

Peter Godfrey & Seal.

RICHARD LEWELLEN of Southern branch of Norfolk
  County . . .

Will Book —— p. 4.

Dated 20 Oct. 1722.

Proved 18 May 1723 by all the witnesses.

> . . . Appoint my . . . wife Eliz^a . . . Sole Extx
> . . .
> . . . to my . . . Son Richard Lewellen my plantacon
> and all the land belonging to it (Except the land I have
> —(torn)— my Son Aabel . . . —(torn)—Son Rich^d
> Should dye wth heirs then the sd pl —(torn)—to return to
> my Son Lemuel . . .
> . . . my Children . . .
> . . . my Little Gunn and Sword . . . to my Son Lem^l
> . . . alsoe my Little pot that was his brother Edwards
> . . .
> . . . my five daughters . . .

witnesses: *John Oerngs.*

> Richd Taylor.   his
> —(torn)—ph Fenly. Richard + Lewellen & Seal.
>   mark.

————

WILLIAM WHIDDON Senr . . .

Will Book —— p. 5.

Dated 18 Feb. 1720.

Proved 16 June 1721, by W^m. Maund & Wm. Gray.

> . . . unto my Son Wm. Whiddon my plantcon where on I
> now live, and a hundred and fifty Ackers of land Called by
> the name of the Little ragg the sd. lands the whole Con-
> taining two hundred Ackers . . . if in Care my Son
> . . . Sauld not make Sale of the sd. land in his life
> time and her Should . . . dye wth out heir or Issue
> then to fall to my Cosen John Whiddon Senr and male
> heirs . . .
> . . . unto —(torn)— er Marg^t Cason . . . steare
> . . .

. . . Appoint my Son Wm. Whiddon and my Cosen John Whiddon . . . Exo^{rs}

witnesses :

his

George + Sugg.

mark

Wm. Maund.

Wm. Gray.

Wm. Whiddon & Seal.

ROBERT LANE . . .

Will Book —— p. 6.

dated 30 Apr. 1721.

Proved 17 Nov. 1721, by John Fulford & James Warden Senr

. . . unto my Son Robert Lane all the land lying on the west ward side of the Creek and on the East ward side of a Crooked run where the Conoes were made . . .

. . . for want of Such Issue to the next in line and there Issue to the worlds End, after the decease of his mother

. . .

. . . unto my Son *Jasper* Lane part of that land lying on the East ward side of the Creek begining at the Crooked runn where the Conoes was made along the Creek Soe as the line of marked trees goe, to a pine being a corner tree Standing on the bare Garden Ridge by the side of the gum Swamp . . . for want of Such Issue to the Next in the line . . . to ye worlds End . . . my house and what he is already possest wth . . .

. . . unto my Son Augustus lane all the rest of my land begining at the pine being a Corner tree Standing by the gum Swamp side, being the End of Jasper Lane's land Soe runing along the Bare Garden ru—(torn)—l land of ffrances Jones, all that Land Com—(torn)—y the name of the wood yard . . . for want of Such Issue to Next in Line . . . to the worlds End, and if any of my sons doe offer to sell or make sale of these Land then it Shall be free for the next of ye line to Enter and possess it

. . .

. . . three youngest Children that is Augustus lane Ann Lane and Lydia Lane . . .

. . . wife *Morger* Lane . . . Sole Exerx . . . in Case She Should dye then my Son Robt Lane to be my Ex^r . . .

witnesses: Wm. Miller Senr.
John Fulford.
James W. Worden Senr.

Robt Lane & Seal.

KEADER CONNER of Norfolk County in Virg^a gent . . .

Will Book —— p. 7.

Dated 19 Aug. 1721.

Proved June 17 —(torn)— by Capt. Wm. —(torn)—

. . . desire is that Soon after my death that all my Lands be it of what Nature or property Soever be Sold for bills of Exchand to Discharge my Debts . . .
. . . wife Abigale Conner . . .
. . . my Said wife and my brother in law Wm. Craford to be my Execrs . . .

witnesses: Wm. Craford   Keader + Conner.
Jno Westcote.

WILLIAM PERKINS of Norfolk County . . .

Will Book —— p. 8.

Dated 11 Nov. 1721.

Proved 21 Sept. 1722, by John Freeman & Wm. Wallice.

. . . to my Daughter Eliz^a the whole dividend of land that I bought of Wm. Freeman . . . after my own and wifes decease only My will is that my Son John is to have the one Orchard that belongs to the manner plantation . . . if my daughter Eliz^a Dyes wth out heire then to fall to my Daughter Sarah . . .

witnesses: his
John + Freman.
mark
his   his
Wm. + Walice.   Wm. + Perkins & Seal.
mark.   mark.
Thom^a Hobgood Junr.

WALTER BAILEY of the western branch of Elizabeth river
. . . Carpenter . . .

Will Book —— p. 8.

Dated 8 *Jan* 1721.

Proved 18 May 1722, by all witnesses.

. . . my oving —(torn)— Mary Baley . . .
. . . Daughter Betty Baley . . . to the age of
Eighteen years . . .
. . . son Wm. Baley . . . when . . . twenty one
. . .
. . . unto my wife Mary Baley . . . the manner plantation whereon I now dwell . . .
. . . my daughter Marg^t Baley . . .
. . . my daughter Sarah Baley . . .
. . . to my Said Son Wm. Baley all my lands in Norfolk
County . . .
. . . wife . . . Exrx . . .

Walter Baley & Seal.

WM. BOULTON

Will Book —— p. 10.

Dated 3 March 1722.

Proved 15 March 1722, by all the Witnesses.

. . . to my Son Aaron Boulton after his mothers decease the
plantation houses and orchards that I now doe live upon
. . .
. . . my daughter An Boulton . . .
. . . my daughter Sarah Boulton . . .
. . . my dearly beloved wife E—(torn)— . . .
. . . wife Eliz^a Boulton . . . Sole Extx . . .
. . . my Estate Divided . . . by three men that I shall
name that is Eleazer Tart & John Bowers and Thom Taylor and According as they shall divide (it shall be) . . .

witnesses: John Bowers.
Robt Johnson.
Eleazer Tart.

Wm. Boulton & Seal.

STANHOPE BUTT of the County of Norfolk in Virginia
. . .

Will Book —— p. 11.

Dated 21 Apr. 1722.

Proved 16 Nov. 1722, by John & Thom⁸ Wilson.

. . . to my Son John Butt my plantacon that I now live
on including Seventy five Acres . . .

. . . to my Son Henry Henry Butt Seventy five Acres Including that Cleared ground on the Cypress branch . . .
all yᵉ rest of my land I give to be Equally divided between my two Sons Benjamin Butt and Radford Butt
. . .

. . . appoint my Son John Butt my whole . . . Exr
. . .

witnesses : John Wilson.

Thom⁸ Wilson.

Samˡ Cuningham.

Stanhope Butt.

NATHANIEL LUDGALL of the County of Norfolk . . .
weak . . .

Will Book —+— p. 12.

Dated 4 Feb. 1717.

Proved 20 Nov. 1719 by JoSeph Willey & 18 May 1822 by
ffaithfull Cherry. Sworne to by John Ludgall Exʳ therein
named . . .

. . . Appoint my beloved Son John Lugall . . . Sole
Exʳ . . .

. . . to my beloved wife mary . . . two Iron pots wᶜʰ
was her own by her former husband John Ivey . . .
. . . a pare of fire tongs . . . an Iron Sadle
. . .

. . . to my Daughter ann Ludgall . . . a Chesht of a Mid-
dling Size . . . Sixty acres of Land a plantacon wᶜʰ
was formerly Robᵗ Tuckers wᶜʰ Robert Tucker was possesst wᵗʰ in his fathers life time Lieing above the manner
plantacon and Joyning on Thom Tucker . . .

. . . unto my Son John Ludgall all the remainder part of my Estate boath person[i] and Real . . .

witnesses: Jos[h] Willey.

      John + Eastwood.

      Faithfull Cherry.

                        his

          Nath[ll] + Ludgall & Seal.

                mark.

JOHN MORRISS . . . Virginia Norfolk County . . .

Will Book —— p. 13.

Dated "gber y[e] 21 :17"—(torn)—

Proved 15 Feb. 1722, by Wm. Hunter & Rob[t] M[c]nely . . .
    Swore to by the Ex[r]x . . .

   . . . unto my Loveing frend Mr[s] Ellenor Britt wife of M[r] John Britt Eight pounds Cash.

   . . . unto M[rs] Mary Ann Britt Daughter of M[r] John & Ellenor Britt thirty five pounds Cash.

   . . . frends John Britt Juner & Mary Ann Britt ffrances Britt, Apphia Britt Rob[t] Britt and Hannah Britt twenty Shill[s] a peace to buy a ring.

   . . . unto my loving frend Mr[s] Eliz[a] Britt Daughter to M[r] John and Ellenor Britt all the rest of my Estate . . .

   . . . appoint M[r] John Britt and Eliz[a] Britt . . . Sole Exec[rs] . . .

witnesses: Robert M*cKarey*.

      Mary *Gromill*.

      Wm. Hunter.

              John + Morris & Seal.

ALICE TART . . .

Will Book —— p. 13, etc.

Dated 28 Aug. 1721.

Proved 18 July 1723, by Eliz[a] Collins.

. . . my Son Joseph Tart . . .
. . . Elnathan Tart Son of Thom⁸ Tart . . . his Mother
Mary Tart . . .
. . . my Daughter mary *Costwld* . . .
. . . my Grand Children Thomas —(torn)—Tart each of
them . . .
. . . —(torn)— of Thom⁸ Tart deced —(torn) . . .
—(torn)—
. . . my Son John Owen . . . Sole Exeʳ . . .

witnesses: Eliz⁸ Collins   Signum,
          Wm. Hasil*d*   Alice A. Tart & Seal.

JOHN SMITH . . .

Will Book —— p. 14.

Dated 12 Dec.—(torn)—

Proved Jan. —(torn)— 1733.

—(torn)— a Weatherland a Gunn, —(torn)—
. . . my Son Levy . . .
. . . yᵉ Gunn called Godby . . .
. . . my Daughter June . . .
. . . my Daughʳ Rachel . . .
. . . unto John Smith and Matthew Godfrey —(torn)— and
Sons, all my part of the Stock at *Nuce* river Excepting a
Steer . . .
. . . yᵉ Rest . . . divided among —(torn)—Six Children that are here . . .
. . . divided by my Son John and Peleg —(torn)—Miler.

witnesses: Wᵐ Drake.
          Willis Miller.
          Abraham Etheredge.

                    Jnᵒ Smith + his m—(torn)—

LEWIS CONNOR . . . weak . . .

Will Book —— p. 14?

Dated —(torn)—

Proved —(torn)—

. . . my Daughter Clare . . .

. . . to my Son Roderick . . . negro . . .

. . . to my Sons Dempsey John, Thorogood, my Negro
. . .

. . . to my Daughter M—(faded)— . . . negro . . .

. . . my Daughter Margrett . . .

. . . my Daughter Mary Teresr . . .

. . . to my Daughter Charlott . . . negro wench Hannah wth my mothers good leave . . .

. . . to my Daughter Clotilder . . . at ye age of Sixtcene
years or Marriage . . .

. . . my Dear Wite . . .

. . . to my Son Lewis my Negro Fellow Pompey And after
my Mothers decease . . .

. . . my Son Anthony . . .

—(rest missing)—

RICH^d ALLISTON—(Nuncupative)—Norfolk County—

Will Book —— p. 14.

The Deposition of Giles Randol Aged thirty-five years or
thereabouts . . . being at the House of Richd Alliston
in the time of his Sickness whereof he died heard the sd
—(torn)—Say this his Son Paul Should have the hand
mill after his wife's decease . . . each of his daughters . . . 21 Feb. 1723 . . .

Giles Randolph.

—(Same)—

Arthur Godfrey.

ROB^t STEWART of Norfolk County in the Collony of Virg^a

. . .

Will Book —— p. 14.

Dated 7 Dec. 1723.

Proved 17 July 1723, by Jonathan Godfrey & Joseph Russell

. . . Swore to by Ex^r . . .

. . . unto my Sons Joseph and Robt Stewart my now Dwelling plantation being all the Land I bought of Benjn Hollowell . . .

. . . unto my Son Joseph Stewart that fifty acres of Land
bought of Jno Coats . . .

. . . unto my Son Lovey Stewart all my Lands in Moyock in the Province of North Carolina . .

. . . my Daughter Eliz* . . .

. . . my Loving wife Eliz* my whole . . . Exe'x . . .

witnesses: Jos^h Russsell.

Henry Roberts.

Jonat^n Godfrey.

Robt Stewart & Seal.

WM. ROE of the County of Norfolk . . .

Will Book —— p. 15.

Dated 28 Oct. 1720.

Proved ————(torn)—

. . . my plantation Containing two hundred and Sixty Eight Acres be Equally divided between my two Sons Wm. and Coleman Roe by any four Honest men Chosen by my two Sons aforesd . . .

. . . my lot where now I live shall be Equally divided between my two youngest Sons *Kiheley* and John Roe . . .

. . . my daughter mary Roe . . .

. . . the remaining part of my Estate boath real and personal unto my deare and Loving wife mary Roe and——(rest missing)——

ROBERT TUCKER . . .

Will Book —— p. 20.

Dated 9 Nov. 1722.

Proved 21 Dec. 1722, by Richd Cheshire, Eliz* Thruston, John Watkins and Maximillian Boush/and Swore to by Mr^s ffrances Tucker and Geo. Walker Taking the Tuckers affermation/being Exors/

——(torn)——rest of my Sloops and boats to be Sold by my Exers . . . (Except my Keel boat and Appurtenances wch I give unto my wife] and the Sloops agreed and now building by Mr Frances Thellaball and Mr Thom^s Herbert

to be finished . . . money then due from Capt. Peter
Wills for one and Danl M^{c}arty Esqr for another . . .
Biggest Sloope Building for my Selfe Capt John Phripp
will bidd for and purchase . . .

. . . my apprentice boy John Walkins . . .

. . . Notwithstanding I have Appropriated the money wth M^r
Lewis Connor Stand indebted unto me towards purchasing
the fee simp—(torn)—the Land mortgaged for Securing
the payment of three hund—(torn)—said mortgaged
premises is obtained for my Son Robert.

. . . rings necklaces Jewels &c . . .

. . . my Loving Brother Mr John Tucker . . .

. . . Four Pounds Ster^l be Laid out in mourning rings
. . . Laid out in England . . .

. . . wife Guardian to all my Children . . . and in Case
of her death my worthy good friends Mr Geo. Walker,
Mr Th—(torn)— Thomas Nelson and John Clayton Esq*
are to Succeeds her in that trust.

. . . my Trusty and well beloved wife M^{rs} ffrances Tucker
my Worthy friends Mr Geo. Walker & Mr. Thom^s Wythe
Exers . . .

. . . my wife and four Children . . .

witnesses: Richd Cheshire.

Eliz^a Thrustone.

Elenor E Brett

Jon Watkins

M. Boush.   Robt. Tucker & Seal.

(Evidently a part of the above Will).

. . . in ye possession of Mr. Robt Hall of the County of
Prince George . . .

Item whereas I have made provision for building a house for my
Son Robert on One of the Lots at ye Eastmost End of
Norfolk Town . . .

. . . my two youngest Children John & Sarah.

. . . my sister Mrs Sarah Cock . . .

. . . my Daughter Courtneys Eldest Child . . .

. . . Messrs John Hyde & Comp^y merch^{ts} in London . . .

—— BAILY . . .

Will Book —·— p. 21

Dated 3 Aug. 1723.

Proved——(torn)——

   . . . unto my Son Joseph Bailey all my lands houses and
   appurtenances whereon I now dwell . . . if in Case
   my Son . . . dye without Issue then . . . to fall
   unto my Eldest Daughter Elizth Bailey and if she dyes
   without Issue to my youngest daughter mary *Ki Ki*wise
   . . .
   . . . my wife . . .
——(rest torn)——

   No wills were found in Wills & Deeds Books F and G.
covering a period from January 19, 1721 to June 16, 1730.

   A careful search was made in the old clerk's office of the
Circuit Court of Norfolk County and the abstractor found a
package of wills marked "1722 to 1741," which seem never to
have been spread on the books or possibly the old books for
this period have been lost.

   Immediately following will be abstracted the original
wills found in package marked 1722-1741, which have not been
spread or recorded in the books found for this period.

WILL BAYLEY . . . Western branch of Elizabeth
   River, in ye County of Norfolk . . .

Original Will.

dated 8th——(torn)——

docked 1722.

   . . . to my Loveing daughter Mary Bayley one Negro Girl
   . . . when she is arrived at the the years of eighteen
   . . .
   . . . also I give——(torn)——William Bayley, one Negro
   girl Called dinah . . . one Large Book Called Jose-
   phus . . . when he is arrived to ye Age of twenty one
   . . .

. . . I give and——(torn)——Mary Bayley four Negroes
. . .
. . . son William Bayley . . .
. . . unto my wife Mary——(torn)——I now dwell with all yᵉ houses orchards and all things also thereto A—— (torn)—To my daughter Margaret Bayley one Shilling
. . .
. . . to my——(torn)——In Norfolk County to him and his heirs for ever Lawfully bego——(torn)——Said Son Wᵐ Bayley . . .
. . . wife Mary Bayle all——(torn)——Estate ungiven away for ever . . .
. . . Constitute and ordain My Loving Wife Mary B——— (torn)——of this my Last will & Testament . . .

witnesses: Thomas Bruce.

William Stafford.

Samⁱⁱ Willard.

(Signature torn out)

FRANCIS WILDER of Norfolk County in Virginia . . .

Original Will.

dated 27 Feb. 1722/3.

proved 19 Feb. 1723/4, by James Toomoth & Henry Mason.

. . . unto my Son Samuell Wilder the plantation where he now dwelleth and all the land on the West of the reedy Branch . . . likewise . . . my Silver headed Cane.

. . . unto my Son Jeremiah Wilder my Plantation where I now Dwell with all my land on the Eastmost Side of the reedy Branch . . .

. . . unto my Daughter Sarah Wilder one Leather Trunk . . . all the dunghill fowls of her raising . . .

. . . to my Son Michael Wilder my Gun . . .

. . . to my Son in law Thomas Voss one Small Check . . . that was his mothers. and one great Bible if he learns to read.

. . . the remaining part of my Estate be Equally divided Amongst all my Children in Such proportion that they which had the least may be made Equal with the rest in

Movables   .   .   .

.   .   .   my Sons Samuell & Jeremiah Wilder my Exec^{rs} .   .   .

witnesses : John Pearce.

Henry Mason.

James Toomoth.

Francis Wilder.

GILES RANDOLPH of Norfolk County   .   .   .

Original Will.

dated 1 Sept. 1724.

proved 15 Jan 1724, by Mary Halet, Thos. Cherry & Sarah Wilkins.

   .   .   .   to my beloved Wife Mary Randolph the plantation and Land I now Live on as far as the West Run During her naturall Life   .   .   .   after   .   .   .   to my Daughter Ann Randolph   .   .   .

   .   .   .   to my Son Giles Randolph The plantation he Now Lives on and all my Land of the North Side of the West Run   .   .   .

   .   .   .   to my Son William Randolph the Two Hundred and odd acres of Land I bought of Henry Dale on ye South Side of ye north west River   .   .   .   with the promise he Doe to pay his Mother Eight pounds In Current Commerritys when She demands It.

   .   .   .   to my Son John Randolph one Hundred and thirty odd acres of Land I bought of John Barnton & John OSea lying In the Fork of ye Norwest River   .   .   .

   .   .   .   to my Grand Daughter Sarah Mercer one feather bead.

   .   .   .   wife Mary Randolph & My Son William Randolph ffull and whole Executrix   .   .   .

witnesses : Thos Cherry.

John Davis.

her

Margett Hewlett.

mark.

Lemuel Wilkins.

Sarah Wilkins.

his

Giles Randolph.

mark.

DENNIS MACCOY Planter in y* County of Norfolk . . .
Original Will.

dated 21 Feb. 1721/2.

proved 19 June 1724, by Peter Taylor & Henry Etheredge.

. . . unto my well Beloved Son Hugh Maccoy y* plantation tion which I now Live upone called Chincapin Neck containing Sixty Acres more or less . . .

. . . unto my well Beloved son Dennis Maccoy y* plantation called Piney Ridge Containing forty Six Acres more or Less to be Run with a Line Just across y* sd Ridge & to Joyn with my Son Richard . . .

. . . unto my well Beloved son John Maccoy y* remaining part of y* Piney Ridge containing forty Six acres more or Less with a Line Run y* same Course.

. . . unto my well Beloved Son Hugh Maccoy y* plantation comonly called by y* Name of Stones Ridge containning forty six acres more or Less adjoyning to y* Land which was formerly called Mr John Edwards . . . when he arrives at Twenty . . .

. . . unto my Well Beloved son William Maccoy one Drawing Table a gun . . .

. . . if any of my four Sons Richard, Dennis, John or Hugh Maccoy should Die without Isue that then their parts or Lotts of Land may fall unto my youngest Son William Maccoy.

. . . wife Elianor Maccoy Executrix . . . Son Richard Maccoy . . . Executor . . .

witnesses : Peter Taylor.

>   his
> Edward Etheredge
>   mark.
> Henry Etheredge.

>   . Dennis Macoy.
>   Seal.

MOSES PRESCOTT of the County of Norfolk in Virginia
. . .

Original Will.

dated 9 Feb. 1723/4.

proved 19 June 1724, by Wm. Ballance & John Smith.

. . . to my Loveing Sonn Robert Prescott my new Store house with fifteen foot of Land square whereon it stands . . . to my Said Sonn Robert one peace of Land Known by y⁰ name of Rubin tree Branch neck begin at a gum standing in my Line and So runing Southwest down to the north branch Containing one hundred & Eight acres of Land more or Les . . .

. . . to my Loveing Sonn John Prescott my plantation whereon I now Live beginning at a Water Oake a Corner tree of my Line & So runing a Southwest Cost to a branch & So down the Said brach to the north branch of the norcwest River . . . Two hundred and forty Acres more or Les . . .

. . . to my Loveing Sonn Moses Prescott the plantation whereon he formerly Lived begining att a White Oke Corner tree & So runing due South to the norwest river Containing two hundred Acres more or Les . . .

. . . to my Loveing Sonn Thomas Prescott the Remainder part of my Land where on I now Live Containing one hundred and Eaighty acares more or Les & . . . unto my Sonn Thomas Prescott the Land I bought of Gabrell Holms . . .

. . . to my Loveing Sonn William Prescott the Land on wheare he formerly Lived none by the name of *Crickmors* I land . . . .

. . . to my Grand Children the Child of my Dafter Ann Twenty Shilins *apes* . . .

. . . Dafter I*asebll* . . .

. . . my Sonn Tho. prescotte . . . Sole Exetor . .

witnesses: John Wilson.

John Smith.

——————— *Boyce.*

Wm. Ballance, his mark.

his
Moses Pre*scott*
marke.

———————

SIMON JACKSON of Norfolk County . . .

Original Will.

dated 12 Mch. 1723.

proved 18 Dec. 1724, by Lem. Simmons & *Ex*ʳ.

. . . my well beloved wife Jean Jackson my bed . . .
. . . to my beloved Son Israel Jackson one feather bed
. . .
. . . to Loveing Daughter Elizabe^th Jackson one years
Schooling . . . She may board at her aunt Mary
Jacksons . . .
. . . my wife and Children . . .
. . . my brother James Jackson . . . Sole Executor*s*
. . .

witnesses : Lemuel Simmons.

     her
   Margery Jackson
   mark.

          Simon Jackson.

ROBART SMITH of Norfolk County . . .
Original Will.
dated 20 *July* 1724.
proved 21 May 1725 & 18 June 1725.
. . . wife Mary Smith the one third . . .
. . . unto Jacob mash . . . Cow . . . att his house
. . .
. . . unt my well beloved daughter Mary Cocks all the Rest
. . .
. . . five pounds of it be put to the Edeation of my Gran
Son Edword Cocks . . .
. . . makeing William ballance my hole Exector . . .

witnesses : Moses Linton.

   Joseph bateman.

          Robard Smith
          marke

J. JOHNSTON Senr . . .
Original Will.
dated 6 Apr. 1721.
proved 21 May 1725, by Eleazor Tart & Sarah his wife.

. . . to my Son Johnston one hundred Acres of Land Lying att the South East End of the dwelent . . . my *Clothes* and part of the or Chad that my father gave mee . . .

. . . to my Son William Johnston one Cow . . .

. . . to my Son Thomas Johnston the plantion I now Live on Contaning one hundred Acres . . . after his mothers deces . . .

. . . to my Son Robert Johnston Small gun . . .

. . . to my dafter Sarah——(*cant read*)—— . . .

. . . to my dafter Ann Smyth foure hundred and fifty pounds of tobacco . . .

. . . to my Son Joseph Johnston All my Cupers tules . . .

. . . to my Sone Benjaman Johnston one Cow . . . when he Coms to Age . . . Eighteen . . .

. . . to my dafter Elizabeth Johnston one febather beed . . . when Shee Comes to Age . . .

. . . to my wel beloved Wife Rebaco Johnston all the Rest . . .

. . . wife Rebco Johnston ad my Son Thomas Johnston . . . Sole Executors . . .

witnesses: William Boulton.

  Elezar Tarte Senr

  his marke.

  Sarah Tart

  hir marke.

his

John Johnston

marke.

JONAS CAWSON of ye County of Norfolk in Virg^a . . .
Original Will.

dated 29 Aug. 1726.

proved 18 Nov. 1726.

. . . unto my well beloved Son Christopher Cawson after ye Decease of his mother all my Plantation I now live upon ye Plantation I bought of Moses Linton and the plantation I bought of John Pricket . . . give to my Son Christopher my Plan——(torn)——I bort of Edward Wynn and a Tract of Land I also bought of John Sylwent adjoining to it called Rich Neck likewise a Track of Land I bor^t of Capt. John Ryall called poynt lookout all lying in Mattche Pungo River in Bath County North Carolina

. . . unto my well beloved Son Argall Cawson my houses and Land Lying at ye Southern Branch great bridge with ye plantation I bou^t of William Bishop called Possum Ridge

. . . unto all my well beloved Children as Christopher Argall Jonas Kesiah Ann Abigall and Jennit Cawson all my goods Chattells . . . after the Decease of their mother

. . . unto Thomas Nash Junr half my Corn*ece* . . .
. . . Wife . . . Sole Executrix . . .

witnesses: Peter Taylor.
         his
     James Edward
       mark.
       her
     Mary Portlock
       mark.

                           his
               Jonas Cawson. Seal. Wax.
                   mark.

PETER CARTWRIGHT . . .

Original Will.

dated 7 Mch. 1726.

proved 19 May 1727.

. . .to my waif Mary Cartwright on negro woman . . .
. . . to my Dafter Margritt Cartwright my graitt Brick hous & To thirds of tha lots *that stands* upon . . . that stands in Noroflk town *Again* . . . Peter Malbons this hous & part of the Kitchen is to bee lett out for the *Scholin* or maintaing of my darter margritt . . . when Shee Come to bee of the Aige of sixteen or marys but if dies without ishau T*henst* must goa to Cartwright Butt . . . & if hee dies without ishau then itt falls to Ele *bitt* . . . neest of bloud to mee the giver.

. . . to my dafter margritt Cartwright fifty Ackers of land

next to the hors Bridge out of this tract *of* of Land whair
I now live . . .
.   .   . to Afia—(can't read)—hundred Acres of Land Joyning
to the East—(torn)— . . .
.   .   . to my Cosin P*eter sayard* . . . the rest to be devided—(torn)—between my two Dafters—(torn)—ibell
butt and margritt Cartwright . . .
.   .   . to my grand son—(torn)—*butt all* That Pees of a lot
of land I bought of Cosin *Job Dibbs* lott in Norfolk town
.   .   .
.   .   . frends Captn. John Whiddon and Richard Whitehust
Senr . . . Soul Axators . . .
.   .   . my two dafters Ciball & Matgritt . . .

witnesses: John Whiddon

     Elizb^th Sunky her mark.
Wm. Sunky.
     Eliz:^th Voilintin her mark.

                    Peter Cartwright
                    Wax Seal.

RICHARD BUTT the Elder of Norfolk County . . .

Original Will.

dated 8 Sept. 1724.

proved 18 Aug. 1727, by Edwd Lem^l & Wm Etheredge.

.   .   . Unto my Loveing wife Sarah Butt, the land & plantacon whereon I now live. known by the name of timber
neck . . . during her natural life, and after her decease . . . Untc my Eldest Son Thomas Butt . . .
& for want of Such heir . . . Unto my Son William
Butt . . .

.   .   .
.   .   . Unto my Son Thomas Butt, my Land or Plantacon
called Burchen Neck, to be devided half way between the
plantacon whereon I live, & burchen Neck . . . & for
want of Such issue, then . . . Unto my Grandson
Richard Butt (Son of Richard Butt) . . .
.   .   . Unto my Son Robert Butt, the plantacon whereon he
now liveth upon the branches of the northwest river,
begining at a Marked white Oak, wch Stands on a branch
call'd the TarrKill branch on the South side of ye Said
plantacon So bounding ye Said bra: an Eastward Course,

& On the North Side of the S^d plantacon begining at a Marked poplar wch Stands by a Cyprus Swamp Side, So runing an Eastward Course, to aline of marked trees, wch devides my land from the land of Henry Halstead wch Said land included within ye Said bounds & Courses I give . . .

. . . Unto my Son Henry Butt, the plantation & Land whereon he now lives, Called the long beach ridge, and also the land call'd round beach ridge, which Said lands bounds on my Cosen Henry Butt's land on the South Side, and on my Cosen Thomas Butt's land on the north side, & on the branch or Run, which devides the Said lands & Timber Neck, on the east side, and also Give Unto my Son Henry Butt, the plantacon at the Gum Swamp with ye one half of the land between the Gum Swamp & the North side of the Cyprus branch, being the half of the land On the Said Swamp Up to Mundens line, wch three percells of land &^c I give . . .

. . . Unto my Son Richard Butt, the plantacon & land whereon he now lives, according to the Known bounds . . .

. . . Unto my Son John Butt, all the Remaining part of the South end of my Said land from the poplar ridge bra^n Unto Henry Halsteads land . . .

. . . Unto my Son Lemuel Butt, all my land on the South side of the Cyprus branch down to Munden's land . . .

. . . Unto my Son Willm Butt, all the Remaining part of my land Northwardly from the Land I have Given my Son Robert Butt, to a Cross line that parts my land from Henry Halsteads . . .

. . . Unto my daught^r Elizabeth Butt my Negro woman named bess . . .

. . . Unto my daughter Mary Butt my Yerb Still . . .

. . . Unto my daughter Sarah Munden one feather bed . . .

. . . Unto my Several Children, Namely Thomas, Robert, Henry, Richard, John, Anthony, Lemuel & William Butt, Elizabeth & Mary Butt, & Sarah Munden, the Several things formerly possessed them of, and now by this will Given . . .

. . . my Loving wife Sarah Butt, and my Son Henry Butt, my whole & Sole Execut^rs . . .

. . . all the Remaining part of my estate . . . be equally devided between all my Children . . .

witnesses: Thomas Etherige.

Edward Etherige.

Lemuell Etheridge.

Wm. Etherdge.

Richard Butt. Wax Seal &
Arms.

FAITHFULL CHERRY of the County of Norfolk of the Southern Branch of Elizabeth River . . .

Original Will.

dated 28 July 1727.

proved 16 Feb. 1727/8.

. . . my beloved wife to be my hole and Sole Executrix . . .

. . . unto my beloved wife full priviled of all my Land During her Life . . . not hindering my Son Luke Cherry to build or Cleare any where upon the wood land ground and after the death of my wife I give all my Land to my Son Luke Cherry . . . when he Come to the age of One & twenty . . . all my Coopers Tools . . .

. . . unto my Daughter Ruth Cherry one feather bed . . .

. . . unto my Son Faithfull Cherry one Hefer . . . when he Come to the age of Eighteen . . . I Desire that Thomas Culpeper Shall have him and keep him . . . Shall put him to School as Long as he Shall See fitt . . .

. . . Unto my Son Titus Cherry one gunn . . .

. . . unto my Daughter Patience Cherry one Large puter Dish . . .

. . . to my Son Job Cherry one Iron pott . . .

. . . my five Children Luke Cherry, Ruth Cherry, Patence Cherry, Faithfull Cherry and Job Cherry . . .

witnesses: Thomas Culpeper.

Thomas Eastwood.

David Dale.

Faithfull Cherry. Seal Wax.

WILLIAM NICHALSON Sen[r] of Norfolk County . . .

Original Will.

dated 24 Feb. 1728.

proved 17 May 1728.

. . . unto my Loveing Son William Nichalson the manner plantacon & houses whereon I now Live Together with all houses and Land on the westerne or westward Side of the holly Boush branch Excepting the now brick Roome which I Shall hereafter direct and dispose of . . . after the Decease of my Loveing wife Alice . . .

. . . unto my Loveing Son *Thomas*—(torn)—Nichalson all my Land on the Eastward Side of the Holly Boush branch . . . my gun called my short Gunn . . .

. . . unto my Sons George Nicholson and Lemuel Nichalson all my Land Lying and being on the North Side of the Gum Swamp Run in princes Anne county *To be* devided in the manner following that is to Say, Marking a Line of trees from a place on the Said Land called the Cow Ponns unto another place called the Little Run: and that part of the Land on the North Side of the Said Line be it more or Less I Give unto my Son Lemuel . . . and the South Side of the Said Line Lett the Same be more or Less I give unto my Son George . . . the true intent and meaning of this my Last will & Testament that Neither of my said Sons George Nor Lemuel Nicholson Nicholson Shall Sell or Dispose of any part of the sd Land to any out of the name of the Nicholsons & Likewise that my Son William & Thomas & John Nicholson Shall have priviledge to Drive on and of the Said Land there hoggs . . .

. . . unto my Son John Nichalson a Negro man named Fortune . . . & my painted Stock Gun . . .

. . . unto my Grandson Joshua Nicholson the Son of my Son William Nicholson the first Child that my negro Girle Kate brings that Lives to be Twelve months old . . .

. . . unto my Daughter Elizabeth Nicholson my Negro Girle called Kate . . .

. . . unto my Daughter Anne Butt my Negro Girle called Unity . . .

. . . unto my Daughter Mary Langley a Negro boy . . .

. . . unto my Daughter Abigall Nichalson my Negro Girle . . .

. . . unto my Daughter Dinah Wilson my Negro Girle
. . .
. . . unto my Daughter Sarah Nicholson my Negro boy
. . .
. . . unto my three Daughters that is to say Elizabeth Abigall and Sarah Nichalson after the Decease of my wife
Alice Nichalson my New brick houss for them all To Live
in untill they are Married.
. . . wife Alice Nichalson my Executrix & my Son William
Nichalson my Executor . . .

witnesses: Tho⁰ Butt.

      Nath¹¹ Tatem.

      George Sparrow.

      Peter Lowe.

                William Nichalson & Wax
                        Seal.

DIODATUS THRELKELD of Norfolk County in Virginia
Mariner . . .

Original Will.

dated 26 Aug. 1728 and in yᵉ first year of yᵉ Reigne of our Sov-
ereigne Lord King George yᵉ Second.

proved 16 May 1729 by Martha Scott & Eliz. Scott & by Sibell

    Thellkeld admr wᵗʰ the will annexed.
. . . to my well Be Loved Wife Sibbelle Threlkeld one half
of my Reall & parsonall Estate as Long as She Shall Live
. . . yᵉ Other half I give & bequeath to my Son Diod:
Thelkeld . . . & at his Mothers Death I give yᵉ Other
half that was his Mothers . . .
. . . my Gun & Sword Shoos buckels & my Sleve Buttons
. . . But if my Son Diodatus Should Dye before yᵉ Age
of one & twenty or be Married then yᵉ half that was Diodatus Threlkeld Shall com to John Threlkeld yᵉ Son of
Jimima Burrows in Bermuda & if Jnᵒ Threlkeld Should
Dye before yᵉ Age of One & Twenty or Maryed to cum to
yᵉ Children of Elizᵗʰ Edwards yᵉ Wiffe of Isaac Edward⁰
. . .

. . . my Frends Thom⁸ Scott & Jn⁰ Tucker be Executors
. . .

witnesses: Martha Scott.
           her mark.
      Mary Ballingtine.
           her mark.
      Elizabeth Scott.

                              Diod⁸ Thrlkeld. Wax
                                      Seal.
                            . . .

RICHARD TAYLOR of Elizabeth River in the County of
    Norfolk in Virginnia . . .

Original Will.

dated 26 Sept. 1729.

proved 19 Feb. 1730/1, by John & Wᵐ Owens.

   . . . to my Son William taylor on Short gune . . .
   . . . to my Son John taylor my *bible* ·. . . three wigs
   . . .
   . . . to my Son Edward taylor my . . . gune . . .
   . . . to my Dafter Mary taylor . . . larg puter basson . . .
   . . . to *yon* Dafter Margret taylor one Larg puter basson
   . . .
   . . . to my Dafter Richal taylor one Large puter basson
   . . .
   . . . wife J*an* Taylor be Excutʳ⁸ . . .

witnesses: John Owens.
      Willa Owens.
      Thomas Owens.
         his mark.   Richard Taylor
                                   his mark. (Scroll).

SOLOMON HODGIS . . .

Original Will.

dated 14 Aug. 1730.

proved 19 *Mch* 1730/1.

. . . my Plantation and tract of Land where *on* I now do
Live to my brother Thomas Hodgis . . . and if my
brother Tho˙ Hodgis Should die without heirs . . .
my brother Robert hodgis Shall have my Plantation
and Lands belonging to it . . . and if my brother
Robert hodgis Shall Die without heire then my will is that
my brother William hodgis Shall have my Plantation with
the Land belonging to it . . .

witnesses: *Peter* White Sener.

      Arthur Godfrey.

      Joseph hodgis.

      mark.

                        his

              Solomon hodgis. Scroll.

                      mark.

FRANCES HODGIS of Norfolk County . . .

Original Will.

dated 20 Apr. 1730.

proved 17 July 1730, by Jno. Watkins & Mr. John Tucker.

   . . . my Son in Law M˙ Edward Thruston my Hole Executor . . .

   . . . unto my Afectionate Grandaughter Courtney Walker
my bed . . . A Gold Ring a Small Silver Cupp & A
Ambur necklaces.

   . . . Unto my Afectionate Grandaughter Mary Thruston
y˙ bed up in y˙ Chamber . . . A Gold Ring . . .

   . . . Unto my Affectionate Grandson Jn˙ Thruston one Cotton Hammock . . .

   . . . unto my affectionate Grandaughter Elizabeth Thruston
A Large Seal Skin Trunk . . .

   . . . Unto my Affectionate Grandaughter Frances Thruston
a black Trunk . . .

   . . . Unto my Affectionate Grandaughter Susanah Thruston
a black Trunk.

   . . . unto my affectionate Grandson Thomas Thruston Six
Silver Spoone's Mark (*T. F.*)

   . . . Unto my affectionate and Dityfull Daughter Frances
Nelson one pare fine Cotton Sheets . . .

   . . . Unto my affectionate & Dutyfull Daughter Elizabeth

Thruston one Cold Still . . . and one Mourning Ring wch was my Deceas^d husband Mr Thos Hodgis.

. . . Unto my Affectionate Son in Law Mr Thomas Nelson one Ginina To buy him A Mourning Ring.

. . . Unto my Affectionate Grandson in Law Mr. Jacob Walker one Sizable Mourning Ring.

. . . Unto my Affectionate Friend Jno Tucker Sizable Mourning Ring.

. . . Remaining part . . . Devided following to my Grandchildren by Each of my t—— Daughters (Vz) Courtney Walker Mary Thruston Jno. Thruston Elizabeth Thruston Frances Thruston Robt. Tucker Jno Tucker Susanah Thruston Thomas Thruston Sarah Tucker & Sarah Nelson.

witnesses: Jno Tucker.

Mary Thruston.

Jno Watkins.

her

Frances Hodgis. Wax Seal.

marke.

RICHARD JOHNSON of Norfolk County in Virginia , . . Original Will.

dated 26 Feb. 1729/30.

proved 18 Sep. 1730, by John May & Ann Johnson Exc^{rx}.

. . . unto my son in law Thomas hamton one hundred acres of Land which I bought of Thomas presend Called by the name of homeses and its my will that if the abovesaid Thomas Hamton Should at any time have a mind to sel it to his brother John Johnson to have The Refusen of it . . .

. . . unto my Son John Johnson my maner plantation whereon I now Live . . .

. . . Rest of my Estate . . . to my Loveing Wife Ann Johnson . . . hir . . . Sole Executrix . . .

witnesses: Richard Linton.

Daneill Glasco.

John Moy.

Richard Johnson

Wax Seal.

JOHN DALE of the Towne & County of Norfolk . . .
Original Will.
dated 23 Jan. 1727/8.
proved 20 Jan. 1731/2, by Willis Wilson.
. . . wife Mary Dale . . . all my Estate reall & personal
. . .

witnesses: Thomas Tryan.
     Peter Mallbon.
     Willis Wilson.

            John Dale.
            Wax Seale.

PETER ROBERTS . . .
Original Will.
dated 22 May 1730.
proved 21 May 1731, by Geo. Writeing, Michael & Ann Wilder.

. . . Samuell Roberts the Son of my Brother James Roberts
Should have my Gunn . . .
. . . my wife Elizabeth Roberts Should have Every thing
after my desease . . . my Land and my Hoggs
. . . for her Life Time and after . . . to Let
James Roberts the Son of my Brother James Roberts
have the Land . . .

witnesses: Michale Wilder
     his marke.
     Ann Wilder
     her marke.

            Peter Roberts.

JOHN BACON of Norfolk County in Virg[a] . . .
Original Will.
dated 29 Nov. 1730.
proved 16 July 1731.

. . . unto my Daughter Hanah Bacon my plantation that I
Live on, and my water mill, Both Land and mill . . .
. . . unto my Daughter Eliz[a] Bacon one feather bed . . .
at Eighteen . . .

. . . unto my Daughter Sarah Bacon one feather Bed
. . . at Eighteen . . .
. . . Unto my Daughter Beththeba Bacon Two Iron pots
. . . at Eighteen . . .
. . . wife Eliz⁴ Bacon . . . Sole Executrix . . .

witnesses: John Jolliff Senʳ
John Jolliff, Junʳ
Richard baker.

John Bacon.
Wax Seal.

ROBERT LEANE of Virginia in the County of Northfolk
Original Will.

dated 14 Oct. 1730.

proved 16 July 1731.

. . . to my Son John Leane my plantation Containing
Seaventy five acres Lying and being in prencess Ann
County in Virginia . . .
. . . unto my Son Robert Leane my neigro Garl . . .
. . . wife Ann Leane my neigro woman . . .
. . . my two Loveing and Trusty Brothers Jasper Leane and
Augustes Leane my Overseers . . .
. . . wife Ann Leane my hole and Sole Executrix . . .

witnesses: James Warden.
John Moy.
John Simmons.
William par.

Robert Leane.
Wax Seal.

THOMAS MASON, Planter of tanners Creek presenks of yᵉ
County of Norfolk . . .

Original Will.

dated 28 Nov. 1731.

proved 17 Xbr 1731, by Cooper & Banks.

. . . to my loveing Son George Mason the one half of my land I now live on & yᵉ Other half of my land I give unto my loveing Son William Mason . . . Equally Devided . . . by three neighbours & the plantasion I now live on I give to my Son William Mason & if in Case my Son William Mason dies without heir . . . unto my Daugter Ann Mason & if in Case my Daughter Ann Mason Dies without heir . . . unto my Daughter Mary Broten . . .

. . . to my Son Lemuell Mason one Shilling . . .

. . . to my Daughter Mary Broten one Shilling . . .

. . . to my Daughter Ann Mason . . . my hand mill . . . only Reserving yᵉ Use of her for my Wife . . .

. . . to my Son Henry Mason one Shilling . . .

. . . to my Daughter Dinah Mason one Shilling . . .

. . . to my Daughter Spring Mason one Shilling . . .

. . . to my loveing wife all thee Rest . . . dureing her Widdowhood . . . wife— (torn) — Sole Executrix . . .

witnesses: John Langley.

Edward Cooper.

John Banks
mark.

his
Thomas Mason
mark.
Wax Seal.

WILLIAM FOREMAN, Senʳ of Norfolk County . . .

Original Will.

dated 20 Apr. 1731.

proved 16 July 1731.

. . . to my Son Alexander foreman the Land Called yᵉ Rowling tree ———— . . .

. . . to my Son William foreman one Hefer and the Rugg I bought of Mʳ Daulays . . .

. . . to my Son Jeremiah foreman Twelve pounds ten Shillings . . . my *Ginnie* pen Chest and all my Coopers and Carpenters Tooles . . .

. . . to my Son Richard foreman the plantation I now live on . . . one Set of Shoemakers Tools . . .

. . . my Loveing Wife Elizabeth foreman . . .

. . . my Grand Children ten Shillings a peace . . .

. . . to my Son Richard foreman the Thirds of the Land I bought of Archable Grimes and my Entrey on the *Ginnipper Swamp* . . .

. . . Wife Elizabeth foreman & my Son Jeremiah . . . Exec^rs . . .

witnesses: J. ffife.

      Benjamin Foreman, his marke.

      Elizabeth Grimes, her marke.

                William foreman.

                Wax Seal.

JOSEPH MILLER of Norfolk County & Colony of Virginia

. . .

Original Will.

dated 30 Dec. 1730.

proved 17 Sep. 1731, by Brooks & Dawley.

. . . to my well beloved Son Joseph Miller two hundred acres of Land which I bought of William Rowe lying on the main roade also one hundred acres of Swamp land joyning on the South Side of my brother Williams Line and the north Sid of the Herring runn . . .

. . . to my Daughter Lavinah *more* one hundred acres of land joyning on Parterick White his line . . . my desire is y^t after my daughter Lavinah her Decease my Grandson Thomas & Miller mor Shall Equally Enjoy ye land . . .

. . . to my Brother Benjn Miler his Son Joseph Miler fifty acres of Land joyning on the West Side of the land left to my daughter lavinah *both* of them runing for breadth upon the Swamp *bed* for length into the wood . . .

. . . to my Daughter providence Miller one hundred acres of Land next joyning on the west Side of the afors^d Land left to my Cousen miler runing for breadth and length as afors^d . . .

. . . to my Son Shadrack Miller three thousand pounds of Good Sound fresh pork att markett . . .

. . . Cipress Chest . . .

. . . unto my well beloved Son Shadrack miler all y⁰ remainder part of my Estate both personal and reyall . . . him to be my whole and Sole Executor . . .

witnesses: William Corbell.

       Lawrance Doyley.

       William Brooks
       his mark.

his

Joseph Miller. Wax Seal.

mark.

WILLIAM NICHOLSON Senr of Norfolk County . . .

Original Will.

dated 19 June 1731.

proved 19 Nov. 1731.

. . . to my Eldest Son Joshua Nicholson all that Tract of Land belonging to me and lying on the East Side of *Salls* Spring neck land . . . that he fully enjoy & possess it when when he comes to the Age of twenty . . .

. . . to my Second Son William Nicholson . . . the Manner House and plantation whereon my Mother Alice Nicholson now lives together wth all houses & Land on the westward Side of the holly Boush Branch and I will and desire y^t he enjoy & possess it w^n he comes to full age.

. . . to my third Son Malachi Nicholson a Tract of Land lying on the north Side of the Gum Swamp Runn in Princes Anne County . . .

. . . to my eldest Son Joshua Nicholson one pair of pistols Holsters and a Silver hilted Sword . . . when he comes of age.

. . . my beloved wife Prudence Nicholson . . .

witnesses: Lem^ll Nicholson.

       Thomas Nicholson.

       Moses Robinson.

Willm Nicholson,

Wax Seal.

WILLIAM COOPER of Norfolk County in Virginia . . .
Original Will.
dated 20 March 1731.
proved 16 Feb. 1732, by Lem¹ Langley & Geo. Wrighting.

. . . to my Son Benjamin Cooper my Plantation whereon I now dwell Together with all Buildings & orchards there upon Except my new Dwelling house & the Buttery and half my Shop which I give to my loveing wife Elizabeth . . . during her naturall Life . . . and Belong to my said Son Benjamin and to the male heirs lawfully begotten of his Body, and for want of Such heir I give the Said plantation to my son Joseph Cooper & the male heirs . . . & on failure of such heirs to the next heir of my sons and not to go out of the name as long any of my sons or their male heirs Shall be living . , .

. . . to my son Edward Cooper the Plantation he now lives upon as it is Bounded Between my said Son Edward and my Son John Cooper by as it is Bounded by a line of markt Trees . . .

. . . to my son John Cooper the plantation whereon he now lives as it is marked between my said Son John and my son Edward . . . to him my said son John and the male heirs lawfully Begotten of his body for Ever and for want of such heirs to the next male heir and to Descend and not go out of the name of the Coopers so long as any shall be living.

. . . to my Two Sons George and Joseph Cooper one piece of Swamp land binding upon Giles Randell.

. . . one great Sermon Book; and all the Rest of my Books I give to my Seven Sons . . .

. . . to my son James Cooper besides what is already given him five Shillings being in full of his portion . . .

. . . to my Daughter Ann Bayly Twenty Shillings . . .

. . . to my Daughter Elizabeth Williamson five Shillings . . .

. . . rest of my movable Estate . . . Equally Devided Between my loveing Elizabeth and Georg, and Joseph and Jacob and Benjamin Cooper . . .

. . . my son Benjamin may have my mill after the Desease of my wife Elizabeth . . .

. . . wife Elizabeth Cooper and my son Benjamin Cooper my whole and Sole Executrix and Executor . . .

witnesses: Lem¹¹ Langley.
              Jas. Toomoth.
              George Righting.   Wm. Cooper. Wax Seal.

JOSEPH HOLLOWELL of the County of Norfolk in the Collony of Virginia . . .

Original Will.

dated 22 Jan. 1732/3.

proved ———— 1732/.

. . . to my Loveing mother my Gould Buttons . . .

. . . all my Cattle to my Loving Grandmother Realing . . .

. . . to my father in Law Joseph Russell and my Loving Sister Marchant One Still and Worm between them.

. . . my Gould Ring to my Loving Sister Sarah William's and her Husband my Gun . . .

. . . my Negroe Garle patience to Grace Russell and Agness and Malachi . . . when Malachi Comes to ye age of fiften years . . .

. . . a Small remnant of OZ: to Stephen Williams . . .

. . . all my Land lying in ye Western Branch to my Loving Sister Merchant . . .

. . . Give Luke Russell all my Wearing Clothes . . .

. . . my father in Law Joseph Russell to be my hole and Sole Executor . . .

witnesses: Richd Church.

John Wilkins.

Joseph Hallowell.
Wax Seal.

———

LAZARUS SWENY of ye County of Norfolk and Coloney of Virginie . . .

Original Will.

dated 21 Oct. 1732.

proved 15 Dec 1732 by Tho. Whiddon & Wm. Tabb.

. . . marke and ordain my Brother Samull Sweny my only and Sole Executor . . . my Loveing wife Elizabeth Sweny Be Equiley Concerned with my Said Brother In ye manigment of all my Estate Boath Real and Persnel . . .

. . . unto my Son Daniel my houses and that Lot of Land at ye Norwest Landing Bought of John *Pesced*.

. . . unto my Son Daniel and my Son James to Be Equily

devided Between them all that Trackt of Land that I have Entered and am now Setting that Lyeth over yᵉ Creek Before my Dore.

. . . all the Remander of my *wifs* Estate Both Rail and persnal to Be Equily Devided Between my *wife* and Children . . . if my wife Be now with Child that yᵉ Child She now Goes with have an Equil part of my Estat with my wife and other Children . . .

witnesses: Willᵐ Tabb.

Thomas Whiddon.

Martha tabb.

Lazarus Sweny.
Wax Seal.

WILLIAM BALLANCE of Norfolk County . . .

Original Will.

dated 3 Mch. 1733/2

proved 18 May 1733.

. . . unto my Son William Ballance my new dwelling plantation with all the land belonging to it . . .

. . . unto my Son Moses Ballance that plantation and land thaᵗ I bought of henary hawely . . .

. . . unto my Son John Ballance all my New Survey at the head of the Swamp Joyning to Henary Etheredge and Andrew Makefashen . . .

. . . to my Son Hasekiah ballance one young hors Called Sparse . . .

. . . unto my sons *and* daughters John and Hasakiah and Ann ballance and bridget ballance and Elizabeth ballance and Marcy ballance and Sarah ballance Each of them a hefer . . .

. . . unto my other two daughters Mary and Esebel Each of them a hefer . . .

. . . one father bed and furnitude to my daughter *Ann* ballance . . .

. . . unto my loveing wife Mary Ballance all the Rest of my moveable Estate . . .

. . . my Son Moses Ballance my beloved Sole Executor . . .

witnesses: Daniel mackfarsen
his mark.
Jonathan mackfarsen.

his
William Ballance.
marke.
Wax Seal.

ROBERT KING, Norfolk County . . .
Original Will.
dated 21 June 1732.
proved 15 Sept. 1732.

. . . to my Daughter Elizabeth one yew & Lam . . .
. . . unto my well beloved wife Elizabeth all my whole Estate till her Deseas & after her Deseas to be Equally Devided amongs my children male & female.

witnesses: Sarah Busten.
Thos Hobgood. Ju.

his
Robert King
mark.

RICHARD FULCHER . . .
Original Will.
dated 29 Aug. 1732.
proved 15 Dec 1732.

. . . one Bead and furnet——— to my uncle Thomas T*wine* . . .
. . . to my Cosen Catern Twine one Gold Ring . . .
. . . unto Edward *Vean* one neagro man . . .
. . . do make Edward *Voan* my hole and Sole Executor . . .

witnesses: *D*avid Ballentine
Abigail Whiddon.
her
mary whiddon
mark

Richard *Vul*her
Wax Seal.

WILLIAM GWIN of Norfolk County . . .

Original Will.

dated 28 May 1733.

proved ————— by Mʳ Mathew Godfrey.

backed: Wᵐ Gwin junʳ will.

recorded, ————— 1733.

. . . to my well beloved Mother Sarah Gwin My Plantation Called and known by the name of Westons being one
hundred acres more or Less . . .

. . . to my mother Sarah Gwin all my Mony Tools & Debts
and all what *enes* Belonging to me I—(torn)—for her
thirds of the Plantation that I Sold to *M*—(torn)—Lowry
She haveing Ecepted of It And doe Apoint—(torn)—Well
beloved Mother . . . Sole Executrix . . .

witnesses: Matth. Godfrey.

Jane Lowry.

Mary Lorey.

his
William Gwin
mark.

———————

"Memorandum of a *Zerewill* will of *Mr.* WM. MARLEYS"
. . .

Original Memorandum.

dated 23 Mch. 1732/3.

proved 18 May 1733, by James Millecent & John Denby & that
Mʳ Lemˡ Langley was desired by sd Marley to write the
above will . . .

. . . all his land . . . to his Cosen Elizabeth Cooper
wife of Tho. Cooper during her naturall Life & att *Her*
deseas . . . to his Cosen John Marly son of his Bro.
John Marly to him & his heres for evert &—(torn)—to
his Bro. Nathan marly he gives a pare of Silver Shoe
Buckels . . .

. . . to Jeems Brambell a Kow & hefer . . .

. . . his Bro John marley Children & Jeams Marleys Children & his sister faith Brambels Children . . .

. . . desirs thatt Lemˡˡ Langley & Edward Cooper one or
Borth of them Shall Be his exicoter . . .

RICHARD *JOELL* of Norfolk Town in Virginia . . .
Original Will. (See also Book 12 p. 18).
dated 2 Aug. 1734.
proved 15 Nov. 1734.

> . . . to my Loving Wife Rebecca Joell all my Estate which
> I am possest of, untill She Changes her Name, But when
> She changes her name then She is to have but one third
> part of my Estate and the rest to be equally devided be-
> tween my Children Susanna Joell, Rebecca, Richard &
> Hannah, and Stafford Joell.
> . . . friend Capt Nathaniel Tatum & my well beloved Wife
> Rebecca Joell to be my Executor & Executrix . . .

witnesses: J. Phripp.
      James Giles.   Richᵈ Jo*ell*.
                                        Wax Seal.

WILLIAM TABB . . .
Original Will.
dated 8 Oct. 1735.
proved 16 Jan. 1735/6.

> . . . my loving wife and loving friends *Mr*. Brodie, Jnᵒ Tabb
> and Thoˢ Tabb be the Executors . . . have full power
> to sell all my houses lands Mills are any other freehold
> Estate that I am now possesd off iff they think proper for
> uses hereafter mentioned . . . the money arising from
> the sails . . . be Equally divided betwixt my Loving
> wife and my two Sons William & Edmund Tabb and in
> case ether of my Children die before they are off the age
> of twenty one years that the Survivor have his part and
> that iff both my Children should die without Heirs and
> before the age off Twenty one years that then these Estates
> that I have bequeathed to the be Equally divided betwixt
> my Loving Wife and the Children off John Tabb James
> *Le Cater* & Jnᵒ Brodies Children . . .

witnesses: Wᵐ *S*hergold.
      Elizᵗ *S*hergold.
      Thoˢ *E*llis.

                                      Willm. Tabb.
                                      Wax Seal.

ELIZABETH PRICE . . .

Original Will.

dated 26 Dec. 1735.

proved 19 Jan. 1735.

   . . . to my Grandaughter Elizabeth Price one Bed . . .
   . . . to my Grandaughter mary Price one hefer . . .
   . . . Give my Daughter Susan one Shilling.
   . . . give my Son Wm Price one Shilling.
   . . . give my Son Edward Price one Shilling.
   . . . give my Daughter Elizabeth one Shilling.
   . . . give my Daughter Elenor one Shilling.
   . . . give my Daughter Ann one Shilling.
   . . . the Rest of my Estate I Give my Son Richard Price
      . . . him to be my whole & Sole Executor . . .

witnesses: John Tart.

        his
      Willm Wakefield.
      mark.   her
                                       Elizabeth Price
                                         mark

THOMAS TUCKER of Norfolk County . . .

Original Will.

dated 19 Mch. 1734.

proved 16 Apr. 1736, by Solomon Cherry & Jon Ludgall & Swore

      to by the Exts . . .
   . . . appoint my Dearly beloved wife and my Son Thomas
   Tucker to be my whole and Sole Executrix . . .
   . . . unto my Son Thomas Tucker one hundred acars of
   Land more or Less part of a tract of Land which I bought
   of henry Bright that part of the Said Land which Binds on
   William Bass and Richard Tucker an^d So by anew made
   line of mark^d Trees which I made my Selfe for bounds
   between my S^d Son Thos Tucker and my Son Marmaduke Tucker and So from that s^d line by a Strait Corse
   to the head or Extent of the S^d Land . . .
   . . . to my Son Marmaduke Tucker the Remainder part
   of that Tract of Land which I bought of henry Bright
   . . . but if my S^d Son Marmaduke Die without Law

full Issue then the Sd. Land to goe to my Son James
Tucker . . .

. . . unto my Son James Tucker . . . *one* Raper and
if he die before he Come to the age of one and twenty
all to be Equly Devided among all my other Children

. . . unto my Daughter Darkes Tucker one year old heffer
. . . to Run on for her till She Come to age . . .
my Seven Children . . .

witnesses: Solomon Cherry.
         John Ludgull.
         William Bass   his
         his mark.   Thomas Tucker.
                                        mark.
                                        Wax Seal.

JOHN TUCKER of Norfolk County in Virginia . . .
Original Will.
dated 12 Feb. 1731/2.
proved 20 May 1736.

. . . I give what money I have in the hands of Capt Hyde
Merch^t in London two thirds to John Cooke and ye other
third to Robert Cooke in case either die before they
are of lawfull Age . . .

. . . my four Nephews Robert Tucker, John Tucker, John
Cooke & Robt Cooke . . .

. . . I give w^t money I have in Mr Isaac Millners hands to
Jno Tucker . . .

. . . Mr Jacob Walkers Children . . . they come of
age . . .

. . . Whatever John Watkins is in my debt in Virg^a I
freely give him . . .

. . . to Mary the Daughter of Mary Botton two hundred
pounds to be raised out of my Westindie goods . . .
She comes of Age . . . Negro Girle . . . lodged
in hands of Saml Boush jun . . .

. . . to Mary Botton fifty pounds . . . & my Negro
boy Munmouth ye boy after her decease to go to Mary
her daughter.

. . . my Sloops . . . my Sloop Phenix be disposed of
. . . Effects I have in the hands of Mr Willm Bloomes
Exec^{rs} to be disposed of Viz^t Twenty pounds to my
friend John Phripp, Twenty pounds to Mr Jacob Walker
and Twenty pounds to ffrances Thruston and fifty pounds
more to Jno Watkins also Twenty pounds to Eliz^a Boush
. . . my Negro man Cezar his freedom & five pounds
Curr^t money and like wise give my Negro boy Whithaven
his freedom & five pounds Curr^t money . . .
. . . all my land in Norfolk Town to my Nephew Jno
Tucker . . . Mary Botton have ye use of ye same
untill he comes of Lawfull Age . . .
. . . to my ffriend Saml Boush jun^r my Sorril horse and
a doz Gold rings to be disposed of among my ffriends.
. . . appoint my ffriends Mr Jacob Walker & Mr Saml
Boush jun^r to be my Exec^{rs} . . .

witnesses: Paul Portlock.
       Jno Livingston.
          his
      Thos Walker.
        mark.

                        Jno Tucker.
                        Wax Seal.

WILLIAM RANDELL of the Norewest *River Par^{sh}* &
County of Norfolk . . .

Original Will. (Also Book I p. 32).

dated 15 *June* 1735.

proved 20 May 1736.

. . . Appoint Thomas *W*oring of Norfolk County to be my
and Sole Execetrix . . .
. . . to my beloved Son William Randall one hundred and
three Acres of Land . . . two hundred and Six Acres
. . . to my beloved Son Josiear Randell one hundred and
three Acres of Land . . . two hundred and Six Acres
in my Tract Whear fore I would Desir that My Land
May be Ealekill Devid between them as It Can.
. . . my wife Shall Keep the Reste of My Esteate Duearing

of her Widerhud and the Reste of My Esteate to Equelly Devided among all My Children.

witnesses: John Randell.

his

W——— Nasen.

mark.

his

Thomas N———

mark.   Willm Randell.

———

MARY HODGES of Norfolk County . . .

Original Will.

dated 10 Jan. 1734/5.

proved 21 May 1736.

. . . unto my dafter francis hodges one Cow . . .
. . . unto my dafter Elisebeth hodges one Cow . . .
. . . unto my grandson William *battle* one hafar . . .
. . . to my Dafter Dinah won Shillen . . .
. . . to my Dafter mary *Eckels* won Shillen . . .
. . . to my Son Caleb hodges too Cows . . .
. . . to my Daftar ann wornar one hefer with Caf if She Comes hear to Live . . .
. . . to my Son Edward hodges my grin Stone . . .

. . . my Son Caleb hodges Execter of all my wordly afairs.

witnesses: James Wilkins.

Nathanal *nosay*.

mark.   Mary hodges.

mark.

———

EDWORD HODGES of Norfolk County . . .

Original Will.

dated 14 Apr. 1736.

proved 21 May 1736.

. . . unto my Loveing brother Caleb hodgeis my plantation Lying one ye River and all the Land yaying to it . . .

unto my Loveing Sister Dinah *ues*tree my plantation and
fifty acrys of Land more or Les Lying over the west
Swampe . . .

. . . unto my Loving Sister ann worner the Remainer of that
tract of Land Lyine the west *Semp* . . .

. . . to my *tow* Sisters frances hodgeis and Elizabeth hodgeis
all the Remaner part of my Estate both Rail and pasanell
. . .

. . . make my brother Caleb hodges holy and Soly Execut^r
. . .

witnesses: Lem^{ll} Butt.

Wm. Hodgis.

James Wilkins.   Edward Hodges.

                                                          Scroll.

WILL^m BALLANCE of the County of Norfolk Virg^a . . .

Original Will.

dated 9 Jan. 1733/4.

proved —— 1736, by —— Miller & And ^w M^cpherson.

. . . unto Loving Wife Elizabeth Ballance all my Estate Both
Real & personal (Except the child she now goes wth Lives,
then to be Equally Divided between them) making my
said Wife the . . . Sole Executrix . . .

witnesses: Andrew Mackfarsen.

Evan Miller.

Signum

Mary Ballance.   William Ballance.

                                                          Scroll.

HENRY NICHOLLS Senr of the Western Branch of Eliz^a River and County of Norfolk Virginia . . .

Original Will.

dated 28 Jan. 1735/6.

proved 16 *Ap.* 1736.

. . . bequeath my Short Musket call^d Jasper to my Son Henry Nicholls.

. . . Bequeath my Trading Gunn to my Son John Nicholls.

. . . Bequeath my Cast Gunn to my Son Nichoilas Nicholls.

. . . all the rest of my Estate, as well wth in as w^{tb} out my Beloved Wife Eliz^a Nicholls Whom I also appoint my Whole & Sole Executrix . . . & after her Decease to be Equally Divided amongst all my Children . . .

witnesses: Peter Dale.

Lemuell Veal.

his

Morris Veal.

mark

Henry Nickols.

Wax Seal.

SAM^l BOUSH . . .

Original Will.

dated 18th day of Octo^{br} 1733.

proved 17 Dec. 1736, by Henry Miller.

backed 19 Noov^r 1736 proved by 2 Witnesses.

. . . to my Son Saml Boush my Riding horse & my best Bridle Sadle & furniture & whipp.

. . . to my said Son my land at the head of the Western Branch that I bought of Wm Willoug—(torn)— . . . in full of his part of my Estate . . .

. . . unto my Grandson Saml Boush all ye rest of my land & Negroes Male & female . . . to him and the Male heirs of his body . . . & for want of such Male heir to Goodrich Boush & his Male heirs forever & for want of such Male heirs to John Boush & his Male heirs forever and so the Male heirs of my Son Saml Boush forever.

. . . to my said Grandson Saml Boush$s$ all my household plate & my Silver hilt^d swoard & belt belonging to it wth my Case pistols Capt quard'd & loops of plate wth my powder flask done wth my best Watch w^{tb} my Gold Seal all my Gold Rings & gold buttons.

. . . give unto my Son Saml Boush my Daught^r Anne Boush my Grandson Saml Boush to Each of them a mourning Suit of Cloaths . . .

. . . & ye rem^r of my Cloaths I give to Mr Thomas Nash the Elder . . .

. . . Appoint Capt. Willis Wilson to receive my Debts & to to accountable to my Son for ye same . . . desire is that all that I am in debted to may be paid without any trouble or law suit . . . that my wife Alice Boush have a good maintenance out of my Estate that my Exec^r take great Care of her during her life & that Care be taken for ye good Education of my Grandson Saml Boush.

. . . appoint my Son Saml Boush Exec^r . . .

witnesses: Mary Miller.

Marg^t Haire.

Henry Miller.

Sa Boush. Red Wax
Seal & Arms.

THOMAS BRUICE Senr of the Western Branch of Norfolk County . . .

Original Will.

dated 20 Jany. 1735/6.

proved 15 Jan. 1741/2. (the wid^o being present and Refusing to accept any benefit by the s^d will) . . .

. . . unto my Wife Mary Bruice the plantation whereon Aron Grimes now Lives w^t the woodland—Grount Joyning to it As it will Make up her full thirds of All my land And in full of her thirds, for and during her Naturall life and after her decess to my Son Thomas Bruice & his Heirs of his bodie but in case that he Should depart this life without Issue that then I doe give and bequeith the Sd. plantation Soe far as the church Road unto my Daughter Dinia

. . .

. . . unto my Son Thomas Bruice . . . My plantation whereon Thomas Grimes Now leives But in case that my sd Son Thomas Bruce Should depart this life w^{t}out lawfull Isue that then . . . unto my Daughter Bettie . . .

. . . unto my Son Thomas Bruice all the Rest of all the Rest of my lands not given . . . with all Reversion or Reversions of all My Other lands and plantations belonging unto me in this county Nansemond or ells where whatso-*more*^{r} But in case my s^d son Thomas Bruice should depart this life w^{t}out lawfull Issue that then & in that case I doe give . . . all the same lands Excpting whats— given unto my daughters Bettie & dinia unto my son Abram Bruce . . .

  . . .

. . . I doe give my son Thomas the liberty to sell and dispose of all that land in Nansemond belonging to me as he shall Recover by law or other wayes . . .

. . . apoynt My son Thomas Bruice and my son in Law Lemuell *poweli* to be My Execotrs . . .

. . . if my Son Thomas Should die w^t Issue . . . . . my daughter Dinia shall have & hold the plantation whereon my son in Law James Danes now Leives during the life of my wife Mary and noe longer . . .

. . . the severall tenants . . . Shall hold the —(torn)— plantation for the same Rents as now they hold them for and during *theire* life . . .

. . . bequeith My plantation whereon Thomas ward now Leives unto my Son Abraham Burce when he Shall atain the age of twenty one yeares . . . —(torn)—

witnesses :   his
      Joseph Waterworth.
          mark.
          his
      William Beaverly
          mark.
      Lemuell Powell.

                      Thos. Bru*ce*.

ARCHIBALD McNEIL of the County of Princess Anne in Virginia . . .

Original Wills.

dated 13 Aprill 1741.

proved 17 July 1741, by Wm. *Visnon.*

. . . It is my will and desire and I here by appoint That all my Estate both Real and personall in Virginia and in Scotland be Sold for Ready money and put out to Intrest in Scotland on Good Security According to this will by the direction and Oversight of my friends Daniel McNeil of Collinsay Alexander Campbell Mechant in Norfolk Virginia, Archibald Campbell of Barnacarci Neil McNeil

my Brother, Ronald Campbell *Tack*sman of B*u*liehaven
and Duggal Mctarrish of Dunardie or the major part of
them then living whom I request to be Overseers & Trustees of my Children herein after mentioned.

. . . In Case my wel beloved wife Elizabeth Mc neil shall return to Britain to live Then in that Case . . . unto her
. . .during all the days of her Natural life one Yearly
Annuity Intrest or Annual rent of the Just and Equal half
of my estate aforsaid . . . In Case my . . . wife
. . . shall Keep maintain Cloath & Educate my Children
Malcolm and Alexander Mc neils in Scotland with the Consent of their Overseer and Trustees . . . That Then
So long She Shall have receive & Enjoy the Annual rent
or Interest of all my Estate aforsaid.

In Case my well beloved wife Elizabeth Mcneil Shall choose
to remain and live in Virginia or any other part of America In that Case . . . unto her and her heirs for Ever
One hundred pounds Virginia Currency to be raised and
paid out of the first and readiest of my Estate . . . the
Service of the two maid Servants Bettie and fflorie Mc neils
during the time of their Indenture, And that in full of all
her right to my Estate real and personal.

. . . unto my Eldest Son Malcom Mc neil . . . two third
parts (the Same in three parts to be devided) of all the
Remainder of my Estate Real and personal both in Virginia
and Scotland not herein before given and devised; and the
other Remaining third part of my Said Estate . . .
unto my Son Alexander Mc neil . . . But in Case both
my said Sons Should die in their minority before their re-
spective ages of twenty one years and unmarried Then In
that Case I give and bequeath their parts aforsaid of my
said Estate unto Hector Mc neil Second Son of my Brother
Neil Mc neil . . .

. . . Nominate and Constitute John Taylor, Alexander
Campbell and Andrew Sproull Merchants in Norfolk Executors . . . So far as concerns that part of my Estate
that Shall be in Virginia . . . and appoint the before-
named Daniel Mc neil, Archbald Campbell, Neil Mc neil,
Ronald Campbell and Duggall Mc*Tarrish* To be Trustees
and Overseers.

witnesses: William *Nimmo J*—.

Arche McNeill.

Archibald McColl—(cant read)—

Wax Seal & Arms.

JOHN CORPREW, Senr of the County of Norfolk . . .
Original Will.

dated 31 May 1739.

proved 19 June 1741, by Mr. Wm Nimmo, Ja^s Timberlake & Jos^h
Russell & John & Mary Corprew.

. . . unto my Son John Corprew all that Messuage and Plantation whereon I now live with all Land and appurtenances
. . .

. . . unto my said Son John Corprew two hundred Acres of Land more or less being the Computed half of a Patent of four hundred Acres Lying & being in Norfolk County up on Simons Creek Swamp . . . in Lieu an Recompence of Some Land Exchanged by my said Son John with me Lying in Black: water and hereafter given to my Son Johathan.

. . . unto my Sons John Corprew, Joshua Corprew & Matthew Corprew. . . . Equally divided between them All my Swamp Land adjoining on John Murdens Land upon this condition always that my said Son John Corprew or his heirs acknowledge assure & convey unto my Said Son Matthew . . . a Certain piece or parcel of Woodland *ground* by Estimation about Eight or ten Acres Lying between the old field of the plantation wherein I now live and the Old field commonly called Dickssons old field But in Case my said Son John or his heirs fail or Refuse to Convey the said Woodland ground to my said Son Matthew . . . Then it is my will and deisre & I declare it to be my Intent & meaning That John's part of the Swamp land given as afors^d fall and Remain to my said Sons Joshua and Matthew . . .

. . . to my Son William Corprew the Plantation he now lives upon with Two hundred Acres of Land belonging my said Son William Should happen to die Without any Child or Children or their Issue living at the time of his decease or in Ventre Sa Mire, Then . . . to my said thereto be the Same more or less . . . But in Case Sons Joshua and Matthew Corprews . . .

. . . to my Son Thomas Corprew the Plantation he now liveth upon with the Land thereto belonging being contained in two patents together also with fifty Acres of the Land purchased by me of James Tooly the Same to be taken next adjoining to the said plantation untill the quantity is Compleated . . .

. . . unto my said Son Joshua Corprew the plantation he now

liveth upon with the Land thereto belonging to a line markt a Cross the Ridge . . .

. . . unto my Son Jonathan Corprew the Plantation and Land which I bought of Henry Simmons as also the plantation & Land which I purchased of James Tooly containing by Estimation two hundred Acres more or less Except fifty Acres thereof given to my Son Thomas as aforsaid . . .

. . .

. . . unto my Son Samuel Corprew my Plantation in North Carolina *Pamplico* River . . . my said Son Samuel paying yearly & each year to my beloved wife Mary four barrels of good Merchantable beef . . .

. . . unto my Son Matthew Corprew the Old Plantation whereon John Dickson formerly lived from my Son Joshua's line that goes across the Ridge and adjoining on the Old field of the Plantation whereon I now live Straight Across the Ridge . . . likewise . . . all my Land and Houses Lying on the South side of the Casway at the Great Bridge in Norfolk County . . .

. . . unto my Daughter Eleanor Peyton five pounds . . .

. . . unto my Sons John, William, Thomas, Joshua, Jonathan and Samuel Corprew all —(torn)— my Land with the Appurtenances Lying at the Great Bridge and not hereby already given . . .

. . . appoint my well beloved wife Mary and my Sons John, & Thomas Corprews Executrix & Executor.

witnesses: William Nimmo, *Jr.*

Abraham Robertson.

James Timberlake.

Jos Russell.
Jesse Sikes.   John Corprew.
                                                    Wax Seal.

ELIZABETH LAWSON of the County of Norfolk . . .

Original Will.

dated 23 Aug. 1740.

proved 19 June 1742.

. . . to Catherine Walke • three negroes To witt Dick, Charles and Nell . . . But in case the s^d Catherine

Walke Should Dye before She attain the age of Twenty one years or marriage then . . . to my Grandchild Elizabeth Sawyer wife of Arthur Sawyer . . .

. . . to my grandchild Catherine Walke my Bed & furniture where I used to lay.

. . . to my daughter in Law Abigall Conner one Chest that Stands under the Window and a Cubard . . .

. . . to John Conner the Son of Kedar Conner a negro woman named Judith . . .

. . . unto my Grandaughter Monica Conner . . . one Chest of Drawers . . .

. . . unto my Grandaughter Cloetilda Conner . . .one negro woman named Ruth . . . Black Chest . . .

. . . unto Lewis Conner Son of Kedar Conner Six Silver Spoons marked L B C.

. . . unto Mary Teresa Wisher . . . one negro boy named Toney . . .

. . . unto my grandaughter Sharlott Conner . . . one Negro woman named Hannah . . .

. . . to Kedrick Conner . . . negro boy named Tom . . .

. . . to my Cousin Henry Deans Son of Richard Deans . . . one negro man named Silvester . . .

. . . to Sarah Shaddock . . . one negro woman named Jenny . . .

. . . to my Grandson Anthony Conner one negro woman Phill . . .

All the rest of my Estate not here to fore given I give unto Anthony Conner, Monica Conner, Sharlott Conner, Cloetillda Conner & John Conner son of Kedar Conner . . .

. . . appoint my Trusty & well beloved Friend Coll. William Crawford . . . Sole Ex^r . . .

witnesses: Christopher Jackson, Junr
          Chisto Jackson.   Elizabeth
                                             Lawson.
                                                Seal.

JOHN TUCKER Senr of Norfolk County . . .

Original Will. — (See fragment in Book I p. (153)—(torn)— —)—

dated 8 Jan. 1749/50.

proved Apr 6^t 1750, by Maning & Spring.

App^{rs} Slaz^h Tart, Aaron Boulton, Wm. Powell & Ja^s Jollif or any three.

. . . to my Loving wife Jane Tucker one feather bed . . . one punch bowl . . .

. . . to my daughters Tamer Tucker one high bed and the furniture . . . two pewter porringers . . . two punch bowls . . .

. . . to my daughter Judith Tucker one high bed with the furniture . . . one old still . . .

. . . also give my Loving wife the thirds of my Land . . .

witnesses: Elisha Manning.

John Spring.

William Ivey.

John Tucker.
Wax Seal.

MATHEW MATHIAS of Norfolk County . . .

Book 11 p. 49.

dated 29 Oct. 1731.

proved 17 Mch 1731/2.

. . . unto my Son Joshua Mathias my Plantation I now Live on . . .

. . . unto my Son Mathew Mathias all that Lands over the North west River wch I have A Bill of Sale for from Willm Linton . . .

. . . unto my Daughter Sarah Matthias one feather Bed wth furniture to it . . .

. . . to my Three Daughters mary Portlock Elizth Portlock & ann halstead to Each of Them one Cow & Calf . . .

. . . the Rest of my Estate within Doors & wth out Doors I give & bequeath to my Loving wife Sarah Mathias to be my hole & Sole Executrix . . .

witnesses: Simon Halstead.

Richd Whitehurst.

Willm Portlock.

his
Mathew Mathias & Seale.
marke.

AMBRUS SHIPWASH of Norfolk County . . .

Book 11 p. 49.

dated 22 Oct. 1725.

proved 18 Mch 1725/6.

. . . to my Loving wife Eliz[th] Shipwash five pewter Dishes & Nine Pewter Plates . . . my great Earthen Punch Bole

. . . unto my Son augustin Shipwash my young horse Called Prince . . .

. . . to S[d] son Ambrus Shipwash my young *hack* horse to be In his mothers *Chur* Till he Comes of age.

. . . to my Daughter ann Shipwash one Cow Yielding . . . when She Comes to age . . .

. . . wife Eliz[th] Shipwash whole and Sole Ex[r]x . . .

witnesses: J. ffife.

Sam[l] Hanbury.

his
Ambrus Shipwash.
marke.

JACOB TALBUTT of the County of Norfolk In the Presents of Taners Creek . . .

Book 11 p. 50.

dated 16 Apr. 1732.

proved 21 July 1732.

. . . to my Loveing wife margrett Talbutt all my four negros as followeth . . . In Case my Loveing wife marrys then I Give . . . Murmoth . . . to my lovin Son William Talbutt . . . moll to my Cosen Tho[s] Talbutt but my will and Desire is that If this Negro wench Should Bred that my Two Cosens Cader Talbut and absolum Talbutt Shall have the Two first children . . .

. . . to my Cossen James Talbutt all my wareing aparrell . . . to these my Cosens afores[d] named being the Sons of my Brother John Talbutt . . . to my Cosen Sheadrack Talbutt the Negro boy Called *Urepe* . . . to my Cosen Israel Talbutt The negro Boy Called *mericah* . . .

. . . to my Cossen James Talbutt all my wearing apparell

. . . to my Cosen Eliz^th Talbutt Two heffers . . . my part of the *horse* & in acres that is Between Capt. Thos Willoughbey and me In his woods . . .

. . . al the rest of my Estate Not all ready given . . . to my Loveing wife Marg^t Talbutt She . . . my Sole Ex^rx . . .

witnesses: John Langley.

his
Robt. x Wooddy.
marke.
his
Edward x Hews
marke.   Jacob Talbutt & Seale.

JOHN BUTT . . . Virginia Norfolk County . . .

Book 11 p. 51.

dated 4 July 1731.

proved *18* Sept. 1731.

. . . unto my Cosen Rob^rt Butt my Plantation and Land belonging to the Same . . .

. . . unto my Cosen Sofiah Butt my Negro man Called Jack . . .

. . . to my Cosen Lidia Butt one feather Bed . . .

. . . unto my Cosen pricila Two Cows . . .

. . . unto my Cosen John Butt one white mare . . .

. . . unto my Cosen Caleb Butt one black mare . . .

. . . unto my Cosen Solo^m Butt Sen^rs Daughter Sarah Butt one mare and Colt running in *Elbrwood.*

. . . unto my Cosen Arther Butt my Riding horse . . .

. . . to my Cosen Saml Butt my gun.

. . . unto my Brother William Butt all my Sheep.

. . . unto my Brother Roberts Two Children—that is *Danil* all my Crop . . . my Bible . . .

. . . to my Sister Eliz^th Butt widdow of of robert Butt

. . . apoint my Cosen *Lem* Butt my hole Ex^er . . .

witnesses: Richd Butt.

Sol^o Butt.
Richd Church.   John Butt and Seale.

ROBERT BUTT Senr of Norfolk County . . .

Book 11 p. 51.

dated 5 Sept. 1730.

proved 21 May 1731.

. . . unto my Loving Son Lem^l Butt all the South End of my Land adjoyning upon my Brother Richrd Line and Land begining for the Bounds on the North End thereof at a marked white oake standing neare the Beaver damb Syprus Swamp a Little to the north ward of a house my Said Son Lem^{ll} built neare The Said Swamp a Soe Runing a Strait Line to a marked red oak Standing by a Tarr Kill formerly Burnt by Said Son Lem^{ll} neare the flat Swamp and from thence and Easterly Course to the Line that Devid^{es} This Said Land from healsteads Land . . .

. . . to my Loveing Son Arther Butt all my Land on the North Side of the Branch that Divides the Same from the maner plantation whereon I Now Dwell Quite up adjoyning up on my brother William Butts Line and Land . . . Likewise . . . my Smallest Gun my Pistols holsters and Sword . . .

. . . to my Loveing Son Robert Butt the maner plantation whereon I now Dwell wth all the Land adjoyning there to from the first Mentioned Line made Between my Son Lem^l Land and this S^d Manor Plantation and the Branch that Devides the Same from my So^o Arthurs Land . . . Likewise my Largest gun . . .

. . . Neither of my Said Sons Lem^l Nor Robert Shall Sell there Land herein . . . Except it be to one or the other . . .

. . . apoint my Loveing wife Elizth and my Son Lem^{ll} Exec^{rs} . . .

witnesses : Thos Butt.

Richd Butt.

John Butt.

Willm Butt Junr   Robert Butt & Seale.

HENRY BUTT now Senr of Norfolk County . . .

Book 11 p. 52.

dated 10 June 1731.

proved 17 Sept. 1731.

. . . unto Willis Butt Son of Richd Butt all my Land both the maner Plantation & my Land Called the gum Swamp after my wife ann Butt her Deceas . . .

. . . to arthur Butt Son of Richd Butt my negro man Called Boomer . . .

. . . to my kins woman Martha Dun the bed & blankets & Sheets that She Now Lise one . . .

. . . bequeath Penelope Butt the young Black mare that is In my Pasture . . .

. . . all the Remainding part of my Estate Not herein Before given unto my wife ann Butt During her Life and after her Decease . . . the Same To be Equally Devided Betwixt all my Brothers & Sisters Children . . .

witnesses: Thos Butt.

Sol^o Butt.

Lem^l Butt.

Henry Butt & Seale.

SIBALL THREADGALL of the County of Norfolk . . .

Book 11 p. 52.

dated 3 Jan. 1730.

proved 15 *Jan* 1730, by Mary Veale & Rebecca Somersell &

Sworne to by Maj^r Wm Craford the Ex^r . . .

. . . unto my Daughter Eliz^{ht} Edwards one gold girdle Buckel & Gildel and one gold Ring . . . & after Her Desease the girdle buckell and Ring to her Children . . . one half of my Parsonall Estate In Virginia . . .

. . . to my Son Deodatus Threadgall one Negro Boy Named Peter when he Shall Come to the age of Twenty one . . . all the Remainder half of my personall Estate In Virginia . . .

. . . unto my Daughter Elizth Edwards the on third part of my Estate In Burmuders both Reale and Personal . . .

. . . unto my Son Deodatus Threadgall all the Remainder part of my Estate In Burmuders both real and personal . . . one gold Ring . . .

. . . my Trusty friend William Craford to be my Sole
Ex^r . . .

Test: William Craford.
> her
> Rebecka Summer*ett*.
> marke.
> her
> Mary Veale
> marke.

> > her
> > Siball Threadgill & Seale.
> > marke.

MARY HEBDON . . . (Nuncupative) . . .
Book 11 p. 53.

William Portlock and Prudence Barte both being off att
age Sath at the Dweling house of mary hebdon widow
(the Twenty third Day of Jan^{ry} one thousand Seven hundred and Thirty, thirty one) the Said Mary Lying on
her bed In her Last Sicknes where of In a few Days
after She Dyed . . . Speaking to us Did utter these
following words I give moll meaning her Negro *moll* to
andre Colling*timas* & sall meaning her son ardregan
Bartee and alsoe these few Sheep or the Sheep or the
Likewords I give Joney meaning her son John Hebdon
them few young hoogs . . . was In perfect Sence
and Memory to the Best of our Judgm^t and furthe
Saith Nott.

> William 'Portlock
> her
> Prudence Bartee.
> marke.

. . . made oath one The holy Eavangilus . . . and Sub-
scribed . . . 30th Day of Jany 1730.

> George Newton.

William Portlock further Sayeth at the Time of the makeing the
above will the Said Prudence Bartee In Presents of her
mother the above said mary hebdon Did Tell this Depo-

nent that her mother had in Presents of one witness Som Small Time Before given her all the flax and Cotton and other Things . . .

William Portlock.

Sworn to before me this 30th of Jan^{ry} 1730/1.

George Newton.

GEORGE BALLENTINE Senr of the Southern Branch of Eliz^a River of Norfolk County . . .

Book 12 p. 1.

dated 14 Nov. 1733.

proved 18 Jan. 1733.

. . . unto my Daughter Mary Deale one large pewter dish . . .

. . . unto my Daughter Frances Cherry one looking glass . . .

. . . unto my Daughter Susan Bishop one large pewter dish . . .

. . . unto my Grandson John B——— Chest . . .

. . . unto my Daughter Dorothy Tucker one box smoothing Iron . . .

. . . unto my Son Samuel Cherry two hundred acres of Land beginning at the Landing point . . . running as the Branch runns up to the Spring Branch, so running up the Branch to a *pine*, as West Course. to the outside of my Land, and . . . Six months Liberty of my House that I now live in . . .

. . . unto my Son George Ballentine all the rest of my Land and movables . . .

. . . my Said Son George Ballentine my full and Sole Executor . . .

witnesses : John Taylor, *Senr.*

Jo^s M*und.*

George *T* Ballentine.

BENJAMIN HOLLOWELL . . .

Book 12 p. 1.

dated 1 Oct. 1732.

proved 17 May 1734, by Caleb Hodges & Sol°: *Wester* & also by

the Ex^{rx}.

. . . unto my well beloved Daughter Elizabeth Hollowell one parcell of Land that is to Say the Dogwood ridge with two hundred acres for to begin in the Bottom of the thick neck, So running with a Streight & Line to the Gallberry's, So along to the white Oak *noiell*, So Still along that Side to make up the said Land . . .

. . . unto my Welbeloved Daughter Bridgett Hollowell . . . one peice of Land that is for to Say that of Slacks wch now Day*ley Latter* lives on wth two hundred acres thereto.

. . . to that Child as my Wife is with Child wth now, whether Son or Daughter, to it and it Heirs for Ever, two hundred acres of Land it beginning at the mouth of the maple Branch so running the upper side of the said Branch Even against the white oak *noiele* then turning to the road to the head Line to make up the said Complement of Land

. . .

*

. . . unto my well beloved Wife Bridgett Hollowell the use of all my Estate both real and personall during her Widdowhood . . . wife . . . Sole Execut^x . . .

witnesses: Caleb Hodges.

Sol° West*er*.

John C Warner.

Benj^a Hollowell, Seale.

*

. . . bequeath all the rest of my Land with the manner Plantation to my well beloved Son Halsted Hollowell

. . .

WM. MAUND Jun . . .

Book 12 p. 2.

dated 6 Apr. 1734.

proved 17 May 1734.

. . . unto my well beloved Son William my my negro boy called D—(torn)—when he Shall arive to the Age of one and twenty years . . . But if my Son William Should not arrive to the said Age, then it is my Desire that my Well beloved Brother Noah Maund Should have the said negro Dav—(torn)— . . .

. . . It is my Desire that the use of my Said Negro Davy may belong to my wel beloved Father and mother Maund untill Such time . . .

. . . unto my well beloved Son William all my part that now belongs to me and the part thereafter coming to me of a water mill . . . after the decease of his Mother . . .

. . . unto my well beloved Brother Lott Maund One Small Gunn . . .

. . . unto my well beloved Sister Elizabeth Maund One young Brown Cow . . .

. . . all the rest and residue of my personall Estate . . . or any thing wch come due to me in Virg^a or Carolina . . . unto my lov—(torn)—Father . . . him full and Sole Ex^r . . .

witnesses: Peter Taylor,
　　　　　　S. Taylor
　　　　　　mark.
　　　　Isabell Sutherland　　　　　　　　　mark
　　　　　　　　　　　　　　　　　　　　W. Maund. Seale

JOHN GUY of Norfolk County . . .

Book 12 p. 2.

dated 20 March 1733/4.

proved 17 May 1734, by all the Witnesses and also by Jno Guy Surviving Executor.

. . . Imprimis I give the house and half the Lott whereon I now live unto my loving Wife Sarah Guy during her Life and after her decease unto James Guy my Son . . .

. . . unto my two Sons Benj^a Guy and William Guy the Plantation in Tanner's Creek precinct that I bought of Edward Hanson . . . to be Equally devided . . .

. . . to my Son John Guy and my Daughter Eliz^a Guy my

half acre of Land that I bought of Colo. Sam^ll Boush, on the north Side of the Road going out of Norfolk Town . . . to be Equally devided among them w^th, Equall breadth upon the road . . .

. . . unto my Eldest Son John Guy after the decease of my loving wife Sarah Guy a Negro Man called Joe . . .

. . . a Copper Kettle Containing about Thirty Gallons . . .

. . . as to ye rest of my worldly Estate . . . I give unto my loving wife Sarah Guy and to my Son John Guy my Son James Guy my Son Hillary Guy my Son Benjamin Guy my Son William Guy and my Daughter Eliz^a Guy to be Equally amongst them. I desire my Friend George Newton to See this part performed.

. . . my loving wife Sarah Guy Executrix and my Son John Guy Executor . . . and in Case my Son John Guy Should die in his voyage now gon to Barbados and dont return home to Virg^a then . . . I appoint my Son James Guy Executor . . .

witnesses: Geo: Newton.

Wilson Newton

Jenadab Townsend.

Jno Guy
Signum.

SAMUEL CHERRY of the Southern Branch of Eliz^a River

. . .

Book 12 p. 3.

dated 19 Jan. 1733.

proved 16 May 1734, by all the Witnesses and also by the Ex^rx

. . .

. . . unto my Son *Dunn*son Cherry Eighty Acres of Land lying on the north Side of Deep Creek.

. . . unto my Son Samuel Cherry . . . two hundred Acres of Land lying at the head of Indian Creek.

. . . my dearly beloved Wife to be my whole and Sole Executo*rs* . . . likewise to my loveing Wife that two hundred acres of Land that lyes in Indian Creek I give to her so that She may Sell it if She Should Come to Want during her Widowhood and al the rest of my Estate to

her likewise if She marrys after her death or marriage to
be Equally devided among my Children.

witnesses: George Ballentine.

Solomon Cherry.

Sam^{ll} M Cherry. Seale.

MARY J. BRUCE of Norfolk County . . .

Book 12 p. 3.

dated 18 Oct. 1729.

proved 18 May 1734, by all the witnesses & also by the Ex^r
. . .

. . . unto my Son James Bruce the Bed he lys on and Three
Baggs of Feathers that hangs by itt & Eleven Geese
. . . my horse . . .

. . . unto my Son Jonas Bruce the Bed he lys upon . . .
two Woods Barrows and two Shoats one Spotted and the
other White . . .

. . . unto my Son William Bruce One red heiffer . . .

. . . all the rest of my Estate . . . divided among my
three Sons James Bruce and Jonas Bruce and Benjamin
Bruce . . .

. . . one Shill'g to my Son John Bruce and one Shilling to
my Son Abraham Bruce and one Shilling to my Daughter
Elizabeth Avis and one Shilling to my Daughter Mary
Culppeper . . .

. . . my Son James Bruce my whole and Sole Ex^r . . .

witnesses: Joseph Maund.

John Joyce.

Mary M Bruce. Seale.

HENRY DEALE of Norfolk County . . .

Book 12 p. 4.

dated 28 Apr. 1734.

proved 21 June 1734, by all the witnesses & Ex^r . . .

. . . appoint my Dearly beloved wife Mary and my loving
Son Henry Deal to be my whole and & Sole Executors
. . .

. . . to my loving Son Henry Deal my plantation and all the Land belonging to it . . .

. . . to my Son William Deal two hundred acres of Land called white Oak Ridge . . . bequeath unto my Son Henry Deal and my Son William Deale all my Swamp land that lye at the head of Deep Creek to be devided between them two . . .

. . . to my Daughter Dinah one Cow . . . at the Age of one and Twenty . . .

. . . to my Daughter Ann Deale and Margaret Deale Each of them a large Bason and Pewter Dish . . . at the Age of one and twenty . . .

. . . unto my dearly beloved all the remainder part of my Estate . . . as long as She remaineth a Widow . . .

witnesses: Sol⁰ Cherry.

Jo* Manning.

Jn⁰ Cherry.   Henry *H* Deale. Seal.

CONSTANCE MICHASON . .

Book 12 p. 5.

dated 21 Jan. 1730/1.

proved 17 May 1734, by all witnesses & Exʳˢ . . .

. . . bequeath all that I have in the World to my two Daughters Constant* Michason and Ann Newton . . .

. . . my three Small Children under the Care and Charge of their two Eldest Sisters aforementioned . . .

. . . my daughter Ann Newton widdow may cleave her husbands Estate out of my Estate and when so don what is coming in of James Newtons Estate. I desire his widdow my Daughter Ann Should buy her a Suit of mourning . . . those two Exʳˢ . . .

witnesses: James Timberlake.

Jas. Hunter.   Constant* *N.* Michason.

JOHN ANGUISH . . .

Book 12 p. 12.

dated 6 March 1733/4.

proved 16 Aug. 1734, by witnesses & Executrix . . .

. . . to my beloved Daughter Mary Anguish my Negro
woman Kate . . .

. . . my well beloved Wife Ann Anguish . . .

. . . to my Daughter Mary Anguish my plantation called
Edertons Neck and if my Daughter Die without Heir of
her Body lawfully begotten then . . . to my Wel beloved wife Ann Anguish . . .

. . . my will is that my lott of Land and Houses at Newtown be Sold . . .

. . . unto my well beloved Wife Ann Anguish my lott of
Land In Norfolk Town wch I bought of Daniel Godfrey
. . . wife Ann Anguish to be my whole and Sole Ex^{rx}
. . .

witnesses: (none Spread).

Jno. Anguish. Seale.

JOHN BALLENTINE . . .

Book 12 p. 13.

dated 1 Feb. 1733/4.

proved 16 Aug. 1734, by the witnesses & Ex^r . . .

. . . appoint my Dearly beloved Son Richard Ballentine my
Ex^r . . .

. . . to my Dearly beloved Son Richd Ballentine all my full
and whole tract of Land including as well my plantation
whereon I now live and likewise that whereon he ye S^d
Richard Ballentine lives and that whereon Jane Widow
of my Son John Ballentine lives . . .

. . . unto my Daughter Susanna Ballentine my best feather
Bed and Cow . . . and in Case She dies without
Heirs to be devided among my other Children . . .

. . . to my Grandson John Ballentine a Heiffer . . .

. . . to my Daughters Mary Eliz^a Creekmur a Cow and Calf
. . .

witnesses: David Ballentine.
      Jno Porter.
      Paul Ballentine.

Jno Ballentine. Seale.
mark.

JOHN PILKINGTON, &c. . . .

Book 12 p. 15.

dated 10 Aug. 1734.

proved 20 Sept. 1734, by Jnº Levingston and Alexʳ Mcpherson & yᵉ Exˣ.

. . . unto my Daughter Mary pilkington One Moeity or half part of all and singular my Estate of what Nature or quality soever . . .

. . . unto my Dear and loving Wife Mary pilkington yᵉ other moeity or half . . . whole Estate together wᵗʰ my Said Daughter Mary remain under yᵉ Care of of my Said Wife untill my said Daughter attain yᵉ Age of Eighteen years or marry . . .

. . . wife Mary Whole and Sole Executrix . . .

witnesses: Jnº Watkins.

Jnº Levingston.

Jaˢ Timberlake.

Alexʳ Mᶜpherson.   Jnº Pilkerton.

LYDIA McMERRIN . . .

Book 12 p. 16.

dated 6 Oct. 1733.

proved 20 Sepʳ 1734, by the Witnesses & Exʳ

. . . order and appoint that my Exʳ hereafter Named Do Sell and Dispose of the Lott and Houses wᶜʰ I am possessed of in order to pay my Just Debts . . .

. . . yᵉ Overpluss . . . to my loving Sister Agness Mᶜ Nerrin.

. . . my loving friend Robert Brough to be my Whole and Sole Exʳ . . .

witnesses: John Broady.

Elizᵃ Hayword.   Lydia Mᶜ Nerrin.

GEORGE SUGG &c. . . .

Book 12 p. 77.

dated 2 Sept. 1734.

proved 21 Feb. 1734, by all the witnesses & Acquilla Suggs one of the Ex^rs . . . other . . . refused . . .

. . . unto my Son Thomas Seventy Acres of Land be it more or less bounding as follows to Witt begining at a marked white Oak Standing by the Line that bounds the s^d Land . . . If my Said Son Dies without Heirs of his Body imediately after the decease of Said Son, the said Land to return to my Son Acquille . . .

. . . to my Son Acquille ye Plantation y^t Plantation wch my said Son liveth on wth the remaining part of the Land adjoyning thereto wch I parchass'd of Thos Danis deced to him being Seventy acres of the said Land, be It more or less . . . if my Said Son Dies without Heirs the said Land to return to my Son Thos Sugg . . .

. . . unto my Son George, the Plantation and land wch I purchased of Thomas Cuthrall fifty Acres that I Patented adjoyning thereto . . . If my Said Son Die without Heirs the said Land and Plantation to return to my said Sons Thos and Acquilla being Equally Divided between them . . .

. . . to my Daughter Presilla Maund my Water Mill wth Ten Acres of Land & the Houses and Tenements belonging thereto . . . if my said Daughter Dies without Heirs the said Water Mill and Land and Houses and Tenement belonging thereto to Descend to my youngest Daughter Mary Suggs . . .

. . . to my Daughter Sarah Wallace my Negro Wench named Jenny . . .

. . . to my Daughter Mary Sugg my Negro . . . comes to the age of Sixteen . . .

. . . to my Daughter Preccilla Maund, a Feather Bed . . . after the death of my Wife . . .

. . . to my Grand Daughter Ann Beak and Margaret Beake, Rechel Mercer and Margaret Mercer ten Shill^s Eeach in Country productions . . .

. . . to my Dear and loving Wife Sarah for the Suport of her Self and the bringing up of her younger Children . . .

. . . appoint my two Sons Thos Sugg and Acquilla Sugg my whole and Sole Ex^rs . . .

witnesses: Jn° Hanbury.

Ruth Hanbury.

Thos Catton.

Geo: Sugg & Seale.

JOSEPH BACHELLER . . .

Book 12 p. 79.

dated 19 Jan. 1733/4.

proved 21 Feb. 1734/5, by all Witnesses & Ex^rx.

- . . . to my Loving Wife Mary Bacheller free priviledge of my Plantation and Land, and the half of my Water Mill During her Widowhood . . .
- . . . to my Son James Batchellor, after my, Wifes marriage or Death my Plantation including wth it two hundred Acres of Land . . . and one Negro Boy called Cush and after my Son James Bachellors Decease, I give the s^d Negro Boy Cush to my Grandson John Bachellor, and if my Grandson John Bachellor Dies wth out Heirs then I give the s^d Negro Boy to Eliz^a Bachellor, my Grand Daughter . . .
- . . . to my Son Stephen Bachelor, One hundred Acres of Land joyning to my Son James Land, being the upper part, and one hundred Acres of Land, in ye Western Branch joyning to Wm Bass . . . and one Negro Boy called Tony . . . and if my Son Stephen Dies without, Then I give the s^d Negro Boy called Tony to my Grandson James Harbutt . . .
- . . . to my Daughter Ann Harbutt, my Negro Woman called Hayes . . .
- . . . to my Daughter Mary Bacheller one Negro Boy called Pompy . . .
- . . . to my Daughter Eady Bachellor . . . one Negro Boy Called Sharper . . . .
- . . . to my Daughter Sarah Bacheller . . . one Negro Boy called Philly . . .
- . . . to my four youngest Children Stephen Mary Eady and Sarah, all my Puoter . . . if my Wife Deceases before my youngest Children Comes to Age, I do give them to my Daughter Ann Harbert and to my Son In Law Richard Harbut ,. . . .
- . . . all the rest of my Estate not here named to my loving Wife Mary Bachellor, within and without During her life . . . my loving Wife . . . whole Ex^rx . . .

witnesses: Thos Cherry.

        Thos T. Culpepper.

        Ann Tucker.

                 Jo^s Bacheller — Seale.

MARY SMITH Widow . . .

Book 12 p. 80.

dated 3 Jan. 1734/5.

proved 11 Mch. 1734/5, by Witnesses & Exr . . .

 . . . all my moveable Estate to be Equally divided Between my Son Tho⁴ Smith and my Grandson John Smith Son of John Smith D. D. . . .

 . . . appoint my Son Tho⁸ Smith . . . Sole Exʳ . . .

witnesses: John Tart.

 John + Ward.

 Mary *W* Smith.

ROBᵗ ETHEREDGE . . .

Book 12 p. 81.

dated 3 Nov. 1734.

proved 21 Feb. 1734/5, by all Witnesses & Exʳ . . .

 . . . unto my Eldest Son Peter Etheredge the Plantation that my Father Gave me wᵗʰ the Land thereto belonging wᶜʰ he my Said Father Gave to me . . .

 . . . unto my Son Robᵗ Etheredge my Plantation I now live on wᵗʰ what Land lyes on yᵉ Side of a Branch dividing the Land of my Son Peters, and that of my Son Roberts . . .

 . . . unto my Son Peter a Gun and a Sword.

 . . . my loving Wife Easter Etheredge . . . Wife . . . to be my Executrix . . .

witnesses: Wᵐ Portlock.

 John + Hebdon.

 his mark
 Robᵗ = Etheredge. Seale.

JNº. McCOY . . .

Book 12 p. 81.

dated 11 Nov. 1734.

proved 21 Mch 1734/5, by all Witnesses & by Exʳˢ . . .

. . . unto my Brother Hugh McCoy and to my Brother William Maccoy my Whole Estate within Doors and without . . . They . . . Sole Ex^rs . . . and all and Singular my Land and Messuages and my land to be divided between my two Brothers Hugh McCoy and William McCoy . . . to my Brother Hugh McCoy the half of my Land that part binding upon his Line and the other part or half . . . to my Brother William McCoy . . .

witnesses: James Timberlake.
    Rich^d *M*. McCoy.

          John Maccoy. Seal.

JOHN WAKEFIELD . . .

Book 12 p. 82.

dated 4 Jan. 1734.

proved 21 Mch. 1734/5, by all the Witnesses & the Ex^rs . . .

. . . to my Well beloved Wife Dinah Wakefield my best Bed . . . and my Negro Fellow During her Widowhood and after . . . to be Sold ad ye money to be Equally divided between Wife and Three Children . . . . . . Wife Dinah Wakefield and my Brother George Wakefield . . . Sole Ex^rs . . .

witnesses: Thos Willoughby.
    Geo. Wakefield.

        Jno Wakefield + Seale.

JAMES COLLWELL . . .

Book 12 p. 82.

dated *17* Apr. 1735.

proved 18 Apr. 1735, by Witnesses.

. . . I give Thirty Odd pounds I have in Col^o Alex^r Mackenzies hands to Mr Thos Martin and Mr Archibald Williamson . . . chest and Trunk . . . Being at Darby Skinners . . . . . . to Mr Thomas Martin and Mr Archibald Williamson

all my Cash and all the rest of my Estate let it be in what
nature soever, and I appoint Mr. Tho⁸ Martin and Mʳ
Archibald Williamson Exᵣˢ   .   .   .

witnesses: Jnº Fife.

Christº Gardner.

James Colwell & Seale.
mark.

EDWARD MURDEN of Norfolk County . . .

Book 12 p. 83.

dated 16 Jan. 1734/5.

proved 17 May 1735, by all the Witnesses & Exᵣˢ . ..

. . . unto my Eldest Son Maxamelian Murden all my Land
and plantation lying up in the Wood toward the Elbow all
that I formerly held as also that wᶜʰ I bought Since of
Lemuel Butt . . . being his full Share of my Lands
. . .

. . . unto my Son Malachy Murden all my Land and Plantation I now live on, . . . Only Excepting that my
loving Wife Mary Murden, live on and Enjoy the same
during her Life or Widowhood . . .

. . . new Gunn . . . Pistols and Holsters . . .

. . . Fifty head of Cattel . . .

. . . my said Sons . . . when they come of age . . .

. . . I do appoint my freind Jeremiah Murden and my Wife
Mary Murden to be my Exʳ and Exʳx . . .

witnesses: Jnº Murden + mark.

Eliz⁴ Daugherty.

Willᵐ Portlock.

Edwᵈ Murden. mark.
Seale.

ADAM ETHEREDGE . . .

Book 12 p. 85.

dated 18 apr. 1735.

proved 17 May 1735, by all the witnesses & Exʳ . . .

. . . unto my loving wife Eliz⁴ Etheredge the mannor the manner Plantation and Land thereto belonging wᶜʰ I lately lived on, it being the Land I bought of William Taylor, lying and being in the Prescinct of Paspatank in the County of Albamarle in North Carolina . . .

. . . unto my Son Levy Etheredge my mannurel Plantation and Land thereto belonging That I bought of Mʳ Thomas Mason . . . and the *Gun* that he now uses and my Carpenters Tooles and my Coopering Shoomakeing and Bricklaying Tools . . .

. . . unto my Said Daughter Lydia Etheredge and Eliz⁴ Etheredge my Plantation that is in the Southern Branch . . .

. . . my Wife and Three Children . . .

. . . Wife Eliz⁴ Etheredge and my Son Levy Etheredge to be my Exʳ and Exʳˣ . . .

witnesses: Robert Williams.

Prudence V. Williams.

Eliz⁴ Williams & mark.

Adam Etheredge. Seale.

JOHN WILLIAMS . . .

Book 12 p. 85.

dated 19 Mch. 1734/5.

proved 17 May 1735, by the oaths of Two of the Witnesses thereto also by the Exʳˢ . . .

. . . unto my loving Wife Eliz⁴ Williams the whole property of all my Lands and Plantation for her Use During her Widowhood, But if She Marrys then only the third part During her Natural Life, and afterwards . . . to my Son James Williams the mannor plantation that I now live on . . .

. . . to my Son Robert Williams . . . the Plantation that he now lives on and my Land to be divided Between my two sons James and Robᵗ accordingly as I have Directed them, and if either of them my two Sons is minded to Sell their part to sell it to their Brother, and to no Body Else And if either . . . Should Die without Heirs then his Part to fall to my Son Richᵈ Williams . . .

. . . my other Two Gunns one to my Son John Williams
and the other to my Son Joseph Williams . . .
. . . to The Rest of my Children a Shilling Each . . .
. . . the Small Children . . .
. . . my wife Eliz⁴ Williams to me by Exʳˣ . . .

witnesses: Adam Etheredge.
Sarah Wilder.
Jeremiah Langly.   marke
                                          Jnº Williams + Seale.

JAMES SIMMONS of Tanners Creek in the County of Norfolk . . .

Book H p. 1.

Dated 27 Apr. 1741.

Proved 16 July 1742, by John Murry & John Simmons and

Dinah the Widow . . . lettʳˢ of Adm. with the Will
annexed is Granted her . . .
. . . to Anne Patten and Margaret Simmons Each of them
One Shilling a Piece Sterling.
. . . to Dinah my wife all moveables . . . and after
her death to be divided Equally to every Child of her body.

Witnesses: John Morry.
                        his
            John + Simins
                mark.

                        her
            Margᵗ + Simins the wife
                mark.

            of John Simins.   his
                                          James + Simins & Seal.
                                          mark

BEATY BALY of the Southern branch of Elizabeth River and
County of Norfolk Virginia . . .

Book H p. 1.

Dated—(torn)—

Proved 16 July 1742, by Thomas Herbert Junʳ and Henry Her-

bert & Adm. wth the Will Annexed is granted Eliz^a Baly
. . . to my Sister Mary Baly Won Negro Wench Named
Inday and all the Rest of my Personal Estate.

Witnesses: Thomas Herbert Junr

      Henry Herbert.

      John Herbert.

her

Betty + Baly & Seal.

mark.

WILLIS CREEKMUR of Norfolk County . . .

Book H p. 2.

Dated 25 Nov. 1741.

Proved 16 July 1742, by John Taylor & Sol^o Creekmur.

. . . to my Well beloved Son Caleb Creekmur the one half
of my Land that I now live on and the Other half I give
my well beloved Son James Creekmur and if 'Cause that
they should dye without are then this Land to fall to their
Sister Lyda Creekm Princess . . .
. . . my Welbeloved Wife Anne Creekmur . . .

Witnesses: John Taylor.

      Thos Taylor.

      Sollomn Creekmur.

Willis Creekmur.

JAMES SICKES of Norfolk County Virginia . . .

Book H p. 3.

Dated 20 May 1742.

Proved 20 Aug. 1742.

. . . Appoint my dearly beloved Wife Mary Sickes and my
Son Jessie Sickes to be Joynt Executor and Executrix
. . .
. . . to my beloved Son Jessie Sickes that Plantation which
was Given me by John Smith and the Land adjoyning to
it which I bought of Capt Lem^l Wilson, and if my Son

Jessie should die without heirs Lawfully begotten of his body then my Will is that his Land shall go to my Son Jacob Sickes.

. . . to my beloved Son James Sickes the Plantation that I bought of Richard Smith Called Chinpapin Neck and the Land Adjoyning to it which I bought of *Otho* Holland and if my Son James should die without heirs . . . to my Son Jacob Sickes.

. . . to my beloved Son Jacob Sickes the Lott I bought of Col° Sam¹ Boush . . . and if my Son Jacob should die without Heirs . . . to my Son Jonas Sickes.

. . . to my beloved Son Jonas Sickes the Lott I bought of William Wilkins Junʳ . . . and if my Son Jonas die without Heirs . . . to my Son Jocob Sickes.

. . . to my Son Joab Sickes a Negro Girle called Beck . . .

. . . to my Daughʳ Abigail Taylor Ten Pounds in Goods . . .

. . . to my Daughtʳ Mary Sickes a Negro Girle called Sarah . . .

. . . five Sons Jesse, James, Jacob, Jonas and Joab Sickes . . .

Witnesses: James Webb.

      Ralph Fenley.

         her

      Elizᵃ + Fenley

      mark.

                James + Sickes & Seal.

WILLIAM BASS of Norfolk County . . .

Book H p. 8.

Dated 1 Oct. 1740.

Proved 17 Sept. 1742, by Henry Creech & Enos Tart.

   . . . to my Son William Bass on Shilling . . .
   . . . to my Son Edward Bass one Shilling . . .
   . . . to my Son Joseph Bass all my Waring Cloaths . . .
   . . . to my Son Thomas Bass one Shilling . . .
   . . . to my Grandson William Bass my Little Gun . . .
   . . . to my Daughter Mary Bass all the Rest . . . my

Cash and also my Land if she can Save it after my Decease
. . .
. . . my Daughter Mary Bass my whole and Sole Executrix
. . .

Witnesses: Henry Crooch.

> his
> Thomas + Tart
> mark.

Enos Tart.

> his
> William W. B. Bass & Seal.
> mark.

JOYCE LANGLEY of Norfolk County in the Colony of Virginia . . .

Book H p. 9.

Dated 9 Sep. 1742.

Proved 19 Nov. 1742, by all the Witnesses . . . .

Probate granted Sarah Langley Exec^x . . .

. . . unto my beloved Sister Kezia Langley my Negro Girle
. . .
. . . my Mother should have the said Negro Girle . . .
Untill my Sister should attain the age of Twenty One
years of age . . . my beloved Mother Sarah Langley
. . . Sole Executrix . . .

Witnesses: Thomas Langley.

> her
> Eliz^a E L Langley
> mark.

Joyce Langley & Seal.

NATHAN LANGLEY of Norfolk County in the Colony of Virginia . . .

Book H. p. 10.

Dated 4 Aug. 1742.

Proved 19 Nov. 1742, by James Timberlake and Tabitha Langley

. . . Sarah Langley & James Nimmo Gent Exec^{rs}
. . . Refused the Burthen . . . Ordered the Sheriff sell the Estate . . .

. . . to my Eldest Son, named Absolom Langley, my Dwelling Plantation. with all the Houses and Orchards . . .

. . . to my Daughter Joyce Langley One Shilling . . .

. . . the remainder of all my Worldly Estate . . . shall all be sold at Public Sale . . . be Equally divided Between my Dearly beloved Wife Sarah Langley, and my Son Absolam Langley, and my Son George Langley, and my Son James Langley and my Daughter Kesia Langley, and my Son Moses Langley.

. . . Ordain my dearly beloved Wife, Sarah Langley, Capt James Nimmo . . . Sole Executors . . .

Witnesses: James Timberlake.

      Tabitha Langley.

      Katherine + Langley
         her mark.   Nathan Langle & Seal.

JAMES JORDAN MORTALL of the Southern Branch of the Elizabeth River and County of Norfolk Virginia . . .

. . . Calling to mind The Mortallity of my Body . . .

Book H p. 13.

Dated 7 Nov. 1742.

Proved 17 Dec. 1742, by all the Witnesses . . .

Probate granted Martha Hodges Exec^x . . .

. . . Appoint my dearly beloved mother to be my whole and Executrix . . .

. . . My desire is that my Mother shood keep my Money tell the time is Expired that I should bin Twenty One Please God I had Lived . . .

. . . to my dearly beloved Sister Rachall Reade the Melattor Woman Vines and Children . . . at the time of Twenty One If I had lived . . .

Witnesses Joseph Hodges.

      Benj^a Hodges.

      William Hodges.

                  James Jordan & Seal.

JOSEPH MANING of the Southern Branch of Eliz^a River Parish and County of Norfolk . . .

Book H. p. 13.

Dated 27 March 1733 and in the Sixt Year of the Reign of our Sovereign Lord George the Second by the Grace of God King of Great Britain France and Ireland defender of the ffaith.

Proved 17 Dec. 1742, by all the Witnesses.

Probate granted Mallachy Maning one of the Ex^{rs} therein named

. . .

. . . Appoint my Dearly beloved wife Martha Maning and my beloved Son Malichy to be my Joynt Executor and Executrix . . .

. . . to my Beloved Son Malichy Maning my Plantation wherein I now live with one hundred acres of Land . . . when he Comes to the age of Twenty One . . . and to be *Put* to a Ship Carpenter trade . . . my Son Joseph Maning may have the Nurcery on this Plantation to plant him out a Orchard.

. . . to my beloved Son Joseph Maning One hundred Acres of Land be it more or less being the Land which I bought of John Willoughby and Thomas Willoughby . . . if his Mother Marrys before he is of Age that he Chose his Guardian . . .

. . . to my Daugh^r Martha Maning a Feather bed with a Rugg . . .

. . . to my beloved Daught^r Mary Maning a Fether with a Rugg . . .

. . . all the Rest of my Estate Personal and real within and without shall be divided between my Wife and my four Children . . .

Witnesses: Ralph ffenley.

William Wallas.

            his
Willm M Maning Junr
            mark.

            her
Eliz^a E Nash
            mark.

                              Joseph Manning & Seal.

Mrs. SARAH LANGLEY'S Will Verbally before these Evidences under Signed on her dying Bed . . .

Book H. p. 18.

Dated 30 Dec. 1742.

Proved 21 Jany 1742/3, by Elizabeth Sparrow & Prudence Williams . . .

Administration with the said will annexed is Granted Mr James Moore . . .

Ordered Capt Thos Willoughby, Mr William Nash, Capt Wm Ivy and Mr James Thedaball . . . appraise the said Estate . . .

. . to my Son Moses Langley and to my Daughter Kezia all my Estate . . .

. . . my desire is that my Brother In Law James Moor, may have the Care of the two foresaid Children in his Possession to see them both brought up Christianly, this was pronounced by the said Sarah Langley, two hours or more before she departed this Life Decemb^r the 30th 1742.

Witnesses: Charles Smith.
        Saml Power.

her
Elizabeth + Sparrow
Assignment.

her
Prudence + Williams
Assignment.

ROBERT CULPEPER, Senr . . . Norfolk County . . .

Book H p. 19.

Dated 16 Oct. 1739.

Proved 21 Jan. 1742/3, by all the witnesses.

Probate granted Eleazar Tart Ex^r.

. . . to my Son Joseph Culpeper five Shillings . . .
. . . to my Son Benjamin Culpeper five Shillings . . .
. . . to my Daughter Rachael Wilder half a Crown . . .
. . . to my Daughter Ann Wilder half a Crown . . . .

. . . to my Daughter Elizabeth Ward a Ewe and Lamb
. . . to my Daughter Mary Grun a Ew . . .
. . . to my Grandson William Culpeper a Cow & Calf
. . .
. . . bequeath all my Land to my loving Daughter Mary
Tart . . . if my said Daughter die without Heir or
Issue to my Grandson William Culpeper . . .
. . . my Son in Law Eleazar Tart to be my full and Hole
Executor . . .

> witnesses: Henry Grun.
> John Joyce.
> Richard Dale.
>
> > > Robert Culpeper & Seal.

JOSEPH ROBERTS of Norfolk County . . .

Book H p 63.

Dated 17 July 1743.

Proved 19 Aug. 1743, by all the witnesses.

Probate granted Alice Roberts Executrix.

. . . unto my beloved Wife Alce Roberts my Plantation &
all my Land and everything that belongs to it . . .
everything that belongs to me both real & personal
. . .
. . . Ordain Tho⁸ Gaulding & Alce Roberts . . . Executor & Executrix . . .
witnesses: Daniel Godfrey.
> Edwᵈ Caire.   his
> > > Joseph + Roberts & Seal.
> > > mark.

RICHARD CHURCH in the County of Norfolk . . .

Book H p. 72.

Dated 20 Apr. 1743.

Proved 16 Sep. 1743, by Peter Taylor & Henry White.

Probate is granted Abiah Church Executʳˣ . . . Heir at Law
being present & consenting by his Guardian Capᵗ Willis
Wilson Junʳ . . .

. . . unto my well beloved Daught^r Lydia Casson one Negro Boy Called Harry . . .

. . . unto my well beloved Daught^r Julian Church one Negro Boy called Will . . .

. . . unto my well beloved Son Caleb Church a Plantation and all the Land not debaring his Mothers Thirds belonging to it: lying in an Lsland in Curretuck in North Carolina known by the name of White's Island . . . But if my Son Caleb should not live to the age of Twenty one years then . . . to my Son Joseph Church . . .

. . . unto my well beloved Son Thomas Church ye Mannor Plantation were I now live with all the Land belonging to it . . . further more . . . the House & Lott of Land at the North west Landing . . .

. . . unto my well beloved Daught^r Elizabeth Church one Negro boy called Robbin . . .

. . . unto my well beloved Son Joseph Church ye Plantation or Land which I bought of Moses Linton lying over the North west River Bridge . . . Likewise the House & Lott of Land at the Southern Branch great Bridge . . .

. . . my well beloved Wife Abiah Church . . . Exec^x . . .

witnesses: Peter Taylor.
Marg^t Wilson.
Henry White.

Richard Church & Seal.

TIMOTHY IVES of Norfolk County . . .

Book H f. 75.

Dated 27 July 1743.

Proved 21 Oct. 1743, by all the witnesses & Probate granted Exec^{rs} . . .

. . . to my Son James Ives one hundred Acres of Land where he now lives with some part of my plantation & Twenty foot square of Land at my Landing at the Back of my House . . .

. . . to my Son George Ives the plantation I now live on & my House with one hundred acres of Land . . . & one half of sixty-five acres of my swamp Land . . .

. . . unto my Son Robert Ives one hundred acres of Land next joining to my Son George Westerly . . . & half of my swamp Land . . . with my Small House & Land my Landing . . .

  . . . to my Son William Ives my Negro boy called Colley . . . .

  . . . to my Daughter Mary Willy my Negro Woman called Jenny . . .

  . . . to my Daughter Eliz* Wilkins one Negro Girl called Sue . . .

  . . . to my Daughter Rachael Hodgis one Negro Girl called Nell . . .

  . . . to my Daughter Eliz* Halett one Negro Girl called Rose . . .

  . . . to my Daughter Affiah Ives one Negro Girl called Hannah . . . .

  . . . to my Grandson Willis Gregory five Shillings in full for his Portion . . .

  . . . to my Grandson Charles Ives five shillings in full for his Portion . . .

  . . . to my three youngest Children George Ives, Robert Ives & Affiah Ive . . . all the rest of my Estate . . .

  . . . Appoint my Son James Ives & my Son George Ives full & whole Executors . . .

witnesses: Tho* Cherry.

         James Ferebee.

         Tamor Burgess.

                    Timothy Ives & Seal.

EDWARD DAVIS of the Southern Branch of Eliz* River & County of Norfolk Virginia . . .

Book H p. 77.

Dated 17 July 1741.

Proved 21 Oct. 1743, by all the witnesses.

Probate granted John Davis one of the Ex^{rs} the other being so ancient & thereby incapable of attending & the Heir at Law being present . . .

  . . . to my eldest Son Edward Davis my best Suite of Cloathes my Wools Gun & Cain.

  . . . to my Son John Davis my new pattent of Land at the lower end of my great Pasture being sixty two Acres . . . also privilege of all my Pasture Land during his his Life & after his death his Wifes Widow: hood.

. . . to my Son Richard Davis a certain parcell of Land joining on my old pattent begining at the Chickopin Branch
& runing down to the Horse pool & from thence across
the Mouth of Goose point to the next branch being bounded
on the Creek according to the former Courses as it was
formerly marked out being fifty acres more or less
. . .

. . . to my Daughter Mary Davis my best Bed . . .

. . . to my Son in law Benjᵃ Hodgis the great Iron pott that
was his Feathers.

. . . to my daughter in Law Mary Williams one warming
Pann.

. . . Appoint my Son John Davis and my Wife Mary Davis
. . . my whole & sole Executor & Exxecutrix . . .

Test: David Ballentine.

> her
> Elizᵃ + Ballentine
> mark.
> her
> Mary + Ballentine
> mark.

Edward Davis & Seal.

JOHN HUGHLETT of Norfolk County in Virginia . . .

Book H p. 78.

Dated 11 Sep. 1743.

Proved 21 Oct. 1743, by all the witnesses & probate granted them
the Heir at Law being Present . . .

. . . unto my Son Francis Hughlett and to his heirs forever
my Mana Plantation together with all the Land . . .
that I bought of Richard Church . . .

. . . to my Son John Hughlett and to his heirs forever the
Land and Plantation he now lives on Being the Land that
I bought of Peter Adams; and the Land called Green Sea
Plantation . . .

. . . to Still his Sider . . .

. . . unto my Daughter Elizabeth Moseley One Negro
Wench called Rose and a Negro boy, called Adam during
hr Natnrual life and after her decease . . . the Negro
Boy to my Grandaughter Sarah Moseley and the Negro
Wench and her Increase . . . to be Equally Divided

betwixt the rest of her Children .   .   .

.   .   . to my Daughter Prudence Maund .   .   . One Negro Wench called Jeny .   .   .

.   .   . unto my Grandson Thomas Wright .   .   . One Negro Girle Called Lucy .   .   .

.   .   . unto my Grand daughter Agness Mohone .   .   . One Negro Girle called Lavina.

.   .   . unto my four Grandsons Namely Arthur Hezekiah Francis & Peledge Mohone One Negro boy Called Robin to be Equally divided among them.

.   .   . all my Children namely Francis, John, Elizabeth, Prudence, Dinah and Mary.

.   .   . Appoint my wel beloved Wife Marg^t Hughlett and my Son John Hughlet Hole and Sole Executors .   .   .

witnesses: Thos Wright.

      Lem^l Wilkins.

          her

      Elizabeth + Flory

         mark.

                                his

                      John + Hughlett &

                      mark   Seal.

SARAH LOW . . .

Book H p. 85.

Dated 14 Dec. 1743.

Proved 20 Jan. 1743/4, by Edward Pugh and John Davenport.

.   .   .

Probate granted Pugh Ex^r .   .   .

.   .   . unto my grandson George Hensley, my half Lott of Land where on I now Live on with all the Improvements thereon .   .   . he dying without Heir I do give it unto my grand Daughter Sarah Haywood .   .   . she dying without Issue .   .   . unto my beloved Daughter Haywood and Elizabeth alias Betty Eastterd .   .   .

.   .   . unto my Grand Daughter Sarah Haywood my best Bed .   .   . my House and Lott, lying on the North side of Church Street near Town Bridge and John Roberts Land .   .   . she dying without Issue .   .   . unto my Grandson George Hensley .   .   .

.   .   . unto my beloved Grand Daugh^r Sarah Wingate one Bed .   .   .

.   .   . unto my beloved Daughter Sarah Lewelling one Bed
.   .   .
.   .   . unto my Son John Low one shilling sterling.
.   .   . unto my Son Peter Low one shilling sterling.
.   .   . unto my Daughter Mary Meech one shilling sterling.
.   .   . unto my Daughter Sarah Freeman one shilling sterl⁵
.   .   . unto my Daughtʳ Martha Griffin one shilling sterling.
.   .   . appoint Mʳ Edward Pugh to be my only Executor
.   .   .
.   .   . the remainder part of my Mansion House to be reserved unto my Grand son George Hensly shall attain to
the age of Twenty one years .   .   .

witnesses: Edward Pugh.
          Margᵗ Pugh.   her
          John Davenport.   Sarah + Low & Seal.
                                                 mark

ANN BARNEY of Norfolk Borough, widow .   .   .

Book H p. 87.

Dated 21 July 1743.

Proved 20 Jan. 1734/4, by Henry Norkott & Thoˢ Avis .   .   .

Probate granted Francis Hatton Exʳ therein named .   .   .
After my Death and after the Death of my loving Friend Richard
Inkson of Norfolk Borough Barber .   . unto my Brother
Francis Hatton .   .   . all my Land & Plantation scituated and
being upon the North west side of the Western Branch of Elizˢ
River and bounded thereon .   .   . being the same parcell of
Land which I purchased of Thoˢ Walker as may fully appear
upon Norfolk Records & cᵃ .   .   .
     .   .   . unto Ann Hatton Daughter of my Brother Francis
          Hatton my Negro Venus .   .   .
     .   .   . all my Brother Francis his Children .   .   .
     .   .   . my loving Brother Francis Hatton .   .   . Sole Execʳ
     .   .   .

witnesses: Richard Harris.
                      his
          Henry + Norkott.
                   mark.
          Thoˢ Avis.
                                                   her
                                          Ann + Barney
                                               mark.

JOHN HAYES of the County of Norfolk in Virginia . . .

Book H p. 88.

Dated 27 Sep. 1743.

Proved 18 Feb. 1743/4, by James *Cleaves* and Abell Ross.

Probate granted Exec^r therein named . . .

. . . to my Brother Thomas Hayes of the City of London Gent the Sum of Twenty Shillings Sterling as a Barr to his having any Claim or Right to any of my Estate.

. . . to my Daughters in Law Elizabeth and Anne *Clee*ve Twenty Pounds Virginia Currency . . . on their day of Marriage or at their arrival at the Age of Twenty one which shall first happen.

. . . to Elizabeth Ivy Daughter of James Ivy of Norfolk County . . . Twenty Pounds . . .

. . . all the Rest of my Estate both Reall & Personal unto my beloved wife Elizabeth Hayes . . . appoint . . . wife and Samuel Smith of Norfolk Town Gent Executrix & Executor . . .

witnesses: Abell Ross.
   William Pitt.
   James Cle*e*ves.

         John Hayes & Seal.

JOHN PORTLOCK of the County of Norfolk . . .

Book H p. 89.

Dated —— 1742.

Proved 18 Feb. 1843/4, by William Portlock, William Portlock Junr and Thomas Nash . . .

Probate granted Exec^rs therein named . .   ,

. . . unto my Son John Portlock my Land and Plantation whereon I now live with appurtenances . . . my Shooling Gun and Silver Hilted Sword . . .

. . . my Son John shall build a Small dwelling house of Twenty foot long and Sixteen foot wide with Plank flowers and a Brick Chimney on the Plantation lower down the Creek and Put that Plantation Under a Good fence all Round the Same and make a Good Well or Spring fitt for Good Water: that then my wife is to have that House and Plantation wth as much Land adjasient to it as she shall Need for Cultivating and ffence and firewood and in Lieu of her thirds of my now dwelling House But

if my Son John Refuse to Build the said House & c⁴
Then my Wife to have her thirds of my Manner House
and Plantation.

. . . unto my two Daughters (Viz') Mary Hodgis & Anne
Whitehurst to Each of them fifty Shillings.

. . . unto my Son John that Parcell of Land Commonly
Called Gilligas . . .

. . . my Water Mill with the Land & appurtenances and my
Negro Man Peter be sold . . . by my Brother William Portlock and my Son John Eith by their Private Bar-
gain or Publick Sale . . .

. . . unto my Loving Wife Sarah One third Part of my
Estate not yett Given away; and the Other two thirds I
Give to be Equally Divided among all my Children Except
my Son John . . .

. . . my Loving wife Sarah . . . her small Children
. . .

. . . my Son John and my wife Sarah to be my Executor
and Executrix . . .

witnesses: William Portlock.
          Matthew Portlock.
          Thomas Nash.
          William Portlock Junʳ

                    John Portlock & Seal.

BRYAN PENNEY of the East Side of the South Branch of
the County of Norfolk Planter . . .

Book H. p. 91.

Dated 20 Sep. 1741.

Proved *18* Feb. 1743/4, by John Cutrell and the Executrix therein
named & Probate is granted her on the Will of Bryan
Penny . . .

. . . unto my beloved Wife Elizabeth Penny that tract of
Land where in I now live on and at her Decease then to
my two Sons Edward Penney & Thomas Penney . . .

. . . my wife - . . my hole Executor . .

witnesses: Jm. Davisson,
         .Jm. Davisson.

        her   his
John —J C Cutrell   Bryan B Pinne & Seal.
   mark.   mark.

PAUL PORTLOCK of the Borough of Norfolk . . .

Book H p. 93.

Dated 21 Oct. 1743.

Proved 16 Mch. 1743/4, by all the witnesses.

Probate granted Executors . . . Heirs at Law being Present and Consenting . . .

. . . unto my Son Nathaniel Portlock the house I dwell in with all the out houses standing on the same half Lott . . .

. . . unto my Son Charles Portlock my New House adjoyning to my new dwelling house with all the houses standing on the same Lott . . .

. . . I appoint my Loving Brothers William & Edward Portlocks to be my whole and Sole Executors . . . to whom I give & bequeath One Guinea a Piece to buy Each of them a Ring.

witnesses: William Bennett.
   Alex^r Crabin.
   John Portlock Junr

        Paul Portlock & Seal.

PRETTYMAN MERRY of the County of Norfolk . . .

Book H p. 94.

Dated 23 Dec. 1743.

Proved 16 Mch. 1744/3, by Mr Charles Sweny, Mr William Nimmo and James Eitheredge.

Probate granted the rest, Mr William Nimmo one of the Executors having Relinquished the Burthen of the Execution.

. . . all my Lands Tenements houses Buildings and Improvements whatsoever and also all my Goods Wares Merchandize house hold Tools and other Personal Estate whatsoever Lying and being in the County of Norfolk to be Sold by my Executors . . . Overplus . . . to my Son, . JohnMerry When he Arrives at the Age of Twenty One Years or Marriage . . . But in Case my Said Son shall happen to die before he comes to Age or is Married Then it is my Will and I Give Twenty five Pounds thereof to the Eldest Child of my Sister Elizabeth that shall be then living . . . to the Eldest Child of my Sister Mary . . . Twenty five pounds . . . and then Residue thereof to my Thomas Merry . . .

. . . to my said Son John Merry . . . all my Lands
and Stock of Cattle in the County of Elizabeth City
. . .
. . . Negro . . . to Mary Tucker Daughter of William
Tucker in Hampton . . .
. . . Appoint Charles Sweny & Joshua Corprew both of the
County of Norfolk and William Nimmo of the County of
Princess Anne Executors . . .

witnesses: James Webb.
James Etheredge.
Charles Sweny.
William Nimmo.

Prittyman Merry & Seal.

MARY MILLER of the Borough of Norfolk Virginia . . .
. . .
Book H. p. 95.
Dated 22 Mch. 1741/2.
Proved 17 Mch 1744/3, by Capt. John Tucker & Sam¹ Boush
. . .
Probate granted Capt. Mathias Miller one of the Executors
. . .
. . . to my Son Mason Miller my Negro boy Jimmy . . .
. . . to my Son Matthias Miller my Negro boy Jack . . .
. . . to my Grand Daughter Mary Ivy my Negro . . .
Toby . . .
. . . to my Daughter Alice Ivy my Candle Moulds & my
Great looking Glass . . .
. . . to my Son Henry Millers Children Each one Shilling
. . .
. . . the Remainder of my Estate both Real and Personal
to my two Sons Mason and Matthias Miller and my
Daughter Alice Ivy . . .
. . . appoint my two Sons Mason and Matthias Miller
Executors . . .

witnesses: James Ivy.
John Tucker.
Sam¹ Boush.

Mary Miller & Seal.

WILLIAM ODEON of Norfolk County of Elizabeth River . . .

Book H p. 96.

Dated 29 Dec. 1743.

Proved 16 March 1743/4, by all the witnesses . . .

Probate granted Executor therein named . . .

. . . unto my Daughter Patience But five Pounds . . .

. . . unto my Daughter Aan Odeon two Pounds three shillings and Seven Pence . . .

. . . unto my Daught^r Mary Odeon Twenty five Pounds three shillings Cash . . . One Wheel . . . One Silver Dram Cup . . .

. . . unto my Daught^r Elizabeth Odeon Twenty five Pounds three shillings Cash . . .

. . . four bags of Feathers . . . my Weavers Loom . . .

. . . my Loving Wife Patience Odeon . . .

. . . unto my Son William Odeon my Plantation I now live on . . Like wise . . . all the Rest of my Estate both in doors and out doors . . .

. . . appoint my Son William Odeon my hole and Sole Executor . . .

witnesses: Aderegan Bartee.

         her
    Ruth R Etheredge
         mark.
    Robert Bartee.   William Odeon & Seal.

THOMAS TAYLOR . . .

Book H p. 105.

Dated: Reign of our sovereign George the second in the year of our Lord 1743/4.

Proved 18 May 1744.

. . . Bendeybow to be left to Margaret Brown the said Sister of Thomas Taylor, the wife of William Brown, and all the rest of my worldly Goods and Estate to my lawfull wife Mary Taylor . . .

witnesses: Nicholas Boulton.
    Richard Webb.
    Farrill Hughes.   Thomas + Taylor & Seal.

GARRATT PLUNKITT . . .

Book H. p. 110.

Dated 13 Sept. 1744.

Proved 21 Sept. 1744, by all the witnesses.

> . . . unto my well beloved Friend William Toppin residenter of Norfolk County all my Wages and Prize money due to me on board. his Magisties Ship Hastings now lying in the Custody or Hands of my Lord Ranff.

> . . . unto the above mentioned William Toppin the Money due to me on board the Ship above mentioned on acc[t] of Spanish prisoners taken and sent home to Great Britain by my Lord Ranff above mentioned with all my other Effects either in Cash due or wearing apparel on board the said Ship or elsewhere.

> . . . appoint William Toppin my Ex[r] and attorney in full

witnesses: Michael Dean.

his

Tho[s] Z Collins

mark.

her

Marg[t] O Little

mark

his

Garratt + Plunkitt & Seal..

mark

CHRISTOPHER SALTER . . .

Book H p. 111.

Dated 7 Sep. 1744.

Proved 21 Sep. 1744, by William Johnson & John Davenport.

Probate granted Executor therein named.

> . . . unto my beloved Friend Joyce Wilder the Sum of Twenty four pounds Curr[t] money of Virg[a] to her and her heirs for ever . . .

> . . . to my beloved Friend Edward Colly the Sum of Six pounds . . . withall my Debts that is now due to me for to carry on a Suit that is now depending for the Recovering of my Fathers Estate in Negroes that he was possest with all when he deceased.

> . . . unto my beloved Friend Sander Colly Son of Edw[d] Colley, one Negro . . .

. . . my beloved Uncle Edward Colly . . .
. . . unto my beloved Friend John Colly Son of Edward
Colly, one Coat and Breaches, a hatt & Whigg . . .
. . . unto my beloved Freind Edward Colly all my Estate
both real and personall . . . & sole Executor . . .

witnesses: William Johnson,
Salter Colley.
John Davenport.

Christopher Salter & Seal.

JOHN MORROW   (Nuncupative)

Book H. p. 119.

Dated 23 Dec. 1744 in the night.

Proved 18 Jan. 1744/5, & Administration with the Noncupative
Will annexed is granted Caleb Murro on the Estate of
his deced Brother John Murro , . .
. . . at the house of Mr Richd Davis of the County of Norfolk in Norfolk Town and about a Weeke before that time
which was to the best of our reembrance on Satturday the
15th of December 1744 these Dependants herd Mr Richd
Davis ask John Morrow if he Died being then Very Sick
what Should be Done with what hee had the Said Morrow Answers was he would give one as much as another
and further saith not.

Sworn to before me this
3d Day of July 1744/5.   Richard Lewelling.
George Newton & c.   his
                                              Solomon + Deane
                                                      mark.

JOHN HANBURY of Norfolk County . . .

Book H p. 122.

Dated —(none)—

Proved 15 Feb. 1744/5 by all the witnesses.

Probate granted Exr therein named.
. . . to my Son William Hanbury my Plantation down below
that I formerly live on and four hundred acres of Land
belonging to it . . . also . . . a small Gun and
Sword.

. . . unto my Son Job Hanbury my Plantation whereon I now dwell and all the Land belonging to it and a piece of Juniper Swamp Land that I have joining to Capt Wilsons
. . .

. . . unto my Daughter Mary Nosay one feather bed & Furniture . . .

. . . my loving Wife . . . all my Children . . .

. . . my loving Wife and my Son William my two Executors.

witnesses : Ja^s Wilkins.

        his

    John + Valentine.

      mark.

    Sarah Hanbury.

                  John Hanbury & Seal.

JOHN TAYLOR of the Borough of Norfolk Merchant
. . .

Book H. p. 123.

Dated 17 Mch. 1743.

Proved 15 Feb. 1744/5, by Revd Chas Smith, Mr William Nimmo & Doct^r Hopper.

Probate granted Executors therein named on will of John Taylor Gent decd . . .

. . . unto my welbeloved Wife Margarett . . . a Clock expected by John Coupland if it comes . . .

. . . unto my said wel beloved Wife the use & Profitts of all my Houses and Lott of Land in Norfolk Borough untill such time as my Son James, or in Case of his Death, my son John comes to the age of Twenty one years compleat . . .

. . . Children, James, Margaret and John Taylor . . . Sons . . . happen to die before . . . Twenty one . . . Daughter . . . die before . . . Twenty one . . .

. . . my Brothers, James, Andrew, Archimald & Sister Margaret & Isabell Taylor's . . . Brother William Taylor's Children . . .

. . . my Goods be sold . . . money arising . . . be putt to interest either in Great Britain or Virginia . . . my Stock in my Brother Archibalds hands in Company with him be continued in Trade . . .

If my Son James should go to Glasgow in Great Britain for his Education I nominate and appoint my said Brother Archibald Taylor Guardian to him . . .

. . . in Case both my said Sons shall die before . . . Twenty one . ι. . without Issue then living . . . unto my said Brother Archibald Taylor . . . all my said Lott of Land in Norfolk aforesaid with the houses & improvements thereon . . .

I desire that George Logan my apprentice and Book Keeper be paid reasonably to attend my Estate untill his Apprenticeship is out.

. . . appoint my Welbeloved Wife, my Brother Archibald Taylor and William Nimmo Executors . . . and in Case any of my Executors happen to die I appoint my Freind John Willoughby Executor in the Room & place of such Executor so dying . . .

witnesses: William Nimmo.

William Happer.

Jn° Hutchings.

Cha⁸ Smith.

John Taylor & Seal.

RICHARD MIARS of the County of Norfolk Virgᵃ

. . .

Book H p. 125.

Dated 2 Sep. 1744.

Proved 15 Mch. 1744/5, by the witnesses.

Probate granted Executor there in named.

. . . unto my Daughter Mary Taylor five shillings sterling

. . .

. . . unto my Brother Thoˢ Myars thirty pounds Cash to purchase a negro . . . after his Decease . . . to his Son Joshua Miars . . .

. . . unto Mary Ives Widow now my house Keeper my Plantation whereon I now live . . . for and during the Term & Space of Eighteen years if she lives so long . . . negro girl Hannah increase . . . and after her decease one half Vizᵗ her part to be equally divided between her Son Charles Ives & her Daughter Mary Williams & cᵃ . . .

. . . unto the said Mary Ives five Pistols one Guinea and one Gold Ring to purchase a horse . . . likewise

. . . all that Estate which I redeemed for her according
to the appraisement of her decd Husband Timothy Ives
during her Life & afterward to her son Charles Ives and
her Daughter Mary Williams . . .
. . . residue of my movable Estate . .. sold at publick
Sale and the said Money to be also put to Usury & cᵗ
. . . If my Daughter Mary Taylor shall have issue of
her Body lawfully begotten that then my Land . . .
given to Mary Ives . . . after the space and Term of
Eighteen years is expired shall return to the my Daughters
Child or Children . . . and for want of such heir or
heirs the above named Estate . . . unto Joshua
Miars Sons of my Brother Thomas Miars . . .
. . . my loving Brother Thoˢ Miars my sole Executor
. . .

witnesses: Richard Harris.
            Thoˢ T Deans.

his
Richard R Miars & Seal.
mark.

ARTHUR BUTT   (Noncupative)
Book H p. 127.

Norfolk County: Lydia Butt and Presilla Butt of the said
County being in full age saith that some time about the
middle of towards the last of October one thousand seven
hundred and forty four these Deponents saith they and
Each of them did hear their now decd Brother Arthur Butt
say unto his Brother Bobert Butt saying if I should die
before you meaning & then speaking to the said Robert you
shall have my negro Man Jeffry and if you die
before me you must leave me your Land which was agreed
on by the two Brothers . . . and afterwards on the
ninth day of November then following the said Arthur
Butt was drowned as these Deponents have been informed
. . .

her
Lydia + Butt
mark.
her
Prescilla + B Butt
mark.

January the 30th day 1744/5 . . . Oath . . .

Will: Portlock.

Court held the 15th day of March 1744/5, Administration with the nuncupative will annexed is granted L^{e}m^l Butt on his Broth^r Arth^r Butt Est^e Robt Butt ye Legatee . . . repes^e the Burthen of ye Execution . . .

WILLIAM BARRINGTON of the County of Norfolk
. . .

Book H p. 128.

Dated 10 Sep. 1744.

Proved 15 Mch. 1744/5, by all the witnesses.

Probate granted Executrix therein named.

. . . unto my Son William Barrington one Gun now in his own Possession . . . in full of his part of my Estate except such other part of my Estate as I shall further give him . . .

. . . unto my Son Saml Barrington Twenty nine Acres of Land that I took up and patented up *Pocaty* Road . . .

. . . unto my Son Lem^l Barrington all that Land & Plantation I now live on which I purchased of Henry Sharples . . .

. . . unto my Daughter Marg^t Cherry Twenty shill^s . . .

. . . all my Wool & Cotton and Flax and all my Crop of Tob^o . . .

. . . the remainder of my Estate after my just Debts & funeral Expenses paid . . . to be equally divided between my two Sons W^m & Saml Barrington . . .

. . . appoint my loving Wife Judith & my Son Lem^l Barrington to be Ex^r and Ex^{rix} . . .

witnesses: Sarah S Wallis.
Mary M Wallis.
Will: Portlock.

his
William W B Barrington, Seal
mark.

THOMAS WARD of the Western of Norfolk County

. . .

Book H p. 129.

Dated 8 Dec. 1739.

Proved 15 Mch. 1744/5, by Lem¹ Powell & Thomas Grimes.

Probate is granted the Executor therein named.

. . . unto my well beloved Son Thomas Ward my best
feather Bed and furniture . . . my Coopers and Car-
pente^rs Tools . . . my using Gun . . . a flax
Hackle . . .

. . . all my Children . . . they attain to the age of
of Twenty one . . .

. . . my welbeloved Wife Sarah Ward . . .

. . . my Son Thomas . . . his mother the use . . .

witnesses: Lem¹ Powell.

Thos Grimes.

Bennett Britten.

his

Thomas *N* Ward & Seal

mark.

JONATHAN GODFREY . . . Virginia Norfolk County

. . .

Book H p. 130.

Dated 4 Jan. 1744.

Proved 15 Mch. 1744/5, by John Halstead & John Miller.

Probate is granted the Executrix therein named.

. . . unto my Daughter Sarah a Negro boy . . . only
she being indebted unto her Sister Amy five pounds for
the Same Gift of the boy.

. . . give my Daughter Eliz^a a Negro Boy named Kann....

. . . unto my Son John my Plantation & c.

. . . my fellow James and my Wench Dinah to my Son
Mathew & my Daughter Ufan and to my Son William

. . .

. . . my daughter Amy Ten Pounds . . .

. . . appoint my Wife Mary Godfrey my whole Executrix
. . .

witnesses: his
          John —J M Miller
                 mark.
          John Halstead.
                 her
          Abiah A ;M Miller
                 mark.   Jonathan Godfrey.

THOMAS BUTT of Norfolk County . . .

Book H p. 150.

Dated 8 June 1744.

Proved 20 Sep. 1745, by all the witnesses.

Probate is granted Executrix therein named.

. . . my loving wife Mary Butt should hold all the land I have
a Right to except the Sypruss Swamp during her natural
life and afterwards as is directed by my father's Will
& c*.

. . . the Syprus Swamp to be equally divided between my
wife Mary and Maximilian Murden and Malachi Murden
. . .

. . . unto my Son in Law Mallachi Murden . . . my
Pistols and holsters and sword . . .

. . my loving Wife Mary Butt and Maximillion Executrix
and Executor . .

witnesses: William Porter.
           Patience Porter.
           Ja* Langly.
                              Tho* Butt & Seal.

WILLIAM TOPPEN of Norfolk Borough Weaver . . .

Book H. p. 152.

Dated 14 Nov. 1745.

Proved 17 Jan. 1745/6, by "Morick and Wm Hodghons.

Probate is granted the Executrix therein named.

. . . unto my beloved Wife Elizabeth Toppen all that I
am now possest with all during her natural Life . . .

after . . . unto my beloved Son Theophilas Toppen
. . .

. . . appoint my beloved Wife Elizabeth Toppen and John
Drury to be my Sole Executor . . .

witnesses: Morick Meach.
         Wm Mchenary.
         William Hodghon.

                     William Toppen & Seal.

HENRY GRISTOCK of the Borough of Norfolk in the
Colony of Virginia . . .

Book H p. 153.

Dated 6 May 1745.

Proved 19 July 1745, by all the witnesses & ordered Lodged.

Probate 18 Jan. 1745/6, granted Mary his widow (the other two
Ex^rs having refused the Burthen.

. . . desire that my Tenement with the Houses and appurtenances lying on the other side of the Town Bridge at
present in the occupation of Lambert Moore . . . be
sold and the Money arising . . . to my loving Wife
Mary . . .

. . . to the other of my Houses . . . unto my said
loving Wife Mary for and during her Natural Life . . .
under the Restriction following never the less . . .
she also pay unto Ann Munds my Couzen . . . she
bring up my Grand Child Frances Tucker in a handsome
manner suitable to her Condition.

. . . said Grandaughters arriving to the age of Seventeen
. . .

. . . to my said Grandaughter Frances Tucker my Lott
Houses and appurtenances in Norfolk near the Corner of
Church Street, in the possession of the said Richard Inkson

. . . my two Grand Children Henry Tucker and Fre^s Tucker

. . . unto my said Grandson Henry Tucker all my Land
and houses in Norfolk Town at the upper End of the
Main Street whereon I now live with the slipe of Land
adjoining thereto which I lately took upon the North west
End of the dwelling House . . .

. . . appoint Col: William Craford, Col: Sam¹ Boush and
my wife Mary Ex^{rs} . . .

witnesses: Christ⁰ Gardner.
         Nicholas Wonycott.
         Alexander McPherson.

his
Henry H Gristock & Seal.
mark.

JOHN ROBERTSON now in habitant of Norfolk Borough
    in Virginia . . .

Book H. p. 155.

Dated 21 Dec. 1745.

Proved 18 Jan. 1745/6, by Mr George Ramsay.

Probate is granted the Ex^{rs} therein named.

. . . my Son John Robertson in the Parish of Cart Mill in
Lancaster in England shall have the whole and Every part
of my Estate real and personal either in Europe or Virginia
. . .
appoint   Executors of
my Estate of all kinds in Europe and Mr Andrew Sprowle
and Charles Smith of Norfolk Borough my sole Executors
of all and Every Estate real or personal that I have now in
America . . .

Test: George Ramsay.
     Richard Ball.

Jn⁰ Robertson & Seal.

JAMES GILES of Norfolk . . .

Book H p. 165.

Dated 12 March 1741.

Proved 21 Feb. 1745/6, by Chas Smith & John Phripp.

Probate granted Ex^x therein named.

. . . do hereby settle my worldly Affairs and to prevent any
future disputes which might arise about them (between
Brothers or any of my Relations) and my beloved wife
Mary Giles . . .

. . . my Brothers, Cousins, or any other relation or person whatsoever shall have no part of my Estate real or personal . . . my beloved wife Mary Giles shall have all and every part of my Estate both real and personal . . . Therefore I do request the worshipfull the Justices of the peace and Judge of the Court of Norfolk, that they shall not see my said wife wronged nor deprived of any thing that belongs to me at my Death I having given and do hereby give to her & to her heirs for Ever, the whole and every part of my Estate of What kind sover . . .

witnesses: Sam¹ Boush.
Cha⁸ Smith.
Jn⁰ Phripp.

James Giles & Seal.

EDWARD ETHERIDGE of the Western Branch of Norfolk . . .

Book H p. 169.

Dated 20 March 1746.

Proved 15 May 1746, by the Oath of John Jolliff and the solemn affirmation of Peter Draper.

Probate granted the Executrix therein named.

. . . unto my loving wife Martha Etheridge all my plantation that I live on during her widowhood, and half of the said plantation during her life time and if the Child my wife now goes with is a Son, I give the other half of the s^d plantation unto him for Ever and after my Wife's death all the s^d plantation to him for ever and if the Child is not a Son . . . the s^d plantation to my Daughter Pacence Etheridge . . . at the age of 18 . . .

. . . unto my Daughter Elizabeth Etheridge one feather Bed at the age of 18 . . .

. . . unto my Daughter Mary Etheridge one feather Bed . . . at the age of 18 . . .

. . . Wife . . . Sole Executor . . .

witnesses: John Jolliff.
Peter Draper.   mark.
Sam¹ Shepherd.   Edward + Etheridge & Seale.
                                    his

JOHN BRUCE of Norfolk County . . .

Book H. p. 170.

Dated 16 Sep. 1743.

Proved 15 May 1746, by Jonas Bruce & John Joyce.

Probate granted the Executor there in named.

. . . Mr Robert Buries should have my son John Bruce to learn his Trade after the Manner fo an apprentice to serve till he come to the years of Twenty and one . . .

. . . unto my Daughter Sarah Bruce my great pewter dish
. . .

. . . my Brother James Bruce . . . hole Executor
. . .

witnesses: Jonas Bruce.
　　　　　　his
　　　　　Ja^s + Bruce
　　　　　mark.
　　　　　John Joyce.　　　　　　　　his
　　　　　　　　　　　　　　John + Bruce & Seal.
　　　　　　　　　　　　　　mark.

JOSEPH RUSSELL—(Noncupative)—

Book H p. 170.

Dated 12 Mch. 1745.

. . . made a verbal Will before Capt Willis Wilson Junr and William Shergold in the following Words: I give my personal Estate to my son Josiah Russell and Mallachi Russell and my Daughter Mary Richards and if my son Mallachi should not return home or live his part to be divided between Josiah and Mary . . .

witnesses: illis Wilson Junr
　　　　　Wm Shergold.
　　　　　　her
　　　　　Abigail + Hodges.
　　　　　mark.

Proved 21 Mch. 1745/6, by Willis Wilson Junr & lodged.

Admin granted 18 May 1746, to Josiah Russell with Nuncupative will annexed.

HENRY MORRISON of Norfolk County—(Noncupative)—
Book H. p. 171.

The Deposition of Capt Joshua Wilkkinson of lawful age
. . . sworn . . . saith That on the Nineteenth day
fo February in the year of our Lord one thousand seven
hundred and forty five he was at the house of Mr Henry
Morrison of Norfolk County, in Company with s^d Henry
Morrison and his wife Mary Morrison, and Martha Sar-
kitt and that the said Henry Morrison then entertained this
deponent and at several times before that; with Com-
mendation of his said wife, by saying that she was a well
behaved woman & very industrious and careful of his
intent and declared that after his Death it was his desire
that she (meaning his wife) should have every thing
that he had in the world. Save Thirty pounds Virginia
money . . . to Catherine McKay Daughter of Angus
McKay of Elizabeth City County, to whom the said Henry
Morrison said he was Godfather . . . heard Henry
Morrison often say that he had no kindred or relations
in the world . . . that the said Henry Morrison on
the Twenty first day of February in the year above mentioned at Norfolk County in the Colony of Virginia departed this Life without making any will . . . otherwise than that what is herein expressed . . .

Sworn to this 22^d day of February
1745 Before me
          Sam: Smith.   Josh: Wilkinson

. . . 16th day of May 1746 The Noncupative Will . . .
proved before Saml Smith Gent one of his Majestias Justices . . . Administration is granted Mrs Mary Morrison with the Will annexed . . . (Seep page 270)

Book H p. 270.

(Similar Deposition Signed):   her
                                        Martha M Surkit
                    ———————   mark.

WILLIAM BLEDGINDIN of the western Branch of Norfolk
          County . . .

Book H p. 173.

Dated 28 May 1746.

Proved 19 June 1746, by all the witnesses.

"Probatt is granted . . . Ex^r therein named."

. . . unto my God son David Miers my Mare, Bridle and Saddle.

. . . my horse Colt to Thomas Miers . . . constitute Thomas Miers to be my holy and soly Executor . . .

witnesses: her
        Eliz + Miers
        mark.
        Lemuel Powell.

                      William Bledgindin & Seal

FRANCIS HATTON of the western Branch in Norfolk County Virginia planter . . .

Book H p. 173.

Dated 10 Feb. 1745/6.

Proved 19 June 1746, by Kaley Wright & Mary Hatton.

Probate is granted her . . . E^x therein named.

. . . to my Son Joh— Hatton the Manner plantation I now live on and all the appurtenances thereto . . .

. . . unto my Son *Lewes* Hatton the tract of land wth the plantation over the Creek which I purchased of Henry Norcutt in the above said County . . . also my Pistols and Sword & smallest Gun to the above s^d Lewes Hatton and all the rest of my Estate both real and personal Goods and Chattles Gold q*uind* or un*quind* ready money or housell stuff and what silver . . .

. . . said Two Sons . . . the rest of my Children . . .

. . . appoint my loving wife Catherine and my loving Brother Bobert Hatton Executors . . .

witnesses: Kaley Wright
        her
    Mary M Hatton
        mark.
    Alex^r Bayne.

                      his
                Francis + Hatton
                marke.

RICHARD BUTT of Norfolk County . . .

Book H p. 182.

Dated 29 May 1746.

Proved 21 Aug. 1746, by Lem¹ Butt & William Butt.

Probate is granted Frances his wife Exˣ.

> . . . to me well beloved son Joseph Butt Poplar Ridge begin at a branch between my two plantations so runing to marked persimon tree and from thence on East Course to Holstead Line . . . only reserving the use of the said plantation to my son Samuel Butt his natural life.

> . . . to my well beloved son Thomas Butt my Manor plantation and all the Remaner part of my on given Land

> . . . to my well beloved Daughter Frances Butt my Negro

> . . . to my three Sons Joseph, Caleb, Arthur my Negro Girl

> . . . to my well beloved Daughter Abigail Butt one Bed

> . . . to my Son Richᵈ Butt one Two year old heifer . . .

> . . . to my Son Anthony Butt one Two year old heifer

> . . . to my Son Joseph Butt my Gun & Sword . . .

> . . . my last Children I had by my last wife . . .

> . . . appoint . . my well beloved wife . . . Frances Butt . . sole Executrix . . .

witnesses: Lemuel Butt.
William Butt.
Presᵉ Butt.

Richard Butt & Seal.

ELEANOR BRITT . . .

Book H p. 183.

Dated 5 May 1746.

Proved 21 Aug. 1746, by Doctʳ Geo. Ramsey & John Ince Junʳ

Probate is granted Majʳ Robᵗ Tucker & Mʳ Archᵈ Taylor Exʳˢ therein named.

> . . . unto my Daughter Hannah Britt one Negro . . .

> . . . unto my Daughter Hannah & the Children of my Son John Britt decd all my stock of Cattle . . .

. . . unto my gran Daughter Mary Britt one Negro . . .

. . . unto my gran Daughter Elizabeth Britt one Negro . . .

. . . unto my gran Daughter Offelia Britt one Negro . . .

. . . unto my Daughter Affiah Stephens one quart silver Tan Kard . . .

. . . the Children of my Daughter Frances and the Children of my Daughter Aphiar . . .

. . . appoint Maj^r Robt Tucker, Mr Archibald Taylor & Capt John Phripp . . . Executors . . .

witnesses: Ew^d Hack Moseley.

Geo Ramsay.

John Ince Junr

her

Eleanor + Britt

mark.

ARCHIBALD TAYLOR . . .

Book H p. 184.

Dated 25 Aug. 1746.

Proved 18 Sept. 1746, by Mr Wm Nimmo & Mr Robt *Arthur* as in the handwriting of the said Taylor.

Probate is granted Mr John Willoughby one of the Executors.

. . . to Archibald Cocke the Son of Argent Cock the Sum of five hundred Pounds Sterling when he is at 21 years of Age with the interest thereof annually till that time to be bestowed in a virtuous Education . . .

. . . to the Daughter of Mary Hodges at Great Bridge the Sum of Two hundred pounds . . . at the age of 20 . . .

. . . bequeath Two thirds of all my other Estate in whatsoever Kind / whether by Sea or Land or in Wares & Merchandize / being of the Value of about Two thousand pound by Computation / . . . to my loving wife Ann Taylor & her Child or Children by me and the other third . . . to be equally divided amongst my Brother John's three Children . .

. . . appoint Mr John Willoughby and Mr Robert Tucker Junr of Norfolk Town . . . Executors . . . they be pleased to receive each a hundred pounds sterling for their Trouble . . .

. . . written . . . with my own hand.

witnesses: —(none)—   Signature —(none)—

WILLIAM NORCOTT of the Western Branch of Eliz^a River Norfolk County planter . . .

Book H. p. 185.

Dated 24 Aug. 1741.

Proved 18 Sep. 1746, by Richard Harris.

Probate is granted Henry Norcott Ex^r therein named.

. . . unto my Son Thomas Norcott one shilling . . .
. . . unto my Son Henry Norcott all my plantation whereon I now live both twig & Turf & all appurtenances & Priviledges thereunto belonging . . .
. . . appoint my Son Henry Norcott . . . Sole Executor . . .

witnesses: ·his
        Francis + Hatton
              mark.
        Richard Harris.   his
                        William M Norcott & Seal.
                             ' mark.

BENEDICTUS THOMPSON . . .

Book H p. 187.

Dated 3 Oct. 1746.

Proved 16 Oct. 1746, by all the witnesses.

Probate is granted Robt Kilby Ex^r.

. . . my beloved wife Elizabeth Thompson . . .
. . . my beloved Son ——— Thompson . . .
. . . appoint Mr Robt Kilby . . . Sole Executor
. . .

witnesses: Stephen Farr.
        Edwd Henly.
                          his
            Benedictine + Thompson
                        marke.

JOHN LOCKHART of Norfolk County . . .

Book H. p. 188.

Dated 23 July 1746.

Proved 20 Nov. 1746.

"Probat is granted Sarah Lockhart Ex�r"

. . . unto my Son John Lockhart the plantation where on
I now live including one hundred Acres & bounded by
by a dividing line begining at John Smith's Line & running across my Land to Joˢ Sike's line . . . after my
wife's Marriage or removal by Death.

. . . unto my Son James Lockhart one hundred acres of
Land including my upper Clearing . . .

. . . one silver hilted Sword & my Pistols & holsters . . .

. . . unto my Daughter Mary Lockhart one Negro . . .
and for want such heir . . . to be equally divided
amongst the rest of my surviving Children.

. . . unto my Daughter Judith Lockhart one Negro . . .

. . . unto my Son Lemˡ Lockhart one Negro . . .

. . . unto my Son Jesse Lockhart one Negro .. . .

. . . unto my Daughter Betty one Negro. . . .

. . . to my Son Samuel Lockhart one Negro . . .

. . . to my Son Benjamin Lockhart one Negro . . .

. . . unto my Grand Daughter Eleanor Corprew one Negro
. . .

. . . unto my Grand Son John Corprew one Cow & Calf
. . .

. . . my wife Sarah Lockhart . . .

. . . all the Rest of my Estate to be equally divided among
all my Children, John, James, Mary, Judah, Lemˡ, Jesse,
Betty, Samuel & Benjamin Lockhart . . .

. . . appointing my loving wife Sarah Lockhart to be Executrix . . .

witnesses: Mary Wormington.

              her

      Mary X Wormington

          mark.

      Richᵈ Wᵐ Silvester

                  John Lockhart & Seal

HENRY PRICE of the County of Norfolk in Virginia . . .

Book H p. 193.

Dated 7 Oct. 1746.

Proved 19 Feb. 1746, by Willis Miller & Tho⁵ Hodges.

Probate is granted Tho⁵ Hodges one of the Exᵣˢ therein named
. . . the other Exʳ having refused the Burthen . . .

. . . to my Son Mallick my plantation Containing Seventy
five acres more or less . . . one pair of Mill stones
. . . but if my Son Mallick dies with out heirs to
my Daughter Lydia all my whole Estate and if my
Daughter Lydia with out heirs then to fall to my Grandson Henry Bradley the Son of Richard Bradley . . .

. . . thirty shilling to Richard Bradley & making Thomas
Hodges and Malbone Godfrey my holy & soly Exʳˢ
. . .

witnesses: Levy Smith.
Willis Miller.
Paul Elleson.

his

Henry + Price & Seal

mark.

TIMOTHY PEATON . . .

Book H p. 195.

Dated 16 Dec. 1745.

Proved 22 Aug. 1746.

Administration with the Will annexed is granted Sarah Peaton
on her deced Husband's Estate . . .

. . . To James Peaton my first born Son five shillings. To
William Peaton Ten shillings. To Elizabeth Creamur
the Sum of five shillings and to Timothy Peaton five
shillings. There is the young Mare Bonny I give to my
Son Lemuel Peaton . . . then there is the Mill I
give to my dearly beloved Son Lemuel Peaton after
the death of his Mother . . .

. . to my dear Daughter Dinah Ewell after the Death of
her dear Mother . . .

. . . every thing else I give & bequeath to my dearly beloved
wife Sarah Peaton during her Life & after . . . to

b equally divided betwixt my Son Lemuel Peaton & his dear Brother Samuel Peaton.

witnesses: John Critchitt.

        his

Geo: + Creamor

   mark.

                         his

                Timothy + Peaton

                   mark.

THOMAS TAYLOR of Norfolk County . . .

Book H. p. 197.

Dated 18 May 1745.

Proved 19 March 1746/7, by Thomas Hobgood & Eleazer Tart.

Probate is granted to Ex^{rs} therein named.

. . . unto my Son John Taylor all my Dividend of Land as I own after the decease of my loving wife Mary Taylor

. . .

. . . unto my Son Andrew Taylor five shillings . . .

. . . to my Daughter Margaret Brown five shillings . . .

. . . to my Son William Taylor five shillings . . .

. . . to my Daughter Anne Noas five shillings . . .

. . . to my Son Caleb a Negro . . .

. . . for the remainder . . . equally to be divided between my wife and five Children whom I shall Name Richard Taylor, James Taylor, & Joshua Taylor, Sarah Maning and Judith Powers . . .

. . . appoint my wife Mary Taylor and my Son John Taylor . . . sole Ex^{rs} . . .

witnesses: Thos Hobgood.

         Eliz^a Eastwood.

         Eleazar Tart.

                         his

                Thomas + Taylor & Seal

                    mark.

REODOLPHUS MALBON . . . Capt. . . . .

Book H p. 198.

Dated 10 Dec. 1746.

Proved 19 Mch. 1746/7, by Mrs Amy Hutchings & Mathew Godfrey Junr.

Administration with the Will annexed is granted Capt. John
Hutchings.

. . . if please God I shall decease out of this World before
I should come into Virginia again and after if not re-
nued again to stand good.

. . . unto my Brother Francis Malbon the Houses and
Land I bought of Mathew Kinnar and his wife Mary that
did belong to her Father Peter Malbon on the west side of
Church Street . . . and if my Brother Francis should
die without and are lawfully begott of his Body, I give
the said Land unto Frances Hutchings the Daughter of
John Hutchings Merchant in Norfolk Borough . . .
one hundred pounds Currᵗ money of Virginia and one
Silver Cann, and six silver spoons marked R. M. and
one Punch Ladle silver . . .

. . . the remainder to my Broher Francis Malbon . . .

witnesses: Mathew Godfrey.

Trim Tatem.

Amy Hutchings.

Reodolᵃ Malbon.

WILLIAM CREEDLE of the County of Norfolk in the
Province of Virginia . . .

Book H. p. 200.

Dated 9 Dec. 1746.

Proved 16 Apr. 1747, by William Richards & lodged 22 May
1747, by John Monford.

Probate is granted the Executor therein named.

. . . to my Cousin Francis Creedle Two hundred Acres of
Land lying and being upon Hatrass Banks that I bought
of William Browning . . . likewise . . . my brass
Gun . .

. . . to my Eldest Daughter Isabell Creedle two hundred
acres of Land lying upon Arrowmocat Lake the said Land
I bought of Watomon Einry . . .

. . . to my Daughter Ann one hundred acres of land lying
and being up on Arrowmocat Lake joyning up on the said
Land I give to my Daughter Isabell . . .

. . . to my Daughter Mary Creedle one Cow . . .

. . . my loving wife Isabell Creedle . . .

. . . to my loving Brother Francis Creedle . . . my Books . . . my said Brother . . . Sole Executor . . .

witnesses: Gilbert McNary.

his

John + Monford.

mark.

his

William + Richards

mark.

William Creedle & Seal.

CORNELIUS CALVERT of Norfolk Borough, Merchant

Book H p. 201.

Dated 29 May 1746.

Proved 18 June 1747, by Mr Nicholas Wonycott & by Hannah Eady now Ivy and Mary his wife one of the Exrs therein named . . . of Capt. Cornelius Calvert . . . the other two having refused the Burthen . . . Probate is granted her . . .

. . . bequeath amongst all my Children & their heirs for ever as much Land as will make an alley from the Front Street into the back Street: the said alley to begin at the South East Corner of my Store House on the Front Street and to Run from thence, on a straight Line to the South East Corner of my Kitching and from thence along the side of the kitching and my Garden Pails, into the back street, which alley is now measured and laid out, being six foot wide and Two hundred & thirty four foot long or thereabouts.

. . . to Mary my wife the free use & occupation of my dwelling house (at the upper End of Norfolk Borough & nearest to the publick Landing) with the Kitching, Store house, Smoke house, Hen house and new Shade joining to my dwelling house and all the Land belonging to it (according to the several Courses and distances hereafter mentioned) during her life and after her decease . . . th said Land and Buildings (excepting my new Shade) to my Son Cornelius . . . But if he dies without heir . . . to my Son William . . .

. . . my three sons Christopher John and Samuel . . .

. . . my Daughter Mary . . . when she is Eighteen

. . .
. . . my Daughter Elizabeth . . . when she is Eighteen
. . .
. . . my Son Samuel . . . at the age of Twenty one
. . .
. . . one Dozen of Leather Chairs . . .
. . . my Sloop . . .
. . . my new shade joining to my dwelling house . . .
to my Daughters Mary & Elizabeth . . . till the day of
their marriage and after that . . . to my Son Cornelius
. . . But if he does with out heirs . . . to my Son
William . . . to my son Maximillian . . . my
Brick dwelling house with the Kitching, Store house,
Smoke house, Hen house and all the Land belonging to
it according to the several Courses and Distances hereafter
mentioned . . .
. . . to my Son Cornelius and his heirs for ever a small
piece of Land and my Wharf joining to it (lying between
the Front street and my son Thomas's Land) . . . But
if he dies without heir . . . to my Son William
. . .
. . . to my Son Thomas . . . a Piece of Land at the
Upper End of Norfolk Borrough, according to the several
Courses and distances hereafter mentioned, with the Store
house on the same . . . when Twenty one years old
. . . But if he dies with out heir . . . to my Son
Christopher . . .
. . . to my Son Saunders . . . a Piece of Land on the
back Street, according to the several Courses and Distances
hereafter mentioned . . . with a new Store house
now there on . . . But if he dies without heirs to
my son John . . .
. . . to my son Joseph . . . a Piece of Land on the
back street, according to the several Courses and Distances hereafter mentioned & with a new kitching
thereon . . .
at Twenty one years of age. But if he dies without heir
. . . to my son Samuel . ⌣ .
. . . to my Son Maximillian, Pool's Annotations . . .
. . . to my Son Cornelius, the History of the Bible . . .
. . . to my Son Thomas the Works of the author of the
whole Duty of Man . . .
. . . to my wife all the rest of my Books . . .
. . . to my Grand Daughter 'Mary Calvert . . . five
pounds . . .
. . . to my Brother Joseph's Daughter Mary Calvert . . .
five pounds . . .

. . . my Six youngest Children, William, Christopher, John, Mary, Samuel and Elizabeth . . .

. . . my son Jonathan decd . . .

Item the several Courses and Distances of my Land now follows which I have given and divided amongst my five Eldest Sons, Maximillian, Cornelius, Thomas, Saunders & Joseph as before mentioned. The Bounds of Maximillian's Land, Begins at a stone on the north east side of the Front street (which stone lies on the dividing Line between Cap' John Hutchings's Land and mine) Running from thence north easterly 38 Degrees (or thereabouts) 150 foot to another stone, from thence South Easterly 45 degrees 74 foot to another stone; from thence South Westerly 44 degrees 102 foot to another stone; from thence South Easterly 45 degrees 12 foot to another stone; from thence South Westerly 40 degrees 47 foot to another stone on the north East side of the Front street and from thence along the side of the said Street North Westerly 45 degrees 79 foot to the first Station.

The Bounds of Cornelius's Land, Begins at a stone on the north East side of the Front street (which stone is 79 foot on the said Street from Capt. John Hutchings's Lot where he now lives) Runing from thence North Easterly 40 degrees 47 foot to another stone; from thence north Westerly 45 degrees 12 foot to another stone from thence north Easterly 45 degrees 83 foot to another Stone, from thence South Westerly along the side of the alley 99 foot to the South East Corner of my Kitchen; from thence South Westerly 57 degrees 54 foot to another Stone at the South East Corner of my Store house on the Front Street and from thence along the said Street North Westerly 45 degrees 57 foot to the first Station: The Bounds of Thomas's Land, Begins at a Stone, on the South West side of the Back Street and at the South East Corner of the Alley, runing from thence along the said Street South Easterly 45 degrees 110 foot to Dun-in-the-Mire-Creek As it is called by the Feoffois) from thence along the side of the said Creek 202 foot to another stone. from thence North Westerly 45 degrees 37 foot to another Stone near my Ovan, from thence North Easterly 57 degrees 10 foot to the North West Corner of the Store house and from thence along the Alley's side 180 foot to the first Station. The Bounds of Saunder's Land, Begins at a Stone on the back street at the North West Corner of the Alley and runs from thence a long the side of the said Alley 81

foot to another stone; from thence North Westerly 45
degrees 83 foot to another Stone, from thence North Easterly 44 degrees 81 foot to another stone on the Back street
& from thence along the said Street 81 foot to the first
Station.
The Bounds of Joseph Land Begins at a Stone on the
Back street joining to Capt John Hutchins Land and
stable & runs from thence by the side of the said Hutchings's Land South Westerly 38 degrees or thereabouts)
81 foot to another stone; from thence South Easterly 45
degrees 74 foot to another stone; from thence North
Easterly 44 degrees 81 foot to another stone on the back
street; and from thence along the side of the said Street,
North Westerly 45 degrees 77 foot to the first Station.
All which Courses and distances are now mentioned in a
Plan, done by my self and in a Frame hanging in my
house . . . my Load Stone to my Son Maximillian,
for his and all his Brothers use . . .
. . . appoint . . . for my Executors, Col: Samuel
Boush of the aforesaid Borough Merchant; Mr Samuel
Boush of Princess Ann County Gentleman and my wife
Mary . . .

witnesses: Nicholas Wonycott.
Edward Archer.
Hannah Eady.   Cornelius Calvert & Seal.

WILLIAM WILKINS of Norfolk County in the Government of Virginia being in firm as to age . . .

Book H p. 210.

Dated 6 Aug. 1745.

Proved 20 Aug. 1747, by Chas Wilkins & Lem^l Wikins.

Probate is granted Lem^l Wilkins the Ex^r therein name . . .
on Capt William Wilkins Will.

. . . unto my loving Son William Wilkins five shillings
. . .
. . . unto my loving Son John Wilkins five shillings
. . .
. . . unto my loving Daughter Catherine Butt five shillings
. . .
. . . unto my loving Son Anthony Wilkins five shillings
. . .

. . . unto my Grandson Lemuel Hodges five shillings . . .
. . . unto my Grandson Willis Wilkins my Brandy Sill
     . . . after his Father my Son Lemuel Decease.
. . . unto Elizabeth Flora thirty shillings Country Commodities.
. . . rest . . . both real & personal . . . to . . .
Lemuel Wilkins . . .
whom I make . . . sole Executor . . .

witnesses: Tho⁵ Keall.
          Thomas Butler
          Cha⁵ Wilkins.
          Lemuel Wilkins.

                                   W⁰ Wilkins & Seal.

WILLIAM RAVEN . . .

Book H p. 212.

Dated 5 Nov. 1744.

Administration with the Will annexed is granted Abigail Peaton
     . . .

Proved —(none)—

. . . unto my loving Freind Abigail Peaton my Chest with
the Cloathes & Tools as also my Share and a half which
shall be taken untill my return, & also if it should happen
that I should never return, that the said Abigail Peaton
should administer up on my Estate & make it a law ful
Claim as her own . . .

Test: Richard Imkoon.
     Abel Lewelling.
     Tho⁵ Snale.

                              William Raven & Seal.

WILLIAM MORIN late belonging to the Privateer Brig.

Raleigh belonging to Virginia Cap⁵ Walter Codd Commander . . . Nuncupative . . .

Book H. p. 212.

. . . Stephen Farr, John Dewey and William Bryan being
this day sworn . . . before me John Phripp Esq⁵
Mayor of the Borough of said Norfolk Did & do declare

that the said William Morin . . . devised and bequeathed unto Robert Crabbin and Alexander Faulkner all and every of his Goods Chattels, Prize money. smart money and all that he had in the World . . . there was a particular agreement between the s^d Morin, Crabin & Faulkner, to the same purpose & that on the making of the verbal will afors^d the deced did deliver up the Key of his Chest to the said Alexander Faulkner.

Sworn to before me this 29th day of July 1745.

John Phripp.

Administration with the Nuncupative Will annexed is granted Robt Crabbin . . .

EDMOND CUPER MARINER . . . On board the Raleigh Privateer January 14th 1745/6 . . .

Book H p. 213.

Proved 12 june 1746—See Original—

. . . on board The Brigatine Raleigh Privateer . . . after resigning my Soul to God and my Body to the waters or Grave . . . I bequeath to my trusty and well beloved Friend William Cheshire his heirs Ex^{rs} and administrators for ever all my Share or Shares that shall or does belong to me during my stay on board the aforesaid Privateer Raleigh likewise all Lands . . . that shall by any my Kind left to me . . .

Test: Ja^s Russell.
Wm Newton.
Edward Rollins.

his
Edmond + Cuper & Seal
mark.

Proved 12 June 1746, by Mr Ja^s Russell . . . before Geo: Newton, one of his Majestys Justices for . . . Norfolk County . . .

Ja^s Russell.

Proved 12 June 1746, by William Newton . . .

William Newton.

RICHARD DAVIS of Norfolk County, Ship Carpenter . . .

Book H p. 214.

Dated 29 Nov. 1747.

Proved 17 Mch. 1747, by all the witnesses . . .

Probate granted Grace Davis Ex^x therein named . . . the
other Ex^r having refused . . .

. . . bequeath (at the Decease of my loving wife Grace
Davis) unto my Daughter Prudence Davis all my land
missuage and Tenements whereon I now live in the
Borough of Norfolk . . . but for want of such heirs
the same shall devolve unto her Sister my Daughter
Patience Davis . . .

. . . unto my Son Samuel Davis . . . all that Tract or
parcell of Land . . . which I bought of my Brother
John Davis joining to the land of John Wallis and my
Brother Edward Davis . . .

. . . unto my Son Joshua Davis . . . thirty pounds
. . .

. . . unto my Son Edward Davis . . . all that tract or
parcell of Land that my father left me by his Will . . .

. . . unto my Friend Josiah Smith all that tract or parcell of
Land that I bought of my Brother John Davis called the
Range computed about Sixty three Acres to be sold in
Discharge of my Debts . . .

. . . appoint my loving wife Grace Davis & my loving Freind
Josiah Smith Ex^x and Ex^r

witnesses: James Moore.
David Murrey.
David Deans.

his
Richard + Davis.
mark.

THOMAS LANGLEY Senr of Norfolk County in Virg^a

Book H p. 215.

Dated 29 Aug. 1746.

Proved 15 Oct. 1747, by Benj^a Guy & John Guy . . .

Probate is granted Capt Lem^l Langley & George Langley . . .

. . . unto my Son Thomas Langley . . . the Land
whereon he now lives with all other my lands adjoining to
it and also fifty acres of land in the North west Woods

which I bought of John Smith joining on the land of my
Son Lemuel Langley the said Land to begin at the Cyprus
Branch or Swamp and so to run to the head Line of my
Land . . .

. . . unto my Son Thomas Langley . . . my Negro
. . .

. . . unto my Son Lemuel Langly . . . my Negro man
. . . my Gun to be in full of his part . . .

. . . unto my Son John Langly . . . the plantation
whereon he now lives Containing one hundred acres more
or less according to the Bounds of the s^d Land . . .
unto him the said John Langly the Benefit of the old Field
on the South side of the Branch his life time . . . my
Pump Tools . . .

. . . unto my Son George Langly . . . my now dwelling
plantation that I now live upon and the Lands belonging
to it according to the Bounds of the said Land Containing
three hundred Acres more or less . . . unto my said
Son George Langly fifty acres of Land in the North west
woods which I bought of John Smith joining on the fifty
acres I gave to my Son Thomas Langly . . . my Gun,
marked T L, . . .

. . . unto my Daughter Mary Millner my Molatto . . .
in full of her portion . . .

. . . unto my Daughter Abigail Hargrove the Labour of my
Negro Girl Bess . . . one Chest which was her Grand-
mothers . . . in full of her Portion . . .

. . . unto my Grand Daughter Marg^t Smith one Silver wine
Cup . . .

. . . my Grandaughter Abigail Langly my Negro Girl
. . .

. . . appoint my two Sons, Lemuel Langly and George
Langly . . . sole Ex^{rs}

witnesses: Solo: Wilson.
Benj^a Guy.
John Guy.

Thomas Langly & Seal.

TIMOTHY TENNANT . . .

Book H. p. 217.

Dated 17 Aug. 1747.

Proved 19 Nov. 1747, by Henry Hughes & Robert Bayly . . .

Probate granted the Ex^r therein named . . .

. . . unto my Father Timothy Tenant all the wearing apparel I have in Lancashire in England of what kind soever excepting my Shoe and Knee Buckles of Silver which I give to my Sister Eleanor Tennant.

. . . all my other wordly Estate . . . be equally divided between my mother Jennet Tennant and my Grand Mother Isabel Fitzackerly . . . Share and Share alike . . .

. . . appoint my Kinsman Tho⁸ Fitzackerly . . . Sole Executor . . .

witnesses: Henry Hughes.
   Peter Guy.
    his
   Robert R Balley
    mark.
         Timothy Tennant & Seal.

GEORGE GRIFFEN of the County of Norfolk, Planter . . .

Book H p. 218.

Dated 18 Dec. 1738.

Proved 18 Feb. 1747, by Richard Wᵐ Silvester & Wᵐ Wormington . . .

Probate granted Constant Griffin Exˣ therein named . . .

. . . unto Constant Griffen my loving Mother three negroes . . . sole Executrix . . . and singular my Lands . . . by her freely to be possed and enjoyed to her and her heirs for Ever . . .

witnesses: John Lockhart.
   Wᵐ Wormington.
   Richard William Silvester. George Griffen & Seal.

DANIEL LONG now in the Borough of Norfolk, Shoemaker

  . . .

Book H p. 218.

Dated 15 Sept. 1747.

Proved 15 Oct. 1747, by John Hamilton . . .

. . . unto my dear beloved wife Ann Long all the rest

. . . appoint my said dear beloved wife . . . sole Executrix . . .

witnesses: Alex^r White.
John Hamilton.
Wm Cheshire

his
Daniel + Long & Seal
mark.

WILLIAM BALLENTINE in the County of Norfolk Virginia . . .

Book H p. 222.

Dated 14 Dec 1746.

Proved 17 Sep. 1747, by John Maning & lodged . . . 19
Nov. 1747, by Saml Hanbury.

Probate granted Ex^r therein named.

. . . my loving wife Judy Ballentine . . .

. . . unto my loving Daughter Milbro Veal one Shilling
. . .

. . . unto my Daughter Tully one shilling . . .

. . . unto my Daughter in law Susanah Cain one shilling
. . .

. . . unto my Daughter Elizabeth Penny one shilling . . .

. . . unto my Daughter Lydia Wood one shilling . . .

. . . unto my Daughter Alfiah Drake one shilling . . .

. . . unto my Daughter Keziah Ballentine a young Negro
. . when . . . of age . .

. . . . . . unto my Grand Daughter Mary Ballentine, one shilling . . .

. . unto my beloved Daughter Abi Ballentine . . .
Negro . . when she shall arrive of age . . .

. . . unto my beloved Son William Ballentine all my land
. . . when he shall come of age . . . three negroes
. . . at the Death of his Mother . . .

. . . Gun and a new Gun Chest standing in the Hall . . .
& if in Case my Son William should die without Issue then
all his proportionable Estate that he must have to be

equal divided between his two Sisters Keziah and Abi Ballentine . . .

. . . wife . . . sole Ex^x . . .

witnesses: Peter Taylor.

        Jn⁰ Maning.

        Sam¹ Hanbury.   his

               William W Ballentine & Seal

                      mark.

THOMAS CHERRY of Norfolk County . . .

Book H p. 224.

Dated 17 Apr. 1748.

Proved 19 May 1748. by Tho' Cherry, Solo: Cherry & Geo
Ives . . .

Probate is granted Jeremiah Cherry & William Cherry . . .
Ex^{rs} therein named . . .

  . . . to my Son Jeremiah Cherry the plantation I now live
on including one hundred Acres of Land to a Division
already made . . . and the half of one hundred Acres
and twenty five of Land I bought of Marmaduke Etheredge Senr . . . one Gun & sword . . .

  . . . to my Son William Cherry the plantation where he now
lives on being seventy five acres of Land and the other
half of the hundred and twenty five acres which I give to
my son Jeremiah . . .

  . . . to my Daughter Sarah Brown at the death of her husband John Brown the plantation and Land I bought of
Marmaduke Etheredge Junr being 63 acres of Land
. . . and if she dies without heirs lawfully begotten
of her Body then . . . to Jeremiah Cherry . . .

  . . . to my Daughter Mary Tart . . . Negro . . .
during her life and at her Death to her Daughter Sarah
Tart . . .

  . . . to my Daughter Martha Foreman . . . the half
of my Land on the North side of deep Creek . . .

  . . . to my Daughter Faith Cherry the other half of my
Land on the North side of Deep Creek . . . and her
Mothers Chest . . .

. . . appoint my two Sons Jaremiam Cherry and William Cherry my Executrix . . .

witnesses: Thomas Cherry.
    Mary Cherry.
    Lydia Ives.
    Solo: Cherry.
    Geo. Ives.

          Thomas Cherry & Seale.

THOMAS WRIGHT of the County of Norfolk . . .

Book H p. 229.

Dated 17 May 1748.

Proved 21 July 1748, by all he witnesses . . .

Probate granted Robert Burges Ex^r therein named . . .

 . . . unto my Grandson Thomas Wright son of James Wright deced my Mannor plantation in the Western Branch Begining at James Grimes's Line and so Runing up as far as his Land goes, then up a Branch to the upper End of an old Field thickett of pines and thence a westerly Course a Cross my Land to David Southerland's Line including all the Land within those lines to the River . . . my using Gun and silver hilted Sword . . . my Case of Bottles in the Western Branch . . .

 . . . all my Iron & pewter that is at my Son Absolem's be equally divided between my son Absolem Wright and my said Grandson Thos Wright.

 . . . unto my Son Absolem Wright the remainder of my Land not before given that is to say in the Western Branch being a plantation called abigarlos on the Western Branch . . .

 . . . unto my son John Wright the Land and plantation I bought of Thomas Ballentine being the Land he now lives on . . .

 . . . unto my Grandson Malachi Burgess that Land which I bought of Samuel Creekmure . . . only reserving that my Daughter Tamor Burgess to have the use . . untill my said Grandson . . . comes to the age of Twenty one . . .

 . . . my Brandy Still . . . my Tea Ware . . .

. . . The Mark of the plantation I now live on in Southern Branch . . .

. . . my Son in Law Robert Burgess have the Managing and schooling my Grandson Tho⁸ Wright and bind him to what trade he shall think proper . . . .

. . . all my Children namely Absolom, John and Tamor and my Grandson Thomas Wright . . . my part of the Juniper Swamp . . . equally . . .

. . . my Son in Law Rob⁺ Burgess . . . Sole Executor . . .

witnesses: Will: Portlock.
     Rich⁴ Hodges.
     Jn⁰ Burgess.

          Tho⁸ Wright & Seal.

JOHN DAVIS of the County of Norfolk . . .

Book H. p. 235.

Dated 18 July 1748.

Proved 20 Oct. 1748, by all the Witnesses.

Probate granted Bathina Davis Ex˟ therein named.

. . . to my Son David Davis a Gun & Sword . . .

. . . to my Daughter Mary Davis my large Table . . .

. . . to my Daughter Margaret Davis one Sow and Pigs . . .

. . . to my three youngest Daughters Lydia Davis & Rachael Davis and Grace Davis Each of them one pewter pottle Bason . . .

. . . Timber of my Land . . .

. . . wife Mary Bethiah Davis . . . sole Executrix . . .

Witnesses: Henry Green.
      his
    James + Taylor
     mark.
    John Joyce.

          his
        John + Davis & Seal
         mark.

JOHN YAXLEY of the Borough of Norfolk in the Colony of
Virginia Turner and Blockmaker . . .

Book H. p. 237.

Dated 9 Dec. 1748.

Proved 20 Jan. 1748, by all the Witnesses.

Probate granted Josiah Smith Gent. Ex^r therein named.

. , . unto my good Friend Elizabeth Warren for and during her natural Life my Mesuage and Tenement now in
the occupation of John Terry blacksmith and Esther
Thomas, and after . . . unto Josiah Smith, of the
Borough of Norfolk Merch^t . . . to be sold . . .
& the money . . . arrising . . . unto my Kinsman Francis Yaxley Son of my Brother William and Mary
Yaxley, now of the Kingdom of Great Britain . . .

. . . all my mesuages & Tenements in the Borough of Norfolk aforesaid . . . my plate, Linen . . . be sold
. . . by Josiah Smith aforesaid Merch^t . . .

. . . my beloved wife Susannah Yaxley in St. Bennedicts
Parish in the Town of Cambridge in the Kingdom of
Great Britain . . .

. . . appoint the said Josiah Smith Executor . . . he be
allowed five pounds in the hundred . . . in or about
the Execution . . .

Witnesses: John Jones.
   Sarah Drury.
   Jno Drury.

          John Yaxley & Seal.

Codicil:

. . . unto my loving wife . . . all that my Mesuage &
Tenements . . . that I am now possessed of in the
Town of Cambridge aforesaid for & during . . . her
natural Life and at her decease . . . unto my loving
Daughter Mary the wife of Robert Mears of ye County
of Cambridge . . . & for want of such heirs . . .
unto my Kinsman Francis Yaxley Son of my Brother
W^m. Yaxley afores^d . . .

Dated 24 Dec. 1748.

Witnesses: John Jones.
   Sarah Drury.
   John Drury.

         John Yaxley & Seal.

STEPHEN WRIGHT in Virginia in the County of Norfolk, Planter .   .   .

Book H. p. 239.

Dated 16 Apr. 1748.

Proved 20 Jan. 1748, by Alex^r Bayne & Martin Bayne· .   .   .
16 Mch. 1748 by Mr. John Tatem therein name the others refusing the Burthen .   .   . Probate is granted on .   .   . Capt Stephen Wrights' Will .   .   .
.   .   . unto my Daughter Ann Tatem one Negro .   .   .
.   .   . to my Grandson Stephen Tatem one hundred p^{ds} .   .   .
.   .   . unto my Daughter Katherine Wright Two hundred and Twenty five pounds .   .   .
.   .   . my loving wife Pembrooke Wright .   .   .
.   .   . if it please God my wife should die before her mother .   .   .
.   .   . unto my Son Stephen Wright all my Lands .   .   . his Mother in Law .   .   .
.   .   . my Money in Virginia & in England .   .   .
.   .   . my plantations .   .   .
.   .   . they have done sawing for Capt Powell, there should be no more Oak plank sawed till my Son Stephen Wright comes to the age of Eighteen .   .   .
.   .   . what Good I have sent whome .   .   .
.   .   . my Daughter Catherine .   .   .
.   .   . appoint my loving wife Pembrook Wright and Mr Ja^s Nimmo & my Son in Law John Tatem .   .   . sole Ex^{rs} .   .   .

Witnesses: Alex^r Bayne
    Martin Bayne
      her
    Ann + Lewis.
     mark

          Stephen Wright & Seal.

AILCE NICHOLSON of the County of Norfolk in the Colony of Virginia widdow .   .   .

Book H. p. 242

Dated 24 Nov. 1741

Proved 16 Mch. 1748, by Malachi Nicholson .   .   .

Probate granted Geo. Nicholson Ex^r therein named, Lem^l Nicholson one of the Ex^{rs} .   .   . refused the Burthen .   .   .

. . . unto my Son George Nicholson one feather Bed . . .
a Black suit of Cloaths to my Son George's wife . . .
. . . to my Son Lemuel Nicholson . . . one feather
bed . . .

. . . to my Grandson Joshua Nicholson one feather Bed
. . .

. . . to my Grandson William Nicholson one breeding Cow
. . .

. . . my Two Sons George Nicholson & Lem¹ Nicholson
. . . sole Executors . . .

Witnesses: James Timberlake.
    Dinah Nicholson.
    Malachi Nicholson.

her
Alice × Nicholson.
mark.

Codicil:

Dated 24 Nov. 1741.

. . . unto my Grandson Wilson Nicholson one Case with
Bottles which was formerly my Son John Nicholson's now
dec'ed . . .

her
Alice + Nicholson.
assignment

LEMUEL LANGLY of the County of Norfolk in Virginia
  . . . Capᵗ . . .

Book H. p. 245.   D

Dated 10 Dec. 1748.

Proved 16 Mch. 1748, by Ann Nicholson & Wm. Granbery . . .
17 Mch. 1748, by Joseph Bayly; & Mary Langly, Sam¹
Boush senʳ and Lem¹ Langly Exʳˢ therein named granted
Probate . . .
. . . my three Sons Willis, Samuel, Nathaniel and my
Daughter Mary Langley . . .
. . . the Island I bought of John Ivy . . . the Land I
bought of Mʳ Lewis Conner in Princess Ann County
. . .
. . . unto my Son Thomas Langley one hundred acres of
Land at the North west River according to the Bounds
thereof . . .

. . . my said Son Thomas his Children . . .

. . . unto my son Lemuel Langley my Mannor Plantation whereon I now live also the Island lying in Princess Ann which I bought of John Ivy . . .

. . . unto my Son Willis my Plantation at Brushy Neck Containing one hundred acres more or less . . .

. . . the Land I bought of Thomas Henly containing one hundred & Fifty acres be sold (reserving unto my Son Lem¹ Langley forty foot wide from the Green Branch to to the Bridge that leads to the Island for a Road . . .

. . . unto my Son Samuel Langley fifty acres of Land more or less I bought of Col. Samuel Boush . . .

. . . unto my Son Lemuel Langley the thirty acres of Land I bought of Noes and Wilbore be the same more or less . . .

. . . unto my Son Nathaniel Langley all my Land on Tanners Creek I bought of James Moore with all the Land adjoyning being in all about two hundred and Seventy five acres . . .

. . . to my Daughter Frances Wilson . . . Negroes . . . a Chest of Drawers & twelve Chairs I bought of Cap⁺ Wakely . . .

. . . to my Son Willis the Desk his Mother uses . . .

. . . to my Cousin Ann Nicholson Twenty shillings to buy a Ring.

. . . to my two Sons Lem¹ & Willis Langley to be equally divided two hundred acres of Land I bought of Lewis Conner . . .

. . . appoint my trusty friend Col. Samuel Boush and my dear & loving wife, Mary Langley & my Son Lem¹ Langley . . . sole Executors & Executrix . . . (Altertation Clause).

. . . in Case my Son Nath¹ shall dye before he comes to . . . lawfull age that then I give all the Land I gave my said Son Nath¹ to my two Sons Willis and Samuel, on their paying to my Exⁿˢ Twenty pounds . . .

witnesses: his
                 Patrick + Murphee.
                     mark.
                 Joseph Bayley.
                 Wᵐ Granberry.
                 Ann Nicholson.
                 Solo. Wilson.

                                    Lem¹ Langley & Seal.

JEREMIAH LANGLEY of Elizabeth River Parish in the County of Norfolk . . .

Book H. p. 252.

Dated 9 June 1747.

Proved 20 July 1749, by Geo. Langly, Jnᵒ Guy & Jnᵒ Williams . . .

Probate granted Joseph Langley & Wᵐ Langley Exʳˢ therein named . . .

. . . unto my Brother James Langley . . . Twenty pounds . . .

. . . unto my Sister Margarett Johnson . . . Twenty pounds . . .

. . . unto my Cousin Joseph Langley Son of my Brother William Langley . . . my now dwelling Plantation that I now live upon and all the Land belonging to it according to the Bounds of the Patten containing five hundred and Twenty five acres more or less . . . One Piece of Land adjoining to the aforesᵈ Land given to him Containing one hundred acres more or less According to the Bounds of the Patten called by the Name of Homers Tree Swamp . . .

. . . unto my Cousin William Langley Son of my Brother William Langly . . . my plantation and all the Land belonging to it in Princess Ann County Containing Two hundred and fifty Acres more or less of Land according to the Deeds which Capᵗ. John Ellegood acknowledged to my Brother Jacob Langley . . . Fifty acres of Swamp Land which my Brother Jacob Langley bought and gave to me . . . my silver healfted Sword . . .

. . . unto my Cousin Jonathan Langley Son of my Brother William Langley . . . my Plantation and all the Land belonging to it which I bought of Mʳ John Chapman and Martha Thomas Containing One hundred Acres more or less . . . my Plantation and all the Land belonging to it which I bought of Mʳ James Guy Containing one hundred and Ten Acres more or less . . .

. . . unto my Cousin Absolem Langley, Son of my Brother Nathan Langley . . . my Plantation in the North west Woods which my father gave to my Brother Abraham Langley Containing Two hundred acres of Land according to the bounds as my Father gave it . . .

. . . unto my Cousin James Langley Son of my Brother Nathan Langley . . . my Plantation which I bought of John Williamson Containing one hundred and Twenty acres more or less according to the Bounds of the Deeds . . .

. . . unto my Cousin Moses Langley Son of my Brother Nathan Langley . . . my Plantation in the North west Woods which I bought of my Brother Jacob Langley Containing Two hundred acres of Land more or less according to the Bounds as my father gave it . . .

. . . unto my Cousin Kezia Langley Daughter of my Brother Nathan . . . Negro . . .

. . . unto my Cousin Elizabeth Langley Daughter of my Brother William Langley . . . Negro . . .

. . . unto Mr Samuel Bartee who intermarried with my Cousin Signa Langley Daughter of my Brother William . . . Negro . . .

. . . the remainder of my Estate both real and personal . . . unto my aforesaid six Cousins, Joseph Langley & William Langley & Jonathan Langley & Absolem Langley & James Langley and Moses Langley . . .

. . . my two Cousins Joseph Langley and William Langley . . . sole Executors . . .

Witnesses: John Langley.

George Langley.

John Guy.

John Williams.

John Simmons.

Jeremiah Langley & Seal.

JOHN LAMBERT of Norfolk Borough, Marriner . . .

Book H. p. 256.

Dated 22 Jan. 1745.

Proved 20 Feb. 1746, by Mr John Willoughby & lodged 20 Oct. 1749, by Ann Barron . . .

Probate granted Mary Lambert and Andrew Sprowle Exrs therein named . . .

. . . unto my beloved wife Mary Lambeth the use of my house and lot in Norfolk Borough whereon I now live during . . . her natural life . . .

. . . my Son Meredith Lambeth when he comes of lawfull age . . .

. . . unto my Son Meredith Lambeth my house and one half

of my land in Norfolk Borough next adjoining the Street
. . . unto my Son John Lambeth the one half of my land
in Norfolk Borough next adjoining the Creek being the
equal half of the lot or parcel of Land whereon I now
live . . .
. . . my Sloop . . .
. . . appoint Andrew Sprowle & my wife . . . Ex^n
. . .

Witnesses: Jno. Willoughby.
  Cha* Smith.
  —— Barron.

         John Lambeth & Seal.

ROBERT STEWART . . . (Noncupative) . . .
Abstracted from the Original. (See Book H. p. 211).
Dated 23 Aug. 1747.
Recorded 24 Aug. 1747.

. . . Levi Stewart and Nicholas Slack Came before me one
of his majes^t Justices Of the Piece & Made Oath that
Robert Stewart . . . a Small Time before he Dyed
Sayed to his Mother Elizabeth Slack . . . I Desire
you to Sell all my Estate Except my Land & house.
. . . my Child Robert Stewart Take Care of him & my
land & have my house Enclosed this being Said the 23d.
Day of August 1747 & the same day he Dyed.

         W illis Wilson, Jr.

MARGARET HERBERT of the County of Norfolk . . .
  Sick and WEAK . . .
Abstracted from the Original.
Dated 9 Dec. 1749.
Proved Jany. Court 1749/50.

. . . unto my son Markcom Herbert my negro woman
named Phillis . . .
. . . Abigall Herbert Daughter of my son William Herbert . . .
. . . my Grandson John Markcon Herbert son of my son
Markcon . . .

. . . my Daughter Margaret Tucker . . .
. . . unto my grandson James Herbert Son of my Son Henry
Herbert my gold Ring and gold Sleave Button and pair
of Silver Shoe Buckells . . .
. . . appoint my Loving Son Marcon Herbert . . .
Executor . . .

Witnesses: Henry Herbert.
        Margaret + Gardner.
        Will. Portlock.   her
                     Maragret + Herbert.
                       mark.

THOMAS HUMPLETT of Norfolk County, Carpenter . . .

Abstracted from the Original.

Dated 30 Nov. 1749.

Proved ———— 1749/50.

. . . unto my beloved brother King Humplett one Half of
my Lott of Land lying neare Norfolk Towne . . .
. . . Appoint my beloved friend Ebenezer Stevens . . .
Executor . . .

Witnesses: William Poole.
          his
      John + Gould.
        mark.
        her
     Mary + White.
       mark.   his   Red
                  Thomas + Humplett Wax
                       mark.   Seal.

NOTE:—The foregoing three wills were found in Package of
1711 to 1755.

THOMAS S senr of Norfolk County Virginia . . .

Book H. p. 257.

Dated 25 Sep. 1749.

Proved 20 Octo. 1749, by all the witnesses, . . . Their
present . . .

Probate granted John Scott & Wm Scott Ex^{rs} therein named

. . . to my beloved wife Martha Scott priviledge of the house and plantation I now live in till the Twentieth day of March next ondley my Daughter Marg^t is to have her Room . . .

. . . I give the plantation I now live on that is to say one half of all the Land that I am now possessed of excepting that that I bought last of Edward Hughs and that that I bought of John Hollow, Jⁿ, that is in this County to say boundin upon a Branch on ye West so up to my Gate so near South to the hed of all my Lands to make *in* as equal as they can between my son John and be so one East bounded on a Creek so on Munsis and Jonas Taylor to Cornel William Craford's Line to a folkitt Maipll so from that Corner Maipel to South be west Cose to my Relops Land so in Cludin ye Relaps Land as the line runs to my said Son Thos Scott . . . the s^d Land before given containing about two hundred and Fifty Acres more or less . . .

. . . to my Son John Scott the other halfe of that parte of Land before mentision^d joining on his Brother Thomas Scott on the East and on Cornell Crafords on the West so runing & bind on Mr William Hapers and so to the hed of all my land . . .

. . . to my Son William Scott two hundred Acres of Land be more or less that I bought of Edard Ivse last as will appeaire by Deades lying on the Souther Branch Rote . . . allso . . . two hundred and twenty acres of Land lying in Preancis Ann County on the North River which Land I bought of my Brother David Scott . , .

. . . My Daughter Elizabeth Harbard has had her peart all Ready . . .

. . . my Daughter Frances Veal . . .

. . . my Daughter Margret Scott . . . her Mother in Lawe . . .

. . . to my wife Martha Eldsites Sun one Shilling being in full of all heis to have being for Good Reasons the above named Eldist Sun is caled James Scott which is cut of with a Shilling.

. . . to my Daughter Abigall Scott one Negro . . .

. . . to my Sun Samuel Scot the plantation that my Sun Thhomas lives on which abooghte of John Holloway . . . after his Mothers decease.

. . . to my Daughter Agnis Scott Twenty pounds . . .

. . . to my Daughter Dina Scott a negro . . .

. . . to my Son Sollomon Twenty five pounds . . .

. . . to my Gran Sun Thomas Scott Sun of Thomas Scott
Junr a Negro . . .

. . . to my Granson Samuel Veal a Negro . . .

. . . my Gran Daughter Eliz^a Harbard a Negro . . .

. . . Money . . . due from Cap^{tn} Smith at Mr Thomas
Harbards for Plank . . .

. . . appoint my Sun John Scott and my Sun William
Scott . . . sole Executors . . .

Witnesses : Peter Portlock.

      Solo. Ewell.

      Jonas Taylor.

                  Thos Scott & Seal.

THOMAS HERBERT of the County of Norfolk . . .

Capt . . . being aged . . .

Book H. p. 260.

Dated 17 June 1749.

Proved 19 Oct. 1749, by Mr Wm Portlock, Jno Whillon & Win
field Dale . . .

Probate granted Mrs Marg^t Herbert, Mr Markeum Herbert &
Mr Thomas Herbert Ex^{rs} therein named . . .

. . . unto my Eldest Son Markium Herbert the plantation
whereon I now live and the land belonging to it . . .
and one Copper Still now standing on my plantation
. . . Twelve Leather Chairs . . . one Gun a
Bayonet a pair of Pistols and back Sword . . .

. . . unto my Son Thomas Herbert the Land and plantation he now lives on being part of the Land called Digbyes
runing up a large flatt Creek to Thomas Edwards his
Corner Tree the said Creek dividing this Land from the
Land I do give to my Son Hinry Herbert . . .

. . . unto my Son Henry Herbert the Land and plantation
called Basit and with part of the Land called Digbyes being the land that he now lives on runing up a line of
marked trees to the Land I bought of Richard Ballentine
and running up that line to my Corner tree adjoining upon
the Land of Capt Wm Busten Runing from the said Corner tree down to a small Branch being part of the Land
that I bought of Richard Ballentine so runing down the
Branch . . . and the remaining part of the said Land
I give unto my Son Thomas Herbert . . .

. . . unto my Son John Herbert a small plantation with the

wood land Ground thereto belonging which I came by my Father Known by the name of Point of Marsh being at the Mouth of Julians Creek so up the River to a line of Marked Trees dividing this Land from the Land I gave to my Son William so along a line runing nigh South West so far as my Land extends being a Line already made & marked . . .

. . . . unto my Son William Herbert the Land and plantation he now lives on which I bought of my Brother being the remainder of my Land lying between the Land I gave my Son John and the River towards Deep Creek . . .

. . . unto my Son Hillery Herbert the Land that I bought of James Jolly being one hundred Acres more or less, lying on the South side of Paradise Creek . . . one dozen of Virginia Chairs . . .

. . . unto my Daughter Margaret Tucker one Lott of Land in New Town joyning the Lott of Wm Godfrey . . . Six Negroes . . .

. . . unto my Grandson Nathaniel Son of my Son Thomas Herbert one Negro . . . my Grandson Thomas Son of my Son Thomas . . . my Grand Daughter Hannah Daughter of my son Markeum Herbert . . . her Sister Mary . . .

. . . my Grand Daughter Courtney Daughter of my Son Markeum . . . my Grand Daughter Margaret Daughter of my Son John Herbert . . . the next heir of my said Son John . . . my Grand Daughter Elizabeth Daughter of my son Thomas Herbert . . .

. . . my Land and old plantation that formerly belonged to my Uncle Richard Herbert near deep Creek Containing about one hundred and seventy acres unto my Son Markcon Herbert and my Son William Herbert . . .

. . . Son Markium . . . my wife . . . his mother . . .

. . . appoint my loving wife Marg^t Herbert and my two Sons Markeam Herbert & Thomas Herbert . . . Sole Executors and Executrix . . .

Witnesses : Will. Portlock.

John Whiddon.

Simon Portlock.

Winfield Dale.

his

Thomas + Herbert & Seal.

mark.

BETTY GOLFREY of Norfolk County in the Colony of Virginia . . .

Book H. p. 265.

Dated 6 Jan. 1748/9.

Proved 20 July 1749, by Martha Lin*us*, Mary Lavin . . .

Probate granted Eliz* Golfrey & Thomas Golfrey Ex*ʳˢ* therein named . . . all the rest of my Estate which was left me . . .

. . . unto my loving Mother Elizabeth Golfrey my Negroes

. . .

. . . my . . . Brother Thomas Golfrey . . . Negro

. . .

. . . appoint my loving Mother Elizabeth Golfrey and my Brother Thomas Golfrey to be my Executors . . .

Witnesses: Martha Lin*us*.

Mary L*ae*vin.

John Golfrey.

Betty Golfrey & Seal.

SOLOMON CREEKMUR of the Northwest River and County of Norfolk . . .

Book H. p. 266.

Dated 28 Sept. 1747.

Proved 19 Oct. 1749, by Tho* Nosay and Wm Hodges & lodged for further proof . . .

. . . appoint my dearly beloved wife Mary Creekmur to be my whole & sole Executrix . . .

. . . to my beloved Son Forman Creekmur one hundred Acres of Land more or less being the Land I bought of Ostin Shipwash & Elizabeth Shipwash his mother the last Convance maid by John Shipwash . . .

. . . to my beloved Son Wright Creekmur the lower part of my land I now live on beginning at Slab Mark Oak· which is a corner tree between Thomas Williams and Solomon Creekmur and runing a strate Corse into my Pastuer to a sarting Persim on Tree & from thence to a line Beach standing between me and Job Hanberey by the Rode side I give the Land below that said bounds to him and his ares for Ever But if my Son Wright Creekmur should die without lawful are begotten of his Body then for the said Land to fall to my Son Solomon Creekmur . . .

. . . to my beloved Son Solomon Creekmur my Manner plantation and all the Land above the line I mentioned between my two Sons . . . But if either of my Sons should be amind for to sell their part of Land Wright Creekmur or Solomon Creekmur the other shall give or take fifteen pounds Current Money of Virginia for their part of Land and if either my Sons Wright Creekmur or Solomon Creekmur should die without lawfull are begotten of their Body for the longs Liver to have all the said Land I gave them both.

. . . to my Sons Wright Creekmur & Solomon Creekmur one parcel of Land that was called Bens taken up and survaded between Doctor William Happer & Thomas Warring and Edmund Craekmur & Solomon Craekmur . . . equally dived between them . . .

. . . to my beloved Son Foremand Creekmur one Cow & yarling . . . Gun be shouts out on . . .

. . . to my beloved Dafter Martha Creekmur one Cow . . .

. . . to my beloved Dafter Mary Creekmur one Cow . . .

. . . to my beloved Son Wright Creekmur . . . a Gun that his Unkel Wright left to him . . .

. . . my Buckernear Gun . . .

. . . sett my Son Wright and Solomon free at the yare of Eighteen . . .

Witnesses: his
          Solo. S. Creekmur.
             mark.
             his
          Thoᵉ N. Nosav.
             mark.
          Will. Hodges.

                              his
                    Solomon S. Creekmur & Seal.
                         mark.

N. B.—First Eighteen pages torn out of Book I.

JOHN BROWN

Book I p. 3 (States Old General Index).

(Completely torn out of Book I and missing from Original Wills).

AARON ETHEREDGE . . .

Book I p. 19.

dated 28 Jan. 1739/40.

proved 21 Nov. 1740, by Wm Etheridge & Thomas Nash & Ex^r . . .

. . . —(torn)— . . .

. . . only reserving to my Wife Sarah Etheredge her priviledge thereof during —(torn)— Natural Life I also give to my Said Son Lott my own using Gun . . .

. . . to my Son Caleb Ethe—(torn)—fifty acres of Land on ye North or upper Side of that Land which I bought of Thomas (—torn)— . . . also two guns . . .

. . . to my Daughter Fabitha Butt one pewter Dish . . .

. . . to my Daughter Rachel Etheredge one heiffer & on pewter Dish . . .

. . . my five Children y^t is to say Aaron Etheredge Lott Etheredge & Caleb Etheredge & my two daughters tabitha Butt & Rachell Etheredge . . .

. . . my Loving Wife Sarah Etheredge & my Son Aaron Etheredge wholly & Jointly my Executrix & Executor . . .

witnesses: Thomas Nash.
            Jos^l Denton.
            Wm Etheredge.

his
Aaron + Etheredge.
mark.

WILLIAM MAUND of Norfolk County & C. . . .

Book I p. 19.

dated 13 May 1741.

proved 19 June 1741, by Ralph Fenby, Ann Bailey & Thomas Floyd.

. . . to my beloved wife Elizabeth Maund ye Profits benefit & use of a Plantation containing ugh—(torn)— acres which I bought of Mr John Hewlet during her Naturall Life I allso give her ye profits benefit —(torn)— & use of Eighty acres of Land Joining upon ye Land of John Steward John & David Sutherland during her Natural Life I also give her ye right to her own Plantation which was given to her by her former Husband William Foreman . . .

. . . to my beloved Son Lott Ma—(torn)—the Plantation whereon I formerly Lived containing two hundred & fifty acres of Land . . . ye Present Crop in case I die be given to my daughter Elizabeth Sugg . . .

. . . to my beloved grandson William Maund ye Plantation whereon I now Live . . . but in Case he die without heir or offer to sell ye s^d Plantation when he comes of age then in either of these Cases . . . ye s^d Plantation revert or belong to mmy beloved Daughter Elizabeth Sugg . . . containing one hundred & fifty acres of Land . . .

. . . to my beloved Daughter Elizabeth Sugg . . . eighty acres of Land which I bought of John Hewlit

. . . my beloved Son Lott Maund to be whole & Sole Executor . . .

. . . I Order y^t all ye res^t of my Estate not already given away be Sold at Publick Sale . . .

. . . my three Sons Jones Lott & Noah being in full of Jonas & Noah Maunds Portion.

witnesses: Wm Bayley.
        Thos Floyd.
           her
        Ann + Bayley.
          mark.
        Ralph Fenley.   Wm Maund & Seal.

SOLOMON NASH of ye County of Norfolk & c . . .

Book I p. 20.

dated 6 May 1737.

proved —(no date given)—adm^n c. t. a. grant unto Thomas Nash.

. . . unto my Brother Thomas Nash my Land belonging to me by deed of Lease & Release which my deceased Father held & possest & gave ye same To me as ye records of Norfolk County will more fully & Largly appear . . .

. . . unto my Brother William Nash my Large Margin Bible . . . my pistols Holsters and hanger . . .

. . . unto John Mathias twelve & Six pence current Money of Virginia . . .

. . . unto Simon Mathias & Eleanor his wife twelve Shillings & Six pence . . .

. . . unto Samuel Whitehurst & Mary his wife twelve Shillings & Six pence . . .

. . . all the rest of my Estate . . . both real & personal
. . . to be equally divided between my two Sisters
that is to Say Dorcas Whitehurst & Elizabeth Etheredge
. . .

. . . my poor Indulging Mother Ann Nash . . .

. . . my brother Thomas Nash my only & Sole Executor
. . .

witnesses : —(none given)—

—(no Signature or Seal)—

SARAH WILLOUGHBY of Norfolk County & c . . .

Book I p. 20.

dated 19 Jan. 1738.

proved 18 Jan. 1739/40. by all the Witnesses & Ex^r . . .

. . . to my Brother Thomas Wiloughby one *Moidore* . . .

. . . to my Cousin Thomas Willoughby my Negro Woman
named Phill . . . If my s^d Cousin Thomas Willoughby
should dye before he arrives to the age of twenty one
Compleat Then . . . to my Cousin Samuel Willoughby
. . .

. . . to my Cousin William Willoughby one Negro Child
named Pleasant & if my s^d Cousin William Willoughby
should dye before he is twenty one . . . to go to my Cousin
Alderton Willoughby . . .

. . . to my Cousin John Willoughby Robertson Son of
ye Revd Mr Moses Robertson two Negro Boys . . .
one gold girdle buckle two gold rings one p^r of gold ear
rings . . .

. . . appoint ye Revd Mr Moses Robertson my Sole Executor . . .

witnesses : Mary Calvert.
    her
   Elizabeth + Sparrow.
   Richard Sparrow.
   Dinah Nicholson.

       Sarah Willoughby & Seal.

ARTHUR GODFREY & c . . .

Book I p. 21.

dated 10 Nov. 1738.

proved 16 May 1740, by John Millison & Patrick White & the
Executor . . .

. . . unto my beloved Son Arthur Godfrey my Mannor
Plantation wherein I now live containing fifty acres of
Land more or less . . . and if my Son Arthur shall
dye without Lawful Issue then . . . the S^d Land &
Plantation shall descend to my Son Solomon Godfrey
. . .

. . . my Son Arthur Godfrey shall pay unto my Son Malbone Godfrey the Sum of fifteen pounds in Cash to be
paid within three years after Arthur Godfrey comes to
the age of twenty one years . . .

. . . unto each of my beloved Children one year old Heiffer
excepting . . . Son Malbone & my Son Arthur
. . .

. . . my house & Land at ye great Bridge shall be sold
. . . & all belonging to ye Land & marshes shall be Sold
to pay my debts . . .

. . . my well beloved Wife Isabel Godfrey my whole &
Sole Executrix . . .

witnesses: Patrick white.
   Brian Penny.
    his
   John + Milleson.

         Arthur Godfrey & seal.

THOMAS HOBGOOD Senr & c .. .

Book I p. 21.

dated 25 Aug. 1737.

proved 16 Nov. 1739, by Eleazer Tart & Solo^n Manning . . .
to my Son Henry Hobgood two barrells of Indian Corn
. . .

. . . to my Son Thomas Hobgood my Feather bed . . .
. . . to my Daughter Elizabeth Jenkins one Linin Chest &
one Wooling Spinning Wheel . . .
. . . to my Daughter Francis Manning four ewes only

She must give one ewe & Lamb out of them to my
grandson John Spring . . .

. . . to my Daughter Sarah Boulton one square black wal-
nut Table & one pewter pottle Flaggon . . .

. . . to my Son John Hobgood one oval Table . . .

. . . to my grandson Sampson Hobgood one Cow Calf
. . .

. . . all yᵉ rest of my whole estate . . . to my Son
William Hobgood . . . Son William . . . only
Execuʳ . . .

witnesses: Soloⁿ Manning.
              Sarah Hobgood.
                  her mark
              Eleazer Tart Sen.   his hand
                                         Thoˢ T. H. Hobgood.
                                                & Seal.

PHILEMON HAYWOOD & c . . .

Book I p. 22.

Dated —(none)—

Proved 20 June 1740.

. . . unto my wel beloved Daughter Sarah Haywood on
Shilling . . .

. . . Jchiise my well beloved wife . . . whole Exʳˣ
. . .

. . . One Plantation Joining to Colᵒ Craford & the house
& Houses & Land I now dwell in and for her to hold
it her right & title as Long as Please God she shall Live
. . . I Case my dear Wife Should dye before my Son
Jonathan Haywood then . . . to him . . . & if
please God after my dear Wife is dead & my Son Jonathan
Haywood should dye before my Daughter Sarah Hay-
wood then . . . to her . . .

witnesses: Edward Pugh.
                  his
              John + Roberts.
                  mark.
                  her
              Sarah + Roberts.
                  mark.
                                    Philemon Haywood.

MOSES MILLER of Norfolk County & c . . .

Book I p. 22.

Dated 15 Nov. 1739.

Proved 16 May 1740, by Joshua Corprew & Exor . . .

   . . . unto my Brothers Son Benjamin Miller all my Land
     which I now possess . . .

   . . . to John Millers Son Moses Miller one iron Pott
     . . .

   . . . to my Coz^n Isb^l Bennet my horse . . .

   . . . my Cozen Benjamin Miller to be my Executor . . .

witnesses : Joshua Corprew.

       Bernard Bangor.   his

       John B*ains*.   Moses + Miller.

                          mark.

THOMAS MARTIN of the County of Norfolk & c . . .

Book I p. 22.

Dated 19 May 1740.

Proved 20 June 1740.

   . . . to Mr Solo^n Shepherd of Nancemond County five
     pounds Curent Money.

   . . . to my God daughter Elizabeth Ives one Cow . . .

   . . . to my Son in Law Gregory Hammands Annotations on
     the New Testament . . .

   . . . desire is that all my Land in Virginia and Corolina or
     elsewhere . . . be Sold by my Executor & ye pro-
     duce to equally devided between my Son in Law William
     Wright & John Gregory of Nancemond County . . .

   . . . my Son In Law William Wright of Nancemond County
     my whole & Sole Ex^r . . .

witnesses : Henry Creech.

       Richard Powel, his mark.

       John Stamp.   Thos Martin.

JOHN ELLEGOOD of Norfolk Borro^h . . .

Book I p. 23.

Dated 30 Sept. 1740.

Proved 20 Nov. 1740, by all the witnesses & Jacob & Abigail
    Ellegood two of the Exor^s

. . . to my Son William Ellegood the Lott of Land where
James Giles now liveth which I bought of Thomas &
George Mason . . . & likewise that Plantation I
purchased of Thomas & Mary Mason formerly belonging
to Major Newton . . . containing about two two
hundred Acres . . .

. . . to my well beloved wife the house & Lott where now I
Live . . . which I bought of Capt. Solomon Wilson
during the term of her naturall Life & allso that plantation
called Jones Point which I bought of Thomas and George
Mason . . . & after her decease I give the s^d Lands
above s^d in town & County to my Son John Ellegood
. . .

. . . my Silver Tankard to my Son John & my great Looking Glass to my Son William . . .

. . . to my Son Mason Elligood y^t Lott of Land . . .
whereon Thomas Walker now Liveth & also that piece
of Land opposite thereto which I bought of Richd Davis
& Grace his wife . . .

. . . to my Son Jacob Ellegood the two Lotts of land
which I bought of Thomas Martin & Matthew Ellegood
& Margaret his wife . .

. . . my Sea Sloop & all other my Water craft whatsoever to be Sold . . . all my rum & dry goods with
all wares & Merchandize which I now have by me together with Some dry goods I expect from Whitehaven all
to be sold for ready money . . .

. . . my two daughters Rebekah & Furnelia Ellegood three
hundred pounds apiece Current Money of Virginia when
they shall arrive at ye age of twenty one . . .

. . . my wife & four Sons . . .

. . . to my Son Mason Ellegood ye plantation in Little
Creek wch I bought of Thomas—(torn)—Margaret his
wife . . .

. . . appoint my Loving Wife & brother Jacob Ellegood, and
my trusty friends Capt. Edward Pugh & Capt. John Phripp
to be my Exec^rs . . .

witnesses: James Giles.
           Edward Pugh.
           Richd Jell.

                       John Ellegood & Seal.

MARGARET MALBONE of y⁰ Borough of Norfolk in Vir-
  ginᵃ &c . . .

Book I p. 24.

Dated 9 Sept 1740.

Proved 21 Nov. 1740, by all witnesses & Exʳ.

   . . . I give out of my Estate what my Exeʳ shall think Proper
   towards yᵉ Schooling of either of my Sons before they are
   bound out & my desire is they be bound out as he shall
   think proper . . .

   . . . to my Son John Hair my diamond ring & gold Neck-
   lace & my desire is he never sell them also half a doz tea
   spoons . . . .

   . . . yᵉ remainder of my estate . . . among my four
   sons John Porten James & Samuel Hair . . .

   . . . my loving brother Samuel Boush to be my Exeʳ
   . . .

witnesses : Paul Portlock.
            Elizᵃ — *Warins.*
            mark.

                              Margᵗ Malbone & Seal.

EDWARD CREAKMUR . . .

Book I p. 24.

Dated 22 Sept. 1739.

Proved 18 Jan. 1739, by Mr. *pretty*ⁿ Merry & James Hodges.

   . . . to my loving Son Benjamin Creekmur one Lott lying
   near yᵉ Great Bridge wch. I bought of old Richard Syl-
   vester adjoining to a piece of Mʳ Samˡ Smiths . . .

   . . . to my Son Willis Creekmur one piece of Land which is
   called Poplar neck which joins yᵉ old Plantation as far as
   yᵉ running Spring & So thro' to Jollifs Path . . .
   to Edmunds Bridge . . .

   . . . to my Son Son Jonas Creakmur one Peʳ of Land which
   is called Deanses begining at yᵉ running Spring & So runs

   . . . to my Son Thomˢ Creekmur one piece of Land lying
   in yᵉ north West Woods which is called dumplin neck as
   far as a line which Edward Creekmur & DanielM͞cPharson
   made . . .

   . . . to my Son Joseph Creekmur yᵉ remainder of yᵉ Land

from yᵉ Line yᵗ Daniel McPharson & Edward Creekmur which is in yᵉ sᵈ Patent . . .

. . . to my Loving Wife three Negroes . . .

. . . Wife & my Son Willis Creekmur holly and Solely Execʳˢ . . .

Witnesses : —(torn)—n Merry.

—(torn)—heredge.

—(torn)—Hodges.

Edward + Creekmur & Seal.

SAMUEL SMITH of Norfolk Town & c . . .

Book I p. 25.

Dated 19 Aug. 1732.

Proved 21 Dec. 1739, ye last Will & Testaᵗ of Samˡ Smith Gent, Ded, by Solᵒ Wilson Thoˢ Scott & Abel Luelling . . .

by Samˡ Smith junʳ one of yᵉ Execʳˢ Josᵉ Smith & Samˡ Boush refusing yᵉ burthen . . .

. . . to my Brother John Smith eldest Son of John Smith of London one hundred pounds Sterling Money . . . in full of all claims or demands either to my real or personall estate . . .

. . . to my well beloved Cousin & Kinsman Josiah Smith now in Virginia my dwelling house I now live in yᵉ sᵈ Town of Norfolk with yᵉ kitchin ware house & improvements thereon with yᵉ land thereto adjoining & belonging . . . but for want of such heirs to Doctor Hoppers eldest Son he shall have by my Cousin Sarah his wife & for want of such a son to yᵉ eldest daughter of yᵉ sᵈ Sarah . . . Two hundred pounds Current money of Virgᵃ and one hundred and fifty pounds in European Goods at prime Cost . . . & the Land I have near Norfolk Town joining Colᵒ George Newtons & yᵉ Glebe Land . . . unto yᵉ sᵈ Josiah Smith . . .

. . . to my Kinsman Samuel Smith of Lonestoft in yᵉ County of Suffulk in South Brittain all my Lands messuages & Tenements in Lonestoft aforesᵈ . . . two hundred pounds Sterling money . . .

. . . to my Cousin Sarah Fowler of Yarmouth in North Brittain eldest Son or for want of Such a Son to her eldest Daughter fifty pounds Sterling . . .

. . . unto my Kinsman Thomas Godly fifty pounds Sterling . . .

. . . unto my Cousin Happer one hundred pounds Sterling
. . .

. . . to my Cousin Mary Landerfeild eighty pounds Current money of Virg^a . . .

. . . unto my Cousin Margaret Landerfeild one hundred pounds Sterling . . .

. . . all the rest and residue of my real & personal estate of what nature or kind soever ether in Brittain Virginia or elsewhere unto my trusty and well beloved Freind Samuel Smith alias Samuel Coverly & my house in Norfolk Town now in the possession & ocupation of Mr Fife & ye storehouse adjoining to it & ye kitchin with ye houses called by ye name of ye Long house & all ye Land belonging to ye s^d Houses & ye land where William Box now lives & ye house & land where Martha Coverly now Lives after her dec'ase . . .

. . . to ye s^d Samuel Smith alias Coverly ye Land I bought of Mr Scott & Mr John Nicholls being their wives parts of Richard Smiths Land on ye Southern Branch of Elizabeth River and also my Lott of Land In Newtown which I bought of George Kemp of Princess Ann County & my Lott of Land at ye Great Bridge in Norfolk County adjoining to a peace of Land of Col^o Samuel Boushes & William McNarell . . . he attain the age of twenty two years and in case . . . dye before he attain ye ye age of twenty two years then . . . unto my s^d Cousin Josiah Smith . . .

. . . appoint my trusty & well beloved Freinds Brian Blundell of liverool in great Brittan Esqr Samuel Boush Junr gent & my s^d Cousin Josiah Smith with ye s^d Samuel Smith alias Coverly Executors . . .

Witnesses: Sol^o Wilson.
　　　　　Thom^s Scott.
　　　　　Abel Lewelling.
　　　　　John Fife.
　　　　　John Pilkinton.　　　　　Saml Smith & Seal.

(Codocil) :
. . . ye Education & maintenance of ye s^d Samuel Smith alias Coverly untill he attain ye age of Twenty two . . .

Witnesses: Sol^o Wilson.
　　　　　Thos Scott.
　　　　　Abel Lewelling.
　　　　　Jno Fife.
　　　　　Jno Pilkinton.　　　　　Saml Smith & seal.

JAMES WARDEN of Norfolk County & c

Book I p. 26.

Dated 10 Sept. 1739.

Proved 19 Oct. 1739, by Edwd Joyce & Jasper lane & Ex^r

. . .

. . . unto my well beloved Grandson William Warden my plantation lying up ye River which I formerly bought of Edward Jones . . . but if in failure of such issue my Will is y^t ye aforesaid plantation should fall to my Son Samuel Warden . . .

. . . to my well beloved Son John Warden ye plantation he now lives on & ye parcell of land binding between ye Creek and reedy Branch to ye back line of my plantation & my Land that I bought of James Jones my desire is y^t ye above named plantation to Wm Warden wth ye s^d plantation to my Son John Warden ye other side of ye River may be equally divided between y^m and ye lands given to ye s^d Jn^u Warden . . .

. . . unto my well beloved Son Lemuel Warden ye plantation I now live with all ye rest of my lands I now hold . . .

. . . to my well beloved Elizabeth Wickliff five Shillings being in full wth wh^t She has already received of all her Portion . . .

. . .

. . . to my well beloved Daughter Margaret Whitehead my Negro boy Called Jo . . .

. . . to my well beloved Daughter Abigail Simmons five Shillings being in full with what she has already received

. . .

. . . to my well beloved Sarah Merchant one negro Girl called Rose . . .

. . . to my well beloved Son Lemuel Warden all ye rest of my Worldly Estate both real & personal . . .

. . . my Sons John & Lem^l Warden . . . Sole Exec^{rs}

. . .

Witnesses: Edwd Joyce.
Jasper Lane.
Eliz^a E. L. Lane.
her mark.

his
James W. Warden
mark.

JOHN HARRIS of Norfolk County & c . . .

Book I p. 27.

Dated 18 March 1736/7.

Proved 20 May 1737, all yᵉ witnesses & Exʳ . . .

. . . unto my Son John Harris . . . all my land one Feather bed & furniture . . .

. . . to my Daughter Catherine Harris one feather bed . . . .

. . . to my Son Thomas Harris one Cow & Heifer & all my wearing apparel . . .

. . . unto my Daughter Margaret Harris . . . two pewter plates . . .

. . . unto my Son Daniel Harris . . . one Warming pan . . .

. . . unto my Grandaughter Elizabeth Wright two Large Silver spoons . . .

. . . unto my Granddagter Sarah Wright one Small Silver spoon . . .

. . . unto my Loving Wife Elizabeth Harris all my personal Estate goods & Chattels . . . Wife . . . Sole Executor . . .

Witnesses: John Hobbs.

        his

    James + Eastwood

      mark.

    Richard Harris.　　　　　　　John Harris & Seal.

JOHN JOLLEY of Norfolk County & c . . .

Book I p. 27.

Dated 5 Apr. 1736.

Proved 20 May 1736, by all yᵉ Witnesses & sᵈ Exʳˢ also Martha yᵉ late wife of yᵉ decd came into court in her proper person & renounced any advantage by yᵉ sᵈ will . . .

. . . unto my Son John Jolley my plantation yᵗ I now live on & yᵉ rest of my land yᵗ belongs unto it . . . my pistols Sword & belt . . .

. . . unto my Son Richard Jolley one plantation which he now dwelleth on . . . my Short Gun . . .

. . . unto my Son Peter Jolley one feather bed . . . one Long Gun . . .

. . . unto my two Sons John & Richard my *Swon*—(worn)
—Land containing one hundred acres more or less to be
equally devided between them . . . & my Son Peter
to get one thousand staves *to* his Share . . .

. . . my Wife Martha out of her thirds of ye Swamp Land
& every one else but my two Sons . . .

. . . unto my Daughter Elizabeth Bowers one Negro boy
. . . .

. . . unto my Daughter Mary Taylor my Negro Woman
. . . .

. . . unto my Daughter Sarah Hodges one Negro Girl
. . .

. . . unto my Daughter Susannah Bowers my Negro man
. . .

. . . unto my Daughter Rachael Jolly one Negro Girl
. . .

. . . unto my youngest Daughter Mary Jolley one Negro boy
. . . in case she should dye under age y^n this negro
boy Jacob to go to her Sister Ann Jolley . . .

. . . one Dozen of English Spoons . . .

. . . my youngest daughter Ann Jolley . . .

. . . my three sons John Richard & Peter . . .

. . . unto my Grand daughter Lida Jolly one ewe . . .

. . . my flax & Cotton . . .

. . . woolen wheel & one Linin wheel . . .

. . . my two sons John Jolly & Richard Jolly to be my whole
& sole Exec^{rs} . . .

Witnesses: his mark
    Richard + Bacon, Senr
    Edward + E*ver*edges
       mark.
    Richard Bacon, Junr his
               John Joleff +   & Seal
                  mark.

ARGENT COCKE of Norfolk & c . . .

Book I p. 29.

Dated 2 Feb. 1736/7.

Proved 18 Feb. 1737, by all the Witnesses & ye Ex^r . . .

. . . unto Mr Archibald Taylor one Guinea to buy him a
mourning ring . . .

. . . unto my loving sister Mary Brett one Pistole to buy
her a mourning ring . . .

. . . unto John Brett son of y⁰ s⁴ Mary one Pistole to buy
him a mourning ring . . .

. . . unto my Son Archibald Taylor my two negroes & all
my other estate both real & personall . . . when he
comes of age . . .

. . . appoint Mʳ Archibald Taylor my whole & Sole Exeʳ
. . .

Witnesses: Samˡ Smith.
              Margᵗ Hill.
              Alexʳ McPherson.

                                          Argent Cocke & Seal.

Doletre Edings & C . . . Norfolk County . . .

Book I p. 29.

Dated 22 June 1737.

Proved 18ᵗʰ—(torn)—, by Exʳ—(torn)—

. . . unto my grand child John Elks one bed . . .

. . . he helping my Son Richard Edings to tend it whilst it
is done—(torn—

. . . unto my Grandson Phillip Edings one bed & F—
(torn)—

. . . —(torn)—my Son Thom—(torn)—

. . . —(torn)—my Son Richard Edings all y⁰ rest of my
Esta—(torn)—

. . . appoint my Son Richard Edin—(torn)—

Witnesses: Willᵐ Avis.
              his mark.
              Lemˡ powell.
              Thomas Avis.

                                          (Signature torn out).

WILIAM GRANT of Norfolk & c . . .

Book I p. 29. (See Original).

Dated 16 May 1735.

Proved 25 May 1736—by both w—(torn)—by Execʳ . . .

. . . unto my Son John Grant all my Land & my Mair bridle
& Saddle . . .

. . . unto my daughter Sarah Holms my one Lodging bed
& Furniture . . .

. . . to my daughter Ann Pead one Shilling in full of her portion . . .

. . . to my daughter Alse Holms one Shilling in full of her portion . . .

. . . to my daughter Mary Grant one Shilling . . .

. . . to my beloved Wife Ann Grant yᵉ use of all yᵉ remainder of my estate her life & after . . . to my Son John Grant my Mill & Iron Wedges . . .

. . . divided amongst four of my Children — as Followeth my Son John Grant & my Daughter Sarah Holms my Daughter Marthay Grant and my Dafter Mary Grant. I leave my Son John my whole Executor . . .

Witnesses: Thomas Goulding.
          Elizabeth Goulding.

his
Willᵐ + Grant
mark.

WILLIAM —(torn)— unty & c . . .

Book I p. 29.

Dated 22 Mar. 1735.

Proved 20 May 1737, by all witnesses & Executor . . .

. . . I give unto—(torn)—one Chest that is called hers

. . . to my Son Solomon Cherry a Sh—(torn)—np Land

. . . to my Son Eleazer Cherry one—(torn)—Caleb Cherry a Small Gun . . .

. . . to my in Law Joseph Grant a—(torn)—my Son Willis Cherry a Sword . . .

. . . to my Son John Cherry my Plantation yᵗ I now live on

. . . my dearly beloved Wife Elizabeth Cherry to be my whole & Sole Executor . . .

. . . remainder . . . divided between them all my Children . . .

witnesses: Solomon Cherry.
          Joseph Cherry.

his
Wᵐ + Cherry & Seal.
mark.

Edmund Creekmur & C . . .

Book I p. 30.

Dated—(torn out)—

Proved—(torn out)—

. . . to my Son Edmund Creekmur & Job Creekmur my mannor Plantation & all yᵉ Land on yᵉ Side of Mudey Branch to be equally divided between them . . . but if either of my two Sons Edward or Job should die without lawfull Issue then & Such Case yᵉ Survivor to enjoy his halfe yᵉ premises aforsᵈ . . .

. . . to my two Sons Edmund Creekmur & David Creekmur all my Land belonging to Muddy Branch & So to the River Swamp to be equally divided betwixt them . . . but if in case either of them two should dye without lawfull Testes then & in Such yᵉ Survivor is to enjoy his part of yᵉ sᵈ Land . . .

. . . to my Son Solomon Creekmur twenty acres of Land joining to him which sᵈ I bought of Frances Lowery . . . but if he should dye without heirs begotten of his body for it to fall to my Son Edward Creekmur & Job Creekmur & if they or either of them should dye with heirs for it to fall to yᵉ Survivor is to enjoy part of yᵉ sᵈ Land . . .

. . . unto my Daughter Sarah Creekmur all yᵉ feithers that she can raise of yᵉ fowls till gets enough for her abed . . .

. . . to my Daughter Elizabeth Worner & Rachel Smith each of them a—(torn)—bed . . . —(torn)— . . .

. . . Daughter Sarah my wifes wearing Clothes . . .

. . . Conlly & Levi Creekmur to my Grandson Benjamin Coulley—(torn)—years of age & to my Grandson Levi Creekmur a ewe & Lamb—(torn)—

. . . I do nominate my Loving Sons E—(torn)—

Witnesses: Willᵐ Hodges.

James Wilkins.

John Creekmur.

—(Signature torn out)—

—(NAME TORN OUT)—

Book I p. 31.

Dated—(torn out)—

Proved—(tornout)—

. . . to Mary my well bel—(torn)—

—(torn)—Moll during her n—(torn)—

—(torn)—to her my Said Wife—(torn)—

—(torn)—my Child that me—(torn)—

—(torn)—but in case my s^d wife should not have a—(torn)—
. . . to Samuel Brown Son of—(torn)— . . .

—(torn)—Mary my well beloved Wife my Sole Execu^x of y—
(torn)—

Witnesses: Jn° Hutchings.
        Jn° Tucker.
            Christ° Gardner.

                        —(Signature torn out)—

SAMUEL BOUSH & c . . .

Book I p. 32.

Dated—(torn)—1735.

Proved 16 Feb. 1738/9, by Col° Sam¹ Boush jun^r . . .. proved
as Will of his s^d deced Father . . .

. . . first I appoint & Ordain my Son—(torn)—to be my
Exe^r . . .

. . . unto my Son Maj^r Samuel Boush . . . also my new
blew Cloak being in full consideration of—(torn)—

. . . my loving wife be well provided for—(torn)—

. . . unto Mrs Mary Miller &—(torn)—a black suit of
Clothes . . .

—(torn)—randson Sam—(torn)—which is my Godsen all my—
(torn)—ure (excepting y° Land—(torn)—

—(torn)—my powder flask with Silver—(torn)—

—(torn)—Plate . . . —(torn)—Gold Seal all my Gold—

—(torn)—my gold buttons.

        —(torn)—my plantations. I give all y° remainder of my
        Estate—(torn)—Samuel Boush & his heirs. I de request
        my Son to sell—(torn)—

. . . unto George Chamberlain all my wearing—(torn)—

. . . unto Thom° Nash on Suit of black—(torn)—

Witnesses: —(torn out)—

                        —(Signature torn out)—

—(NAME TORN OUT)—

Book I p. 33.

Dated 12th—(torn)—

Proved—(torn)—

. . . unto my Loving daughter Sarah M—(torn)—Swamp joining on Peter Smith & Henry Wood n—(torn)—

. . . bequeath to my—(torn)—that my negro girl Pashant shall have that sh—(torn)—Same at ye Decease of his mother Sarah Mann—(torn)-—

. . . unto my grandson Jonathan Man—(torn)—possesst with ye s^d girl at ye death of his mother—(torn)—

. . . unto my Loving Daugh—(torn)—Great Swamp with ye house & plantation bein—(torn)—

. . . unto my—(torn)—boy named Jacob to be delivered to her at the de—(torn)—

. . . to my Gr—(torn)—named Nel to be delivered him at his mothers—(torn)—

. . . to my daughter Alice Creekmur—(torn)—late Survey taken up in Dixons Neck Swam—(—(torn)—

. . . bequeath to—(torn)—that my Negro woman Moll shall have that—(torn)—

. . . to loveing Son Jerem—(torn)—which, I have not already given away to him—(torn)—remaining part of my personal Estate which—(torn)—with ye same at ye decease of his mother excep—(torn)—my daughter Ann . . .

. . . do appoint my l—(torn)—of this my last Will & Testam^t—(torn)—& appoint ye only to be my last—(torn)—

Witnesses : James Hodges.

John Gammon.

    his

W^m + Nicholson

mark.

(Signature torn out).

N——(torn)— (Tatem)—

Book I p. 33.

Dated 18 Oct. 1737.

Proved——Augt 1739, Wm Godfrey made oath he see Capt. Nathl

. . . & that ye last Paragraph was wrote by ye s^d

. . . & that he saw Wm Wood & James Cox sign ye s^d

Will . . . Ann Tatem relict & Exe^x herein named re-

nounced any benefit . . . y⁰ other Exeʳ named Swore
to y⁰ Same Will according to—(torn)—is accordingly
granted in due form.

Proved in Court, 25 Sept. 1739, by yᵉ Oath of Capt. Wᵐ—(torn)
    —James Cox . . .
—(torn)—hundred & fifty acres of Land with yᵉ man—(torn)—
    in Elizabeth River in Virginia unto my Son—(torn)—&
    for want of Such heirs to next of ki—(torn)—
    and will is that my Loving wife Ann Tatem—(torn)—
    Plantation together without any lett or hindranc—(torn)
    —bequeath all yᵉ Land I have at Crane Island—(torn)—
    about Seven hundred & eighty acres be more—(torn)—
    on that tract thereon standing Scituate lying—(torn)—
    Virginia unto my Son John Tatem & to his heirs—(torn)—
    heirs next of kinn so from generation to generatio—
    (torn)—of Land in Norfolk Town which I bought of Col⁰
    —(torn)—(page 34).
—(torn)—m unto my Daughter Love Tatem . . .
—(torn)—Tom unto my Son Nathaniel Tatum . . .
—(torn)—y Ship Caesar & half yᵉ brigantine Charming & my—
    (torn)—
—(torn)—ndred Pounds Current money of Virginia to be
    equally—(torn)—Viz Nathaniel Tatem John *Ta*imingham
    Love to Share &—(torn)—
—(torn)—Wife Ann Tatem during natural life & after—(torn)
    —& Share all alike among my four Children—(torn)—
    atems & Lastly I do hereby nomonate & appoint my sᵈ
    loving—(torn)—tchings Executrix . . .
—(torn)—Plantation at Crane Island & the Law—
—(torn)—year John *Tr*immingham & as come to—(torn)—yᵉ
    Lott yᵗ lyes in Norfolk I give my—(torn)—yᵉ sᵈ Lott
    bought of Peter Malbone.

Witnesses : —(torn)—   Nathˡˡ Tatem & Seal.
—(torn)—nellings yᵉ Daughter of William Snellings twelve—
    (torn)—

WALTER MOUAT & c . . .

Book I p. 34.

Dated 7 Dec. 1741.

Proved 18 Dec 1741, by all yᵉ witnesses & Execʳ . . .

—(torn)—e paid & discharged by Josiah Smith of yᵉ Borrough
    of—(torn)—nominate & appoint my whole & Sole Exeʳ
    . . .

—(torn)—ds my Ticket for wages due on board his Majesties
s^d—(torn)—two pounds Sixteen Shillings & Six pence
Sterling wh^{ch}—(torn)—full power or by his order to receive ye s^d wages on ye s^d—(torn)— —(torn)—god my
debts & Funeral expences & a reasonable allowance—
(torn)—remainder unto my dear & only Son Andrew
Mouat in—(torn)—rittain . . . revoke & Disannull
all former wills . . .
　. . . Set my hand & Seal in ye Borrough of Norfolk in Virg^a
　. . .

Witnesses: James Pasteur.
　　　　　　John Barney.
　　　　　　John Calverley.
　　　　　　　　　　　　　　　　Walter Mouat & S.

GEORGE ROWSE & c . . .

Book I p. 35.

Dated 25 Oct. 173—(torn)—

Proved—(torn)—

　. . . to my Loving Sister Mary Manning & ye heirs lawfully begott of her Body all my Land in Elizabeth County
in ye western branch . . .
　. . . to my Cozin Moring Hancock one Cow . . .
　. . . to my Cozin George Manning my Chest & one pewter
bason one pate of pewter & Six pewter Spoons & ye remainder of my pewter my will is it be equally divided
betwixt my two Sisters Mary Manning & Martha Hancock
　. . .
　. . . to my Cozin Benamin Manning my Gun . . .
—(torn)—Manning my whole & Sole Exec^r . . .

Witnesses: —(torn)—
　　　　　　　　　　　—(Signature torn out)—

THOMAS MARTIN & c . . .

Book I p. 36.

Dated—(None)—

Proved 16 June 1738, by ye oaths of Richd Harris & that he See
James Libby Sign as a Witness & Sworn to by ye Exe^r
　. . .

. . . unto my Son John Martin one Shilling.

. . . unto my Son Tho⁸ Martin one Cow . . .

. . . unto my Son Willm Martin one Shilling . . .

. . . unto my Son James Martin one Shilling . . .

. . . as for my Daughter Mary Claxton I have given her already her Dowery . . .

. . . unto my Wife Ann Martin my negro Girl . . . & after her decease to my Son Robert Martin y⁸ younger & after his Disease to my grand Daughter Ann Claxton . . .

. . . appoint my Loving Wife afors^d whole & Sole Exec^x . . .

Witnesses: Richard Harris.
         James Libby.

                                        his
                           Thomas + Martin & Seal.
                                       mark

JOHN LUDGALL & c . . .

Book I p. 36.

Dated—(torn)—

Proved—(torn)—

. . . appoint my dearly beloved wife to be my whole & Sole Exec^r . . .

. . . unto my eldest Son John Ludgall—(torn)—ty acres of Land belonging to it . . .

—(torn)—y Ridge—(torn)—

—(torn)—till her—(torn)—

Witnesses: —(torn)—

                           —(Signature torn)—dgall.

JOHN WARDEN . . .

Book I p. 36.

Dated—(torn)—er A. D. 1741.

Proved 20 Nov. 1741, by all witnesses & Exe^r . . .

—(torn)—y beloved Nephew John Collins—(torn)—

. . . unto y⁸ aforsaid Edward Collins my Plantation whereon I now Liveth on Tanners Creek road . . . & for want of Such male heirs . . . unto my Nephew John Collins . . .

. . . unto my beloved Nephews John & Edward Collins all
my household goods   . . .
. . . appoint Edward Collins to be my only Executor   . . .

Witnesses: John Davenport.
          Edward E Collins
            mark.
       James Miller.   his
                    John + Warden.
                       mark.

WILLIAM MILLER & c . . .

Book I p. 37.

Dated—(torn)—May 173—(torn)—

Proved—(torn)—

. . . unto my daughter Guddy Miller three Cows   . . .
at yᵉ age of Sixteen   . . .

. . . unto my Daughter Courtney Miller three Cows   . . .
when she comes to age of Sixteen   . . .

. . . unto my Daughter Abbia Miller three Cows   . . .
when she comes to the age of Sixteen   . . .

. . . unto my Daughter Lucey Miller three Cows   . . .
at age Sixteen   . . .

. . . unto—(torn)—   . . . three Cows   . . .

—(torn)—orse & all my Land at yᵉ great bridge & my mannor
P—(torn)—my beloved Wife to have her thirds in—
(torn)—

Witnesses: Richard Wᵐ Sylv—(torn).
          Robert Hodge—(torn).
                    (Signature torn out).

—(NAME TORN OUT)—

Book I p. 37.

Dated 7 Aug. 1740.

Proved 15 Aug. 1740, by all yᵉ Witnesses & Executor   . . .

. . . Mary Dixon yᵉ Wife of—(torn)—Hampshire yᵉ Sum
of F—(torn)—Margaret Holms yᵉ S—(torn)—Holms
Living in ne—(torn)—Jennet Cawson yᵉ Sum—(torn)—
unto my well beloved F—(torn)—Wright his heirs Exeʳˢ

or—(torn)—Wages & pay Bount—(torn)—as now are & which—(torn)—pensions Salaries—(torn)—(Page 38). at any Time hereafter is or Shall be due to me for my Service or otherwise in any of his Majesties Ship or Ships Frigates or Vessels After ye payment of ye forementioned Debts & Legacys . . .

. . . Constitute my afors^d Friend Capt. John Whiddon Sole Exec^r . . .

Witnesses: Francis Cawsey.

George Manley.

Josiah Nash.

John Brisco & Seal.

RICHARD SPARROW & c . . .

Book I p. 38.

Dated—(torn)—

Proved—(torn)—

. . . my Loving Wife Sarah Sparrow my housen.& Land during her naturall Life & after her Decease to my Son Thomas Sparrow . . .

. . . unto my Son Rodham Sparrow one negro girl Called Betty . . . gun & Sword & one Plane Case of Bottles . . .

. . . unto my Daughter Sarah Sparrow one negro girl Called Racheel . . .

. . . one Japan Case of Bottles . . .

. . . my three Children . . .

. . . Constitute—(torn)—*Bro*ther Sparrow to be my whole (torn)—

Witnesses: —(torn)—

Richard Sparrow & Seal.

—(name torn out)—

Book I p. 38.

Dated 5 Dec. 1733.

Proved 18 May 1739, by Wm Mecoy & Eliz^a Mecoy & ye Exe^r

. . .

—(torn)—bequeath unto

—(torn)—Land belonging to it

—(torn)—John McCoy y° Plantation

—(torn)—beginning at y° Cupress Swamp

—(torn)—dle of y° valley y^t makes out of

—(torn)—to my Son John McCoy &

—(torn)—McCoy fifty foot Square of high

—(torn)—wamp to my Son John McCoy

—(torn)—aniel McCoy y° Plantation y^t

—(torn)—Acres of Land being y° remainder

—(torn)—Hoppers tract of Land at y° head of y° River to my
Son Josiah McCoy . . .

. . . unto my Son Josiah McCoy one hundred foot Square
of high Land joining to his brother John at y° Juniper
Swamp . . .

. . . if either of my three Eldest Sons should dye without
heir y^t my Son Josiah McCoy shall inherit their part
. . .

. . . unto my Daughter Mary McCoy one feather bed
. . .

. . . unto my Living Wife Mary McCoy all y° rest of my
moveable Estate . . . Wife Mary McCoy my Whole
& Sole Exe^r . . .

Witnesses: Joseph Makefarson.

William Mecoy.

her

Eliz^a + Mecoy.

John Mccoy & Seal.

JOHN SHEPHERD & c

Book I p. 39.

Dated 6 Jan. 1741.

Proved 19 Feb. 1741/2, by all y° witnesses & Exec^x . . .

. . . to my well beloved Wife all my personall Estate . . .
for her the bring up of my Son Samuel Shepherd & to
do & Act in all Cases as She shall see proper & if there
be any thing remaining when my Son Samuel comes of
Age it to be equally to be divided between y^m both . . .

. . . Wife my whole & Sole Execut^x . . .

Witnesses: Morick Meack.

　　　Edwd E. Hensley

　　　　his mark.

　　　　her

　　　Mary + Meach

　　　　mark　　　　　　　　　　　John Shepherd.

—(torn)—hard Ballance & c . . .

Book I p. 39.

Dated 21 Jan. 1736.

Proved 18 Feb. 1736/7, by Moses Linton & Samuel Linton Ballance & Exe^x . . .

　. . . to my Son Richard Ballance one Negro fellow . . . after ye Decease of his mother & I like wise give my s^d Son—(torn)—Iron pot to be delivered to him at ye age of twenty years old . . .

　. . . one Bay Colt called Esqr . . .

　. . . Wife Ann Ballance . . .

　. . . Money Due to me from Thos Jewell & Thos Tuly in North Carolina . . .

　. . . to Bridget Ballance one young heifer . . .

　. . . to my well beloved Wife & my Son Richard all ye rest of my Estate ungiven both personall & real to be equally devided betwixt y^m

　. . . appoint my well beloved Wife & Willis Wilson jun^r my Exec^x of this my Last Will . . .

Witnesses: Moses Linton.

　　　Samuel Ballance.

　　　Willis Wilson Junr　　　　　　　his

　　　　　　　　　　　　　Richard + Ballance

　　　　　　　　　　　　　　mark.

HENRY HOLSTEAD & c . . .

Book I p. 40.

Dated 24 Oct. 1729.

Proved 17 June 1736, Sworn to by Exe^r . . . ye oath of Wm But . . . & James Wilson jun^r . . . Simon Holstead heir at Law pray—(torn)—not be admitted as proved . . . Drew Holstead yᵉ Execʳ thereon named moved to take yᵉ oath of an—ᴉ(torn)—Certificate for a Probate be granted him which is by yᵉ Co—(torn)—from wᶜʰ order yᵉ heir at law prays an appeal wᶜʰ is granted he giving Security—(torn)—fifty pounds.

Test Solo Wilson. C. C.

. . . unto my brother Drew Halsted my mannor Plantation with yᵉ equall half of my Land belonging & Joining to yᵉ sᵈ plantation & yᵉ other half of my land to my brother Thomas Holsted.

. . . my Sister Mary Holsted . . .

. . . my two Sisters Sarah & Bridget . . .

. . . unto my brother Simon my part of my Uncle John Holsteads Estate.

. . . unto my brother John my reding mare & Colt . . .

. . to Sister Elizabeth one pewter dish . . .

. . . a pair of pistols a pair of Silver buckles . . .

. . . my brother Drew . . . Sole Executor . . .

witnesses : William Butt.

James Wilson.   H. H.

JOHN BARNEY . . .

Book I P. 69—(torn)—

(Abstracted from Original, See Box 1711-1755).

Dated 13 Feb. 1741/2.

Proved 21 May 1742, by all the Witnesses . . .

. . . it is my Desire to have that plantation that I bought of thomas walker Sould to pay for itself . . .

. . . unto my Loving Wife my half Loot and the house upon it During her Life and after her Decase to Eakwilly Divided between my Cosen Lamuell Godfree Son to Daniel godfree and Cosen Johney Williams Son to James Williams . . .

. . . my wife and her brother Frances hatton Shall administer . . .

his

Test. William + Fife.

mark.

Richard Inkson.

his
John + Barney
mark.

JOHN MATHIAS . . .

Book I p. 128, (States Old General Index).

(Completely torn out of Book I and missing from Original
Wills).

ANDDRYAN BARTU . .

Book I p. 142 (States Old General Index).

(Completely torn out of Book I and missing from Original
Wills).

JOHN TUCKER of Norfolk . . . —(torn)—

Book I p. 153.

. . . (rest torn out) . . . (Original missing) . . .

JOHN NICHOLLS, Senr, of Norfolk County Virginia . . .

Book I p. —(torn)—

(Abstracted from Original, See Box 1711-1755).

Dated 8 March 1743.

Proved Apr. Court 1750

. . . appoint my Dearly Beloved Wife Alice Nicholls and
my Beloved Son William Nicholls to be joynt Executrix
and Executor . . .

. . . to my Beloved Son William Nicholls the Plantation
whereon I now live and likewi.e the Plantation whereon
he lives and all the Land that I am possessed off, to him,
his Heirs or Assigns, after my Wifes Death, And if my
Son John will live with my Son William, then to have my
Negro Harry . . .

. . . my Daugr Sarah Seavell . . . But if my Son John
will not live with my Son William, then William to build
him a house on my Plantation where John likes . . .

. . . my Daugr Elizabeth Creekmur

. . . my Daugr Alice Seavell . . .

. . . my Daugr Mary Nicholls . . .

. . . all my Children (Viz^t) John Nicholls, William Nicholls, Alice Seavells, Elizabeth Creekmure, Sarah Seavells and Mary Nicholls . . .

Witnesses: Ralph Fenley.

John Gaman.

James Taylor.

his

James + Gamon.

mark.

his

John + Nicholls. Red Wax Seal.

mark.

NATHANIELL BUTT . . . Norfolk County . . .

Book I p. 154 (Page taken from Old Index, See Original Wills, Box 1711 to 1755).

Dated 2 Jan. 1749.

Proved 6 April 1750.

. . . to my soon Nathaniell Butt that Plantasion Whereon formerly Livd on with all the land that is Laid of and marcked out by a line of marcked Trees . . .

. . . to my soon James Butt the Plantasion Whereon he now lives on with all the Lands Laid of and marcked by Lines of Trees as it is bounded . . .

. . . to my soon Nathaniell Butt that Plantasion Whereon he now Lives on with all the Lands as it is Laid of and marcked out with a Line of marcked trees . . .

. . . to my soon Thomas Butt that Part of my Lands Called by the Name of the Litel Ridges with all the Lands Laid of and marcked out by Lines of marcked trees . . .

. . . to my soon Wilson Butt That Part of my Land Called bul Ridge as it is marcked and bounded and also the Survay adioyning to the sd. Lands . . .

. . . to my soon John Butt the Plantation whereon I now Live with all the Lands Laid of and marcked out as it is bounded . . .

. . . my Daughter Teresha Butt . . .

. . . my Daughter Mary Murden . . .

. . . to my Loving Wife all the Remaing Part of my Estate or not as yet Givin a way . . .

. . . Appoint my Loving Wife Mary and my soon James Butt To be my . . . Executors . . .

Witnesses: James Wilson.
James Pinkerton.
Jeremiah Wilson.
Tho. *Boid.*

Apprs. Thos. & Jno. Halstead, Jos Church & Edd. Lattimore.

Nathaniel Butt & Seal.

JOSEPH LANGLEY of the County of Norfolk in Virginia . . .

Book I p. 158.

Dated 10 Mch. 1749/50.

Proved 17 May 175—(torn)—

. . . I give the Land Whereon I now live being the Land that was given me by my Uncle Mr Jeremiah Langley decd, to the Child my Wife Elizabeth Langley—(torn)— ors with if a Boy, Otherwise I give the said Land to my— (torn) Fran*ces* Langley . . .

. . . the Land where my Brother William Langley lives

. . . my Children . . .

. . . my Daugh—(torn)—

. . . appoint—(torn)—Loving Wife Eliz^a Lang—(torn)—d Capt. William Ivy m—(torn)—ecutors . . .

Witnesses: William Ivey.
William Langley.
John Williams.
Samuel Boush. Joseph Langley & Seal.

Codicil.

. . . my Brother William Langley

Dated—(torn)—March 1749/50 . . .

Joseph Langley & Seal.

LEMUEL WILES of the County of Norfolk Dominion of Virginia . . .

Book I p. 165—(torn)—(Abstract from Original).

Dated 22 Oct. 1750.

Proved 20 Dec. 1750.

. . . unto my Son Samuel Wiles three hundred akers of Land with the Plantation I now live on . . .

. . . to my Son Seth the Plantation I bought of Samuel Butt, and a hundred & twelve akers of West Side of the Run to William Ederedge Line . . .

. . . to my Daughter aby Wiles . . .

. . . my Daughter Hannah Wiles my Negro Girl . . .

. . . to my Daughter Elizabeth Wiles . . .

. . . to my Amy Wiles my Negro Wench . . .

. . . to my old Aunt Elizabeth Fentry . . .

. . . my Loving Wife Amy Wiles . . .

. . . devided amonge my Six Children Samuel Wiles, Seth Seth Wiles, Aby Wiles, hannah Wiles, Elizabeth Wiles, Amy Wiles . . .

. . . appoint my Loving Wife Amy Wiles and my Brother Thomas Wiles my Executors . . .

Witnesses: Anthony Butt.
        Affia Ethredg.
        Tho* Wiles.

                    Lemuel Wiles & Seal. Red Wax.

ST. LAWRENCE BERFORD . . .

Book I p. 166—(torn)—(See Original Box 1711-1755).

Dated 13 Mch. 1750.

Proved 21 June 1750.

. . . my real Estate in Ireland, but that the same shall descend according to the Rules of Law, all the s^d personal Estate . . . I devise to be converted into money for the sole and separate use, of my truly friendly Frances Webb . . .

. . .appoint my Loving Friends The Reverend William Webb and John Pearson Webb and the Survivor of them to be Executors.

Witnesses: Chris^r Perkins.
        John Langdale.

                    St. Law^{ce} Berford & Seal.

ABELL LEWELLING of the County and Borrough of Norfolk V*intner* . . .

Book I p. 167.

Dated 28 Apr. 1750.

Proved 22 J—(torn)—

> 20 July 1750 Administration—(torn)—tel Capt. John Hutchings.
> . . . unto my beloved Wife Sarah—(torn)—
> . . . Boom & Bobspritt, and a Rudder . . .
> —(torn)—to be equally divided between my said Wife & seven Children—(torn)—*hard* Danai Abell John Paul Elizabeth & Frances Lewelling—(torn)—and two hundred Acres of Land, not touching my son Richard—(torn)—disposed of and then an Equall Devision to be made . . .

Witnesses: William Nash.
George Rouviere.
William Pool.   Abell Lewel—(torn)—

JOHN MURDEN . . .

Book I p. 168.

Dated 28 Apr. 1750.

Proved 20 Dec. 1750.

> . . . to my Son John Murden the Plantation with all the Lands belonging to it where he now lives . . .
> . . . to my Son Jeremiah Murden the Plantation whereon I now live with all the Lands thereto belonging and the Land called the Gum thicketts and all the Part of Land called the Elbow and likewise the Land I bought of William Ackis . . .
> . . . to my Son Robt Murden the Plantation wth all the Lands belonging to it that I bought of Moses Fentris . . . Negro called Jenny . . . fifty acres of Land called the Gum Swamp . . .
> . . . to my Son Jeremiah Murden all the rema^s Part of my Lands as not as yet given away . . .
> . . . to my Daughter Elizabeth Fentris one Negro Girl . . .
> . . . to my Daughter Mary Shipp Negro Girl . . .
> . . . unto my Daughter Fentr—(torn)—one Negro Girl . . .

. . . to my Daughter Ann Butt one Negro Boy . . .
. . . to my Daughter Martha Murden two Negroes . . .
. . . remaining . . . equally divided between my—(torn)—that is, John, Jeremiah. Robert, Elizabeth, Sarah, Ann—(torn)—Martha Murden . . .
. . . Son Jeremiah Murden . . . sole Ex—(torn)—itor . . .

Witnesses: Thomas Butt.
      Isaiah Nicholas.
      Betty Butt.

                          his
                John + Murden & Seal.
                mark.

JOHN CONNER of Norfolk County Virg* Marriner . . . .
Book I p. 169.
Dated 17 July 1749.
Proved 19 July 1750.

. . . to my loving Brother William Conner two Negroes . . .
. . . to my loving Sister Margaret Watkins two Negroes . . .
. . . to my loving Brother E—(torn)—rd Conner two Negroes . . .
. . . to my loving Sister Elizabeth Conner two Negroes . . .
. . . to Abigall Conn—(torn)—Daughter of William Conner one Negro . . .
. . . The rest of my Estate I leave to my Brother Craford Conner to be sold to pay my Debts . . .

Witnesses: John Westcott.
      Martin Baynes.
      Mary Griffin.

                John Conn—(torn)—& Seal.

DURHAM HALL of the Borough of Norfolk in the Colony of Virginia Merchant . . .
Book I p. 179.
Dated 4 Nov. 1750.
Proved 18 Jan. 1750.

. . . first it is my Will & Desire that the Sloop Molly whereof John Ingram is at present Master, and whereof I am two third Part Owner, as soon as possible after her Arrival here may again be fitted out for the West Indies on Freight if possible . . .

. . . It is my Will & Desire that the Sloop Harry whereof John Loyall is at present Master, and whereof I am five twelfths Parts Owner . . .

. . . the Briggantine William lately Launched of which I am to hold three Eight parts my Brother William Hall & Capt James Dickenson to hold the remaining . . . fitted . . . Voyage to Madeira . . .

. . . to my dearly beloved Wife Jane Hall all my houshold Furniture . . . to bring up my Children, William, Henry, Durham and Daniel . . . as they come to age . . .

. . . appoint my said beloved Wife Jane Hall, my Dearly beloved Brother William Hall my Friends Colonel Robert Tucker & Christopher Perkins Executors . . .

Witnesses: James Dickinson.
Archibald Campbell.
Elizabeth Campbell.

Durham Hall & Seal.

Memorandum . . . Desire that a Tract of Land wch I hold in Brunswick County may be sold by my Ex^{rs} likewise a Lott or half a Lott of Land morgaged to me by Edwd Hainly may be sold in like manner.

Witnesses: Archibald Campbell.
Thomas Dickinson.
her
Mary + Hickman
mark.

Durham Hall & Seal.

EDWARD HANSLEY of the Borrough of Norfolk . . .

Book I p. 182.

Dated 8 July 1750.

Proved 16 Aug. 1750.

. . . unto my Loving Daughter Mary Hansley the Sum of fifty five Pounds . . . four Gold Rings Weighing £ 2.

3 S . . . twenty Pounds Part of the Said Fifty five Pounds together wth a Bond of thirty five Pounds being the remaining Part thereof from Tho⁸ Morgan with Robert Todd Security Dated the 18th Day May 1750, I have Delivered unto & committed in Trust to my well beloved Friend Mr James Pasteur to & for my said Daughter Mary . . . during her Minority . . . but if my s^d Daughter should die . . . to my loving Brother George Hansley living in Spotsilvania County of Virg⁸

. . . my loving Wife Eliz⁸ Hansley . . .

. . . my Loving Friend James Pasteur my . . . Sole Executor . . .

Witnessees: James Moore
        William Nimmo ju^nr
        Robert Martindale.

                Edward Hensley & Seal.

JAMES GRIMES of the Western Branch of Elizabeth River Norfolk County . . .

Book I p. 183.

Dated 15 May 1750.

Proved 19 July 1750.

. . . unto my Son Thomas Grimes all my Land and Plantation . . .

. . . unto my Son James Grimes Thirty Pounds Cash . . .

. . . unto my Son Jesse Grimes a Negro Boy called Tony . . .

. . . unto my Daughter Sarah Deans Negro Boy called George . . .

. . . unto my Daughter Mary Grimes Negro Boy called Peter . . .

. . . unto my Son John Grimes Negro Boy called Kelly . . .

. . . unto my Son Samuel Grimes one Negro Boy called Harry . . . .

. . my loving Wife Mary . . .

. . . appoint my Son Thomas and my Wife Mary Execur˟
. . .

Witnesses: Richard Harris.
          her
      Eliz˟ + Wright.
      mark.

                        his
                 James + Grimes & Seal
                     mark

RICHARD MACCOY of the County of Norfolk . . .
Book I p. 186.
Dated 25 March 1750.
Proved 19 July 1750.

. . . unto my Son Richard Maccoy after the Death of my
Wife Eleanor Maccoy my Land & Plantation I now live
on. He my said Son Richard paying unto my Son Thomas
Maccoy Ten Pounds Curr˟ Money when he shall attain
unto the Age of twenty one years . . . But & if my
said Son Richard shall refuse to to pay . . . then
. . . unto my s˟ Son Thomas . . .
. . . unto my Son Keader Maccoy my Negro Boy Attee
. . .
. . . my Coopers Tools . . .
. . . unto my Son Thomas Maccoy my hand mill . . .
. . . unto my Daughter Eliz˟ Carson one Bed . . .
. . . unto my Daughter Sarah Maccoy . . . Bed
. . .
. . . appoint my Son Richard & my loving Wife Ellinor
Maccoy to be my Ex˟ & Ex˟ . . .

Witnesses: Wᵐ Portlock.
          Andrew Carson.
          Caleb Maccoy.
          Cadez Maccoy.

                      his
             Richard Maccoy + & Seal.
                 mark.

JOHN WHIDDON of Norfolk County in Virginia . . .

Book I p. 192 (Checked by Original).

Dated 9 Nov. 1748.

Proved 18 Jan. 1750.

. . . to my Daughter Mary Herbert wife of Marckham Herbert the Dividend of Land with the Plantation thereon that I bought & purchased of William Ballentine Lying on the South Side of Bay Tree Hole . . . being the same Land which I have already made over to the Said Marckom Herbert by & acknowledged in the open Court of Norfolk . . .

. . . unto my Daughter Martha Whiddon one Hundred Acres of Land with the Plantation thereon lying on the Nort Side of the Western Branch of of Elizabeth River being the Land formerly Mossets . . .

. . . And in Case an Heir shall come & Disinherit my said Daughter of the Said Land then . . . my said Daughter . . . shall have one hundred Acres of Land with the Plantation which I bought of William Whiddon . . .

. . . unto my Son John Whiddon the home and Plantation with the Wood land Ground therunto belonging which I now Live on also Fourteen Acres of Land joining thereto called Pedley's . . . also the Land I bought of William Whiddon if not taken by my Daughter Martha Whiddon as before mentioned . . .

. . . all the Rest of my Estate both real & personal within Doors & without . . . unto my Son John Whiddon . . .

. . . my Wife Abigail Whiddon . . .

. . . if it should please God that my Daughter Martha Whiddon should die before she attain to Years of Twenty one or marry then in such Case her Estate both real & personal to fall to my Son John Whiddon . . . And if it should please God that my Son John Whiddon should die before he attain to the Age of Twenty years at which Time I allow him at age or marry then In such Case his Estate both real & personal after my Wifes Decease to be equally Divided my two Daughters viz. Mary Herbert & Martha Whiddon . . .

. . . appoint my Loving Wife Abagail Whiddon & my Son John Whiddon wholly & jointly my Exe[x] & Executor . . .

Witnesses: W[m] Bayley.
           Paul Ballentine.
                her
           Ann + Ballentine
            mark.

                          his
                   John + Whiddon & Red Wax
                              Seal & Crest.
                 mark.

HENRY ROBERTS of Norfolk County in the Colony of Virg[a] . . .

Book I p. 194.

Dated 24 Nov[r] 1749.

Proved 17 Jan. 1750.

. . . unto my Grandson Mordakaia Ballance Roberts my new Dwelling Plantation & all the Land belonging to it if he should live to the Age of one & twenty years . . . but if he should not live till he come of age . . . the Land shall & may be Equally Divided between Richard Ballance two Daughters namely Julian & Caty . . .

. . . unto my Daughter Barthana Roberts any three of my Cows . . . her mothers Side Saddle . . .

. . . unto my Daughter Cateron Ballance my hackle & Spoon molder . . .

. . . unto my Son in Law Joseph Hammond my Gun . . . s[d] Joseph . . . pay unto Elizabeth Slack . . . three pounds . . .

. . . my Brother in Law Francis Credle my whole & Sole Ex[r] . . .

Witnesses: Joseph Stewart.
           Jos: Hamon.
           John Arnal.
           Martha Busly.

                              Henry Roberts & Seal.

MARY GRISTOCK . . . Norfolk Borrough . . .

Book I p. 196.

Dated 19 Dec. 1750.

Proved 18 Jan. 1750.

. . . unto my beloved Neice Ann Franks one black Trunk, on Seal Skin Trunk . . . four pairs of Denlass Sheets . . . a Remnant of blue Tammy . . . Six Plates of Delph Ware . . . one Gold Ring wth the Posey /Let not absence banish Love/

. . . unto good Fiend Christopher Gardner ten pounds—(torn)—

. . . unto my beloved Grand Daughter Frances Tu—(torn)—money . . .

. . . also—(torn)—Grand Daughter Frances Tucker one Gold Ring wth The Posey /—torn)—as Love Debarrd/ . . .

. . . unto my good Friend Christo: Gard—(torn)—and one Gold Ring with the Posey /I have obtained whom God ordained/ . . .

. . . unto my beloved Cousin John Munds . . . five pounds . . .

. . . my Husbands Will or Inventory . . .

. . . my good Friends Mr Saml Boush jun^r & Christopher Gardner my Executors . . .

Witnesses: Alexander Ross.
Chris: Gardner.
Mary Calvert.

her
Mary + Gristock & Seal.
mark.

GILES RANDOLPH of Norfolk County and Parish of Elizabeth in Virginia . . .

Book I p. 210.

Dated 7 Sep. 1750.

Proved 18 Oct. 1750.

. . . to my Son Thomas Randolph the Plantation & Land whereon he now lives containing a hundred acres . . .

. . . to my Son James Randolph the Plantation whereon he now lives in Princess Ann County containing a hundred acres . . .

. . . to my Son Willis Randolph . . . one hundred acres of Land in Princess Ann County being one half of the Land I bought of Benjn Cumings where his Brother James lives . . .

. . . to my Son Giles Randolph the House & Plantation whereon I now live after his mothers Death or Day of Marriage . . . also . . . two thirds of my Water Mill during my Wifes Life and after her Death I give her wholy to him . . .

. . . to my Son Solomon Randolph one hundred acres of Land more or less . . . the which—(torn)—I bought of Benjamin Cumings up Pockoyty Road . . .

. . . to my Daughter Martha Hodges a young heifer . . .

. . . to my Grandson Solomon Hodges my Gun which his Father has in Possession . . .

. . . to my Son Giles my Entry in the Juniper and Cyprias Swamp . . .

. . . appoint my Loving Wife & my Son Willis & Giles to be my Executrix and Executors . . .

Witnesses: Willis Wilson.
           John Williams.
           Charles Wilkins.

his
Giles + Randolph & Seal.
mark

JOHN DRURY, Senr—(Nuncupative)—

Book I p. 212.

Dated 19 Feb. 1750/1.

Proved 21 Mch. 1750.

. . . John Lloyd and John Drury jun^r being in Company with John Drury Senr on his Death Bed, heard the said John Drury Senr say that all he had in this World he gave his Wife Sarah Drury . . .

Norfolk County—(torn)—
Feb^{ry} 26. 1750/1.

John Loyd.
John Drury.

Personally appeared John Lloyd & John Drury before me one of his Majesties Justices of the Peace for Said County & made Oath . . .

> Robert Todd.

THOMAS LANGLEY . . . Norfolk . . .

Book I p. 213.

Dated 20 July 1750.

Proved 21 Mch. 1750.

. . . to my Son Thomas Langley my Plantation & all my Land . . . Reserving unto my dear loving Wife the houses I now live in . . .

. . . unto my Daughter Tabitha . . . after my Said Wifes Decease . . . During her Life or Day of Marriage wth one third of the Said Lands during the said Term which shall first happen . . .

. . . to my Son Thomas my Negro . . . after his Mothers Decease . . .

. . . unto my Daughter Mary Briant one Negro Girl . . .

. . . unto my Son John Langley one Negro boy . . .

. . . to my grandson Tho$^·$ Dunnock my Negro Girl . . .

. . . unto her grand Daughter Katharine Dunnock . . . Negro . . .

. . . my Gun & sword . . .

. . . Wife Katherine . . .

. . . appoint my Son Thomas & my Daughter Tabitha Langley my whole & Sole Executor & Executrix . . .

Witnesses: Absolom Langley.
James Langley.
Solomon Wilson.

> Thomas Langley & Seal.

ROBERT WILLIAMS . . . .

Book I p. 213.

Dated 8 Feb. 1750/1.

Proved 18 Apr. 1751.

. . . unto my Eldest Son Willis Williams my Plantation that I now live on, and all the Land belonging to it . . .

. . . un—(torn)—ungest Son Robert Williams my Negro Girl Pleasant . . .

. . . to m—(torn)—Daughters Mary Williams & Monaca Williams my Negro Girl Ag—(torn)—Molatto between them . . .

. . . appoint my well beloved Wife Prudence Williams and Samuel Bartee my whole and sole Executors . . .

Witnesses: Thomas Willoughby.

Sam¹ Bartee.

Absolom Langley.

Robert Williams & Seal.

WILLIAM WISHART of the Borough of Norfolk and Colony of Virginia . . .

Book I p. 216.

Dated 15 Sept. 1743.

Proved 21 March 1750.

. . . to my two Nephews William and Frances Wishart Sons of my Brothers Tho* and George Wishart of Princess Ann County my houses & Land lying and being in the Borough aforesaid . . .

. . . to my loving Wife Mary Wishart my Negro woman Frank with her Child being a man Child . . .

. . . to my Said Wife all the Remainder Part of my Estate whatsoever shall be found within Doors and without . . .

. . . ordain Mʳ William Nimmo and my Brother George Wishart my Executors . . .

Witnesses: Francis Yarrowwood.

Jacob Langley.

Wᵐ. Wishart & Seal Red Wax.

MOSES PRESCOTT . . .

Book I p.—(torn)—(taken from a fragment of a leaf).

Dated—(torn)—Jan. 1747.

Proved—(torn)—

—(torn)—John Prescot the Land that

—(torn)—y plantation called Sower Wood

—(torn)—beginning the East side and
—(torn)—black Cherry tree & also through
—(torn)—John part of the Land joyning
—(torn)—Wilson's Land begining
—(torn)—Sower Wood Ridge where we
—(torn)—ning a straight Course to a
—(torn)—Maj^r Wilsons and John Halsteads
—(torn)—to my Son Aaron Prescot the Land &
—(torn)—live on with all the Lands Islands
—(torn)—to him and his heirs for Ever, I
—(torn)—the other part of Sower Wood.
—(torn)—Briar Swamp with the Land I bought
—(torn)—Williams and I also give my Son Aaron the
—(torn)—Lands joyning to John Halstead & Maj^r
—(torn)—ath to my two Grandsons Moses & James
—(torn)—dred acres of Land called Rose*s* Ridge
—(torn)—ually between them . . .
—(torn)—ughter Mary Warden one Bay Mare is
—(torn)—mare I bought of John M*assar*.
—(torn)—beloved wife during her natural life
—(torn)— . . .

I give to William Warden—(torn)—I give all the rest of
m—(torn)—and my Daughter Mar—(torn)—them and
their heirs for—(torn)—and lastly I constitute—(torn)—
and my Son Aaron Pr—(torn)—this my last Will and
Tes—(torn)—

Witnesses: William Fairfield.
　　　　　Willis Wilson Junr
　　　　　William Wilson.

(Signature torn out).

WILLIS WILSON Junr of Norfolk In the Colloney of Virginia . . .

Book I—(page torn out).

(Abstracted from the Original Will).

Dated 10 Jan. 1749/50.

Proved 19 Apr. 1750. (See Book I).

. . . Unto my Son Malachi Wilson my plantation and land
that was given to me by my Grandfather Thos. Butt and
allso a Certain piece of land Joining to it that was giv^n
me by my Father and allso another piece of land Joyning

to Woodwards line by Varias Courses for Two hundred acres more Or Less as it is bounded and allso all my land at Ballahack   .   .   .

. . . Unto my Son John Wilson the plantation I now Dwell On and all the land Belonging to it and allso all the land I Bought of Anthony Eathridge and allso a piece of land Commonly Call Wild Horse Ridge Joyning to Ballahack . . . allso my ware house at the great bridge & the land it Stands On   .   .   .

. . . my Daughter Mary Wilson   .   .   .

. . . My Silver hilted Sword & Belt and a book Cald the Exptan: a^n of the New Testament and my Two Dixanaryes   .   .   .

. . . appoint my beloved Wife Mary Wilson and my Brother Josiah Wilson my whole and Sole Execut^s

Witnesses: Joseph Stewart.
  Sam^{ll} Langley.
  Nathaniel Wilson.
  Josiah Wilson.

  Willis Wilson. Red Wax Seal.

ELIZABETH MILLER of Norfolk—(torn)—inia Spinster

.   .   .

Book I p. 217.

Dated—(torn)—March 1751.

Proved 18 Apr. 1751.

. . . unto my loving kinsman Mason Smith vizt Two—(torn) —and one Pewter Dish   .   .   .

—(torn)—to my Cousin Letuticea Miller one gold now in the Possession of—(torn)—

. . . unto my Cousin Elizabeth Miller one P^r—(torn)—Rings now in the Possession of Amy White.

—(torn)—to my Cousins Amy White & Lucy White one piece of Stuff—(torn)—

—(torn)—and Peledge Miller any my Cousin Lucy Miller & I make—(torn)—er, Peledge Miller my whole and sole Executor   .   .   .

Witnesses: Mathew Godfrey.
  Elender Godfrey.

                                 her
                         Eliz^a + Miller & Seal.
                                 mark.

JOHN ASHLEY . . .

Book I p. 219.

Dated—(torn)—

Proved—(torn)—

. . . unto my beloved Daughter Elizabeth Langley one Negro Woman named Dinah . . .

. . . to my beloved Daughter—(torn)—one Boy . . . Barbara to her my said—(torn)—

. . . my Land at Brushe—(torn)—of Daniel Godfrey to him my said Son—(torn)—

. . . unto—(torn)—named Robin, & one half of a L—(torn)——in Norfolk Town from the Corn—(torn)—Ashley Land to him the said Jame—(torn)—

. . . unto my beloved Sons John Ashley James Ashley and Lemuel Ashley . . . the Land & marshes in Coretuck in the Province of North Carolina . . .

. . . appoint Thomas Langley & William Ashley to be my whole & Sole Executors . . .

Witnesses: —(torn)—

John Ashley & Seal.

WILLIAM BUTT . . .

Book I f. 222 (See Old Index).

. . . (missing from Volume & also from Original package of "Wills 1711 to 1755") . . . (Depositions of Lem[l] & W[m] Butt in Original package) . . .

NATHANIEL NASH of Norfolk—(torn)—

Book I p.—(torn)—(taken from a fragment of a leaf).

Dated—(torn)—

Proved—(torn)—

. . . Elizabeth Nash my Plantation whereon . . . my Said Sisters . . . —(torn)—
—(torn)—appoint my Friend Capt.—(torn)—
—(torn)—& jointly my Executors of—(torn)—

Witnesses: —(torn)—

(Signature torn out).

SAMUEL ROGERS of the Borough of Norfolk . . .

Book I p. 225.

Dated 28 June—(torn)—

Proved 16 Aug. 1751.

. . . my loving Wife Mary Rogers . . .

. . . Samuel, William, Matthew, John & Gead . . .

. . . appoint my Friend—(torn)—Tucker & Mr Nicholas Won—(torn)—Executors . . .

Witnesses: —(torn)—

Samuel Rogers & Seal.

WILLIAM NASH of Norfolk County In the Dominion of Virginia . . .

Book I p. 218—(torn)—

(Abstract from the Original Will).

Dated 19 Apr. 1751.

Proved——1751.

. . . unto my beloved Son Nathaniel Nash my Plantation whereon I now Live Lying on Broad Creek . . . appurtenances thereto belonging and all the merch which I am now possessed with on the Sea Side . . .

. . . unto my Said Son Nathaniel Nash all that Tract of Land lying in Princess Ann County which I bought of Capt. John Thorowgood . . .

. . . unto my beloved Daughter Elizabeth Nash all that Tract of Land . . . I bought of Mr Arthur Sayer . . . Round Tea Table that was her Sisters . . .

. . . young Spad mare . . .

. . . my godson William Nash Son of Thomas Nash . . .

. . . Daughter Elizabeth Nash . . . shall attain to the age of Sixteen . . .

. . . Remainder of my Estate . . . not before given . . . unto my Son Nathaniel Nash . . .

. . . appoint my Loving Brother Nash and my well Beloved Son Nathaniel Nash . . . Executors . . .

Witnesses: George Poole.

Natha^l Thedaball.

Matthew Godfrey Junr

Wm Nash. Red Wax Seal.

JOHN MERCER of Norfolk County . . .

Book I p. 227.

Dated 19 May 1751.

Proved 20 Sept. 1751.

. . . to my Daughter Katherine Hughes my. great Table . . . in the Possession of Edward Hughes . . .

. . . to my Daughter Ruth Grimes my large Drawer Table . . .

. . . to my Grand Child Mary Falkner the black Heifer . . . and the Land whereon I now living . . . If my Grand Child Mary Falkner should dye without Heir the Land to my Grand child James Grimes the Son of James Grimes & Ruth his wife . . .

. . . to my Daughter Margaret Owen my Cattle . . .

. . . appoint my Son in Law John Owen to be the sole Executor . . .

Witnesses: Richard Smith.
   David Manning.
    Signum
   Honour + Manning.

        John Mercer & Seal.

WILLIAM BALLANDS of Curratuck Precinct in Albamarle County in the Province of North Carolina . . .

Book I p. 229.

Dated 25 Nov. 1700.

Proved 27 April 1701, by Wᵐ Bateman, John Ward & Andrew Mackfashion.

Exhibited to Court: 4 July 1732.

Proved 19 July 1751 by Mary Creedle & ordered recorded "as far as he Can possibly read it the same being Much defased and torn to pieces."

. . . Ordain and make my Loving Wife Mary Ballands my whole & Sole Executrix . . .

. . . unto my Son Samuel Eight Hundred Acres of Land with my my now Dwelling Plantation Upon it Unto . . .

. . . unto my Daughter Mary One Hundred and fifty acres

of Land Joining unto the said Eight Hundred and at that End Near the Fresh ponds . . .

. . . unto my Son William my Plantation at the Swamp and one half of the Land belonging to it . . . and the other half of the said Tract of Land I Give unto my Son Richard . . . my Desire is that the said Tract of Land be Divided . . . by a Branch Called the Sturrup Branch . . .

. . . unto my Daughter Luretha One half of my Land which Joseph Chur Surveyed . . . And the other half of the said Tract of Land . . . unto my Daughter Ca— (torn)— . . . Desire is that if any of my Children do Die without Such Issue as is aforementioned that then the Eldest—(torn)—his or her Inheritance of Land so Demand or the Eld—(torn)—Heirs . . .

. . . my Wife Mary Ballands . . .

. . . my Daughter Luce . . .

. . . my Desire that Mr—(torn)—hard Brian, Mr William Allen and William Bateman shall see that my Testament Equally fullfiled Amongst my Children . . .

Witnesses: Ardr—(torn)—Mak—(torn)—shion. .

his mark.

John + W—(torn)—

his mark.

William Bate—(torn)—an.

William Ballance & Seal.

his B mark & Seal.

"Memo. The Above Will was plainer to be read than I Expected."

Sam¹ Boush, C¹ C.

JOHN SAUNDERS . . .

Book I p. 232.

Dated 23 Apr. 1751.

Proved 17 Oct. 1751 & Administration with the Will annexed granted Alexr Ross as per Order Book.

. . . unto my Loving Wife Eliza—(torn)—all my Estate both real and Personal wheresoever—(torn)—

Lastly . . . appoint my sa—(torn)—Wife Elizabeth Saunders my Whole and Sole Executrix . . .

Witnesses: Henry Holmes.
             Wm Newboule.
             Francis Dison.

John Saund—(torn)—

. . . , I Eliz^a Saunders do Re—(torn)—administrating on my Deseased Husb—(torn)—that the Court may Appoint Alexander Ross being a gr—(torn)—

. . . October 17th 1751.

Eliz: Saunders.

Test:

William Nimmo.
James Nimmo.

JOHN SCOTT of Norfolk County . . .

Book I p. 233.

Dated 10 June 1751.

Proved 16 Aug. 1751 & Probate granted Willis Scott the 18 Oct. 1751 as p. Order Book.

. . . unto my Son in Law Ebenezar Stevens One—(torn)— Sterling . . . and likewise to his—(torn)—r Anna Stevens One Shilling Sterling . . .

. . . to Sisilia Stevens my Grand Daughter—(torn)— Comes of Age One Negro Girl . . . Case she should Die without Heirs then to my Son—(torn)—ott and his Heirs.

. . . unto my Son John Scott (when he reeturns)—(torn)— Houses in Newport in the Isle of White and three—(torn) — . . . if in Case he dies without Lawful Heirs then to my—(torn)—ce Scott and to his heirs forever.

. . . to my Son Will*ise* Scott and his heirs—(torn)—Lands *& Houses* in and about Norfolk . . . my Whole and Sole Executor . . .

Test: Patrick Murphy.
          her
     Mary M Sparrow,
          mark.
     Elizab: O. Bennett.

John Scott & Seal.

RICHARD HODGES of Norfolk County in Virg^a . .

Book I p. 234.

Dated 10 Feb. 1750.

Proved 21 Nev. 1751.

. . . unto my Eldest Son Richard Hodges my Plantation whereon I now live with three Hundred and Seventy Seven Acres of Land thereunto belonging . . .

. . . unto my Son Thomas Hodges Seven pounds . . . in full of his Part . . .

. . . unto my Son Robert Hodges my Negro boy named Bristol . . . also . . . all my Right to one Negro man named Sunday Now in the Possession of Mary Al— (torn)—Emanuel Burges . . .

. . . unto my Son William Hodges my best Bed . . .

. . . unto my Daughter *I*sabell Godfrey Ten Pounds . . .

. . . unto my Grandson Randolph Hodges . . . Negro . . . and in Case my said Grandson . . . should Die before he Attains the Age of Twenty one . . . to fall to my Grandson Richard Hodges . . .

. . . unto my Daughter Ann *Fitzakery* the Next Child that the said Jane shall bring . . .

. . . unto Mr Thomas Fitzackerly and unto my Daughter Ann his Wife . . . Negro . . .

. . . unto my Daughter Mary Hodges . . . Negro . . .

. . . unto my Grandson Richard Br*own* forty Shillings . . .

. . . unto my Grand Daughter Lydia Price forty Shillings . . . and for all the remaining Part of my Estate not before Bequeathed of what kind soever . . . I leave to be Equally Divided Between my Son Richard Hodges, my Son Robert Hodges and my Friend Thomas Fitzakerly . . . my Executors . . .

Witnesses: Thomas Nash.
George Sparrow.
Wm Brown.
George Holdcroft.

mark
Richard + Hadges & Seal.
his

JOHN IVY of Norfolk County in Virginia . . .

Book I f. 238.

Dated 1 Nov. 1749.

Proved 21 Feb. 1752.

. . . unto my Son William Ivy my House that is On the South Side of the Road with Liberty of Garding and firewood for one year after my Decease . . .

. . . unto my Son John Ivy all my Land . . . all my Cyder Hogsheads . . .

. . . unto my Loving Wife Sarah Ivy my former Dwelling House which my Son John now Dwells in, & John to Keeep it in Repairs for her During her natural Life . . .

. . . unto my Son Lemuel Ivy One Negro . . .

. . . unto my Son in Law Luke Slatter five shillings Cash,

. . . unto my Daughter Charity Slatter . . . five Pounds
. . .

. . . to my Daughter Keziah—(torn)—*v*es and the other Part to my Daughter Patience Foreman . . .
I desire my two neighbours Cap* William Hodges, Henry Creech and John Hollowell to Appraise . . .

. . . Ordain by two Sons John Ivey and William Ivey to be my Whole and Sole Executors . . .

Witnesses: Eleazar Tart.
John Tucker.
James Jolley.

John Ivey & Seal.

KEADER TALBOTT . . .

Book I f. 239.

Dated 26 Jan. 1752.

Proved 16 Apr. 1752.

The Land and House I now Live in I Give and bequeath to my Dear and welbeloved Brother Isaac Talbot . . .

. . . I Give and bequeath my House and Lot and Desk and Rent to my Brother William Talbot . . .

. . . to my Cousin Isaac Talbot One bed and furniture
. . .

. . . to my Cousin Mary Talbot Daughter of James Talbot Six head of Cattle . . .

. . . all the Money that is in Col° Robert Tuckers Hands to my beloved Brother Isaac Talbot.

. . . all the money due for the *Schooner* that is now in the Stocks for Cap¹ Max Calvert . . .
my beloved friend Lem¹ *Covrly* & my Brother Isaac Talbot Execᵣ⁸ . . .

Witnesses: Lemuel *Coverly.*
Samuel Lambard.
John Lowery.

Attestation: . . . Above named Cader Talbot . . . January 26ᵗʰ 1752.

Kadlor Talbott.

JOHN WARREN Sʳ of the Western Branch of Norfolk County . . .

Book I p. 239.

Dated 6 Feb. 1746/7.

Proved 16 Apr. 1752.

. . . to my Welbeloved Son James Warren One Shiling Sterling Money of England.

. . . unto my welbeloved Son John Warren One Shilling Sterling money of England.

. . . unto my Welbeloved Son William Warren one shilling Sterling Money of England.

. . . unto my Well beloved Daughtʳ Elizabeth Hanbury One Shilling Sterling Money of England.

. . . my Welbeloved Wife Ann Warren . . .

. . . my Youngest Daughter Martha Warren . . .

. . . my Wife Ann Warren to be my . . . Sole Executor
. . .

Witnesses: William Bayley.
his
James + El*l*is
mark.

his
John J. W. Warren
mark.

THOMAS WILLIAMSON of Norfolk Borough . . .

Book I f. 240.

Dated 4 March 1752.

Proved 16 Apr. 1752.

> . . . my Body to be Decently Buried at the Discretion of Robert Tucker and Lewis Hansford Who I hereby Appoint & Constitute my Executors.

> . . . after my Affairs in Company with Robt Tucker are settled . . .

> . . . unto my Worthy Friends Robert Tucker and his Wife Ten Guineas Each to Purchase Rings in Remembrance of me. Also to Each of their Children I desire a Genteal Mourning Ring may be Given as also to my Good Friends Robert Campbell of Jamaica Samuel Daviss of *Hanover*, Graham Frank, Willm At*chason*, Hugh Blackburn, Robt *Blows* and Lewis Hansford of Norfolk, John and Elizabeth Holt of Williamsburgh, to all I say I have a Genteel Morning Ring as a token of my regard for them.

> . . . to my Hon^d Father John Williamson of Hanover my Negro boy David and my Horse.

> . . . to my Well beloved Friend Lewis Hansford 400 Acres of Land in Luisa and 400 Acres of Land in Albermarle Countys, or in *share* all the Lands I am possessed of . . .

> . . . to the Presbiterian Meeting House in Hanover Twenty Pistoles to be applyed, by the Minister Mr Saml Daviss towards the necessary Charges thereof. Sixthly, I desire that One Hundred Pounds may be Given into the Hands of my Father Mr John Williamson to be applyed to Charitable Uses in the Parish wherein I was born.

> . . . five Pounds be Paid to Mary McCoy, as an Acknowledgement for her Care of me . . .

> . . . And Whatsoever Remains, or Appertains to me I desire may be paid into the Hands of Mrs Rob. Baker my Good and Loving Friend . . .

Witnesses: George Logan.

           Thomas Randolph.

           Samuel Happer.

                     Thomas Williamson & Seal.

WILLIAM LEWELLING of the Western Branch of Elizabeth River and County of Norfolk Virginia . . .

Bok I f. 240.

Dated 28 Jan. 1751.

Proved 16 Apr. 1752.

. . . Appoint my Dearly beloved Wife Frances Lewelling to be Joint Executors . . .

. . . to my Well beloved Wife Frances Lewelling this Plantation whereon I Liveth During her Widowhood and then to fall and belong to my Dearly beloved Son John Lewelling . . .

. . . my Dearly beloved Children . . .

. . . my Dearly beloved Grandson William Maning . . .

. . . to my Children again John Lewelling. Sarah Lewelling, Franke Lewelling, Annas Lewelling, and Abbe Lewelling, Chloe Lewelling, Leddia Lewelling, and Abbe Lewelling.

Witnesses : Richard Buntin.
       John + Owens.
       Daniel + Culpepper.

his
William + Lewelling & Seal.
mark

EDWARD LEWELLING of Norfolk County Virginia . . .

Book I f. 241.

Dated 10 Jan. 1752.

Proved 16 Apr. 1752 & 21 Aug. 1752.

. . . my Dearly Beloved Wife Marg^t Lewelling . . . if she marry again my Will is that my Son Thomas Lewelling shall Deliver to her the House wherein he now dwells

. . .

. . . my Son John Lewelling and Lettee Lewelling.

. . . my Wife Margaret Leewelling and Thomas Lewelling to be Joynt Executrix & Executor . . .

. . . unto my Son Thomas Lewelling the Manner plantation whereon I now Dwell Which I bought of John Tully . . . and if he the said Thomas Offers to Sell or Transfer the said Lands . . . said Manner Planta-

tion may be Invested in my Son Lewis & if he Die
without Lawfull Heirs . . . said Plantation may
Remain in the Possession of my Son Lewis Lewelling
. . .

. . . Chest of Drawers made of Mahogany, Six Leather
Chairs . . .

. . . unto my Son Benj* Lewelling the Land and Plantation
which I bought of John Green . . . And if my Son
Benj* Offers to Sell or Transfer the Said Land to any person or if he Dies without Lawfull Heirs then . . . to
my Son Edward . . .

. . . to my Daughter Elizabeth Bustin a Negro . . .
also Give her a . . . Trunk which was her Mothers
. . .

. . . to my Godson George Veale a Negro . . . He
not Coming in for any more of my Estate . . .

. . . to my Daughter Lydda Ewell a Molatto Girl . . .

. . . to my Daughter Mary Lewelling . . . a Negro
Wench . . .

. . . to my Daughter Lettissha Lewelling . . . a Negro
Girle . . .

. . . my Sons Edward, Lewis, my Daughters Eliz* Lydda,
Mary, Lettissha, Lettae & John Lewelling . . .

Witnesses: Henry Hughes.
   Jn° Gibson.
   Thomas Campbell.
        Edward Lewelling & Seal.

JOHN JOYCE of the Western Branch of Eliz* River Norfolk
County . . .

Book I f. 242.

Dated 2ᵈ March 1752.

Proved 16 Apr. 1752.

. . . unto my Son Martin Joyce my Gun Sword . . .
all my Carpenters and Calkers tools . . . the Large
Room of my New Dwelling House with two Parts of the
Profitts of the Ordinary . . . my Hone and Razors
. . . my Scripture Books . . .

. . . to my Loving Wife Kezia Joyce two feather Beds
. . . & the Small Room of my house . . .

. . . to my five Daughters, Jane, Rachael, Mary Buntin,
Kezia, Betty Each Forty Shillings Virg* Currency . . .
at the age of Twenty One . . .

. . . my Son Martin Joyce & my Loving Wife Kezia Executor & Executrix . . .

Witnesses: Richard Harris.
  Richard Buntin.
  Courtney + Green.

John Joyce & Seal.

THOMAS ETHEREDGE of the County of Norfolk . . .
  Well Stricken in age . . .

Book I f. 243.

Dated 31 Dec. 1750.

Proved 16 Apr. 1752.

First my Will and Meaning is that fifty foot in Length & Twenty
foot in Breadth on my Manner Plantation where the
Bodys of my Deceased ancestors were buryed be Reserved
for a Burying place and not at any time by any One sold
or Transferred.

. . . my Loving Wife Ann Etheredge . . .

. . . unto my Son Samuel Etheredge . . . all that Tract
of Land with both the Plantations . . . Whereon I
now Live and that whereon he Now Lives . . .

. . . unto my Daughter Dinah Nash One Feather Bed
. . .

. . . unto my Grandaughter Courtney Portlock the Sole
Use and Profits of my Negro . . . the Said Courtneys Children . . .

. . . unto my Grandson Enoch Etheredge my Gun and
Sword and Cat......k Box.

. . . unto my Grandson Thomas William Etheredge . . .
all that Parcell of Land Called Prescots . . . which
I Escheated from Matthew Nichless . . .

. . . unto my Grandaughter Mary Ann Nash my Negro
boy Paul . . . but if in Case the said Mary Ann
should die without Issue then . . . to fall to my
Grandson Robertson Nash . . .

. . . unto my Grandaughter Dinah Nash . . . Negro
Girle Tabb . . . if she should die without Issue then
. . . to fall to my Grandson John Nash . . .

. . . unto my Grandaughter Lydia Nash one Negro
. . . but if she the said Lydia should Die without Issue
then . . . to fall unto my Grandson William Nash
. . .

. . . unto my Grandaughter Anna Nash one Negro . . . But & if she . . . should die without Issue then . . . to fall to Robertson Nash . . .
. . . unto Thomas Portlock Son of Matthew Portlock One Negro . . .
. . . all my Estate not before Given away . . . to be Equally Divided into three Lotts and my Daughter Dinah Nash to have the first choice of one Lott and my Grandaughter Courtney Portlock . . . Second Lott and my Daughter Dinah Nash to have the third & last . . .
. . . Ordain my Loving Wife Ann Etheredge & my friend Thomas Nash to be Executrix & Executor . . .

Witnesses: William Portlock.
          Richard Murray.
          Simon Portlock.
          Seth Portlock.   Thomas Ethereidge & Seal.

WILLIAM AVIS of the Western Branch of Elizabeth River Norfolk County . . .

Book I f. 245.

Dated 22 Feb. 1752.

Proved 16 Apr. 1752.

. . . unto my Grandson Wm Avis Son of John Avis all my Land Situate at the head of Clarks Creek at the Western Branch . . .
. . . unto my Son Thomas Avis one young Heifer . . .
. . . unto my Son Abraham Avis one Heifer . . .
. . . unto my Daughter Sarah Harris one heifer . . .
. . . unto my Daughter Mary Avis my feather Bed & furniture . . .
. . . unto my Grandson William Harris one heifer . . . all the Rest and Remainder of my Estate Goods & Chattels . . . unto my Daughter in Law Frances Avis with whom I now live . . . .
. . . appoint my Son in Law Richard Harris x^r . . .

Witnesses:
                his
          Thos H Hare
                mark
                his
          Rich^d R D Deans
                mark
          Wm Bryan.   William + Avis & Seal.

GEORGE BEVAN[i] of the Borough of Norfolk . . .
Book I f. 245.
Dated 18 Feb. 1752.
Proved 16 Apr. 1752.

. . . my part of the Sloop Dolphin be sold to pay my Debts.

. . . unto my Son William Bevan my Negro Boy Harry, my six large Silver Spoons, my Gold Sleeve Buttons, my Silver Shoe and Knee Buckles . . . and if in Case he should die without such heirs then to his Mother Dinah Bevan . . .

. . . unto my God Daughter Margaret Portlock the Sum of Twenty five pounds.

. . . unto my wife Dinah Bevan the remainder part of my Estate as long as she bears my name and if in Case she should marry to have but the half of my Estate; but if in Case should not marry then to my Son William Bevan . . .

. . . my wife Dinah Bevan Edward Portlock and John Portlock should Ex[rs] . . .

Test: John Paderick.
Pat Murphy
Mary + Bramble.
    her
    mark.

                               George Bevan & Seal.

AARON BOULTON . . .
Book I f. 246.
Dated 21 Jan. 1752.
Proved 16 Apr. 1752.

. . . unto my Loving Wife Betty Boulton one third Part of my Manner Plantation on the side Joining to the Hundred Acres of Land wich I bought that formerly did belong to John Raynor w[ch] Hundred acres I also Give to my Said Wife During her Natural Life Likewise . . . my Water Mill . . .

. . . my two Sons William Boulton and Elisha Boulton . . .

. . . unto my Daughter Sarah Boulton One feather bed . . .

. . . unto my Daughter Mary Boulton One feather Bed

. . . unto my Daughter Betty Boulton One feather Bed

. . . unto my Son Aaron Boulton Fifty Acres of Land as I bought of Josepr *Eollotf* & Joining on John Jolloffs Land

. . . unto my Son Thomas Boulton fifty acres of Land in the same Swamp and Joining to the Aforementioned Land

. . . unto my Son Benj⁴ Boulton fifty Acres of Land in the same Swamp and Joining to the aforementioned Land

. . . unto my Son Jonathan Boulton fifty acres of Land in the said Swamp and Joining on the afore mentioned Land

. . . unto my Son James Boulton Seven Pounds Cur⁴ money of Virginia . . . at the Age of Twenty and One

. . . unto my Son Elisha Boulton *Atf* his Mother's Decease the Aforesaid Hundred Acres of Land as I bought as did belong to John Raynar and Richard Raynar . . .

. . . Eight of my Children as I shall mention hereafter Thomas Boulton, Aron Boulton, Sarah Boulton, Mary Boulton, Betty Boulton, Ben: Boulton, Jonathan Boulton and James Boulton . . .

. . . Wife to be my Whole and Sole Exec^r . . .

witnesses: James Jolloy.
John Spring.
Henry Hapgood.
Eleazar Tart.

Signed by Aaron Boulton & Seal.

JOHN HOLLOWELL of Norfolk County in Virginia

Book I f. 246.

Dated "24ᵗʰ day of the 1ˢᵗ Month 1751."

Proved 16 Apr. 1752.

. . . unto my Son John Hollowell my plantation which I now dwell on with all the Land belonging to it and the

Water Mill that is on it, with the old Mill Stone in
the house . . . my large Bible . . .
. . . unto my Son Thomas Hollowell the plantation which
I bought of my Cousin Tho⁸ Hollowell with all the Land
belonging⁸ to it containing one hundred and Ten Acres &
also the Water Mill that is on it and the Iron Crow and
my whip Saw . . . a Book the History of the Quakers

. . . unto my Daughter Rachael Copeland one Silver Spoon

. . . unto my Daughter Mary Hollowell one Silver Spoon

. . . unto my Daughter Sarah Hollowell one Silver Spoon
and one pair of *Quern* Mill stones.
. . . my loving wife Sarah Hallowell . . . shall not sell,
waste nor imbezzle any of the Estate that is in her Care.
After the experation of my wife Life I then give all my
. . . to be equally divided amongst all my Children
that shall be then living, by three honest men . . .
Vis' Rachael, Mary, Sarah, John and Thomas . . .
I order that my Estate be only Inventoried & not appraised
after proving this Will. In Case my wife should die
before my two Sons John & Thomas be of age to take
Care of themselves I desire my Brother Tho⁸ Hollowell
shall take Care of them . . .
. . . ordain my loving wife Sarah Hollowell & my two Sons
John & Thomas Hollowell my whole & sole Ex˟ &
Exʳ . . .

Witnesses: William Powell.
      Wᵐ Tart
      John Jordan.
                  Jnᵒ Hollowell & Seal.

WILLIAM BUSTIN . . .

Book f. 248.

Dated 20 Feb. 1752.

Proved 16 Apr. 1752.

. . . nominate Elizabeth Bustin my true & lawful wife to
be my sole Executrix and administrator.
To the said Elizabeth Bustin my wife I bequeath &
leave the Plantation and house I now dwell in & after
her Death the said house and Plantation to my Son

Edward Bustin . . . To my Daughter Sarah Bustin . . . one Lott of Ground joyning upon Mr Andrew Sproul's Line from the Water side upward.

. . . to my Daughter Frances Bustin one Lott of Ground joining to Sarah Bustin Line upwards.

. . . to my Son Thomas one Lott of Ground joining upon Sarah Bustin upon the Water Side.

To my Son William Bustin one Lott joining upon my Son Thomas Bustin upwards.

To my Son Christopher . . . all the Remainder part of the said plantation belonging to my Father Wm Bustin senr that is to say runing a straight Line from Henry Herberts Line to the First Branch and from the said Branch runing along the East side of the Branch to my Brother Thomas Bustin's Line.

And the remainder part of the said Land that my father gave unto me I leave and bequeath to my Son Benjamin.

. . . To my Daughter Frankey . . , one Negro . . .

. . . Mr Thos Busto and Mr Thomas Edwards to see the Land divided and measured belonging to me which I bequeath to my Son Christopher . . .

Witnesses: Thomas Burtin.
         Thos Edwards.
         Thomas Lewelling.

                 Willm Bustin & Seal.

JOHN DRURY of the Borough & County of Norfolk . . .
Book I f. 248.

Dated 16 March 1752.

Proved 16 Apr. 1752.

. . . to my loving wife Sarah Drury the house wherein I now dwell together with the Land and premises thereunto belonging / which descended to me by the Death of my late Aunt Elizabeth Warren decd / . . . during her life, And after her Death . . . to my Son Thomas Drury . . .

. . . to my said Son Thomas Drury the house which Reodolphus Higginbottom lately lived in joining the aforementioned house together with the House at Town Bridge and the Lands & premises adjoining & belonging to the said Houses / which also descended to me by the death of my aforesaid Aunt / . . .

. . . to my said wife Sarah Drury all the remaining part of
my Estate both real & personal . . .

. . . appoint my Friend Horatio Stammers and my loving
wife Sarah Drury Executors . . .

Witnesses: Nicholas Winterton.

     W^m M^cE*nnery*.

     her

     Ruth + M^cE*nnery*
       mark

     Ja^s Holt.

                  John Drury & Seal.

NATHANIEL PORTLOCK of the Borough of Norfolk in
    Virginia . . .

Book I f. 249.

Dated 10 March 1752.

Proved 21 May 1752, by Sam: Smith & Alex^r Ross . . .
Rebecca Portlock Ex^x therein named having taken Oath
. . . Probate is granted her . . .

. . . all my Estate both real & personal laying and being
within the said Borough of Norfolk or elsewhere either
in Lands, houses, Messuages or Tenements, household
furniture of all kinds & Negroes & C^a the after mentioned
Legacies excepted . . . be sold at the Discretion of
my after mentioned Executors and the monies arrising from
such Sales to be equally divided among my wife Rebecca
Portlock, my Sons Paul Portlock, & Nathaniel Portlock,
my Daughters Phebe Portlock, and Eliz^a Portlock Share
and Share alike . . .

. . . to my Daughter in Law Nancey Ballard a Negro

. . . my said Children during their minority stay and board
. . .
with their mother & that reasonable Satisfaction be made
to her for their maintenance.

. . . ordain my loving wife Executrix & Messrs William
Portlock and Peter Dale Executors . . .

Witnesses: Sam: Smith.

     Alex^r Ross.

     Thomas Sowell.

              Nathl Portlock & Seal.

MARY CATO of the Borough of Norfolk . . .

Book I f. 250.

Dated 20 Feb. 1752.

Proved 21 May 1752, by Andrew Whyte and Alex^r Ross . . .
    John Scott the Ex^r . . . Probate is granted him
. . .

   . . . unto my loving Son John Cato my house and Lott laying and being in the Borough of Norfolk, as likewise all
my household furniture Real and personal Estate of all
kinds whatsoever . . .

   . . . if my Son John Cato should die without lawful issue
of his Body then & in that Case . . . my said houses
& Lott & all my other Estate unto my beloved Brother
Christopher Pool & Sister Sarah Scott . . & that
two persons be indifferently chosen to value my said Estate
and if my said Brother has *arived* to keep the same in
possession . . . he pay unto my said Sister Sarah one
half of the Value . . . in Cash Six months after said
Estate is valued.

   . . . appoint my Brother in Law John Scott my Executor
. . .

Witnesses: Andrew Whyte.
         Alex^r Ross.
           her
        Frances + Doyal.
         mark.

                       Mary Cato & Seal.

RICHARD DALE of the County of Norfolk . . .

Book I f. 252.

Dated 15 Apr. 1749.

Proved 21 May 1752.

   . . . to—(torn)—Winfield Dale his choice of the plantat—
(torn)—either that where Mr Robert Dyes—(torn)—
Benj^a Buntin lives & after his Mothers decease by her own
Consent to have and possess both . . .

   . . . bequeath the plantation that I now live on to my Son
Richard Dale with Privilege of one half of my dwelling
house and one half of my Orchard & my will is that my
Son shall not barr his mother from the other half during

her widowhood. I further give my s^d Son my Still except a Privilege to his mother & Brother Winfield to still their Liquors . . . and if *it* please God my Son Richard dies without heir or issue . . . his plantation shall fall and belong to my two Daughters Dinah Ow*eins* & Mary Dale . . . and if either of them dies without heirs their part to fall and belong to my Daughter Rachael Dale . . .

. . . give my Son Son Winfield my Cane . . .my Hone and Razors . . .

. . . —(torn)—ghter Susanah Dale Fifty Shillings . . .

. . . to my loving wife Susanah Dale the use of all my old Negroes . . . if please God my wife dies before my two Daughters Mary & Rachael comes to years of Eighteen . . .

. . . my Daughter Susannah comes to the years of fourteen for the use of schooling and bringing her up . . .

. . . Negroes to be sold at publick sale and the money to be equally divided amongst my five Children, Winfield, Richard, Mary, Dinah, & Rachael except Susannah . . .

. . . my five Children . . .

. . . I do appoint my Daughter Mary Dale if please God my Son Richard dies without heir to have that part of the plantation my house is on split from the River side up to the head of the Land . . .

. . . give my loving wife my Ready Cash for to pay my debts & School & bring up my small Children . . .

. . . my wife Susanah Dale and my two Brothers Daniel Dale & Peter Dale and William Dale as Trustees & Executors . . .

Witnesses: John Joyce.
         Dinah Dale.
         Eleazar Tart.

                    Richard Dale & Seal.

JOSEPH COOPER of Norfolk County in Virginia . . .

Book I f. 254.

Dated—(torn)—Feb. 1751.

Proved—(torn)—

. . . bequeath my Land whereon I live to—(torn)—D— (torn)—fe during her widowhood—(torn)—

. . . to my Son Joshua Cooper my Plantation whereon I
live after my mothers decease . . .

. . . to my Son Joseph Cooper the South side of the Road
whereon James Simmons lives after his mothers decease.

. . . to my Son Timothy Cooper a Plat of Land abounding
upon the Western Side of the fresh Run joining upon
Benj⁴ Coopers Line . . .

. . . to my Son Timothy Cooper my Land upon the Southern
Branch of New Mill Creek.

. . . Great Bible . . .

. . . my two Daughters—(torn) *urtny* **Marley** and Abigail Cooper . . .

—(torn)—point and ordain my loving wife Joyce Cooper & my
Son in Law John Marler . . . Exˣ & Exʳ . . .

—(torn)—

Witnesses: —(torn out)—

—(Signature, torn out)—

NATHANIEL LANGLEY of the County of Norfolk in the
Colony of Virginia . . .

Book I f. 255.

Dated 22 Jan. 1750.

Proved 21 M—(torn)—

. . . unto my two Brothers Willis Langley and Samuel
Langley all and singular the Lands & Tenements whatsoever left or given to me in & by the last Will and Testament of Lemuel Langley my Father late of Norfolk County
deceased to be equally divided . . . but in Case either
of my said Brothers Willis or Samuel should die without
heir or Issue that then the longest Liver . . . Enjoy
the whole . . .

. . . but provided both my said Brothers should die without such lawful heirs or Issue . . . to my sister
M—(torn)—

. . . Negro . . . to my loving mother Mary Langley
. . .

. . . to my Sister Mary Langley . . .

. . . all the rest . . . to be equally divided between my
said two Brothers . . . be it real or personal . . .
. . . two Brothers . . . Ex^rs . . .

Witnesses: William Nimmo, Junr
      Richard Jackson.
      Francis *Dailson*.
      Wm Granbery.
      Willaim Hodges.   Nathaniel Langley & Seal

EDWARD COLLEY now Resident in the County of Norfolk and blessed by Almighty God for it . . .

Book I f. 261. (Checked by Original).

Dated 26 Feb. 1750/51.

Proved 22 Nev. 1751 & 23^d Novr 1751. The Widow relinquished
all Benefit by the s^d Will.
. . . to my loving wife Phillis Colley one Bed and Furniture

. . . to my Son John Colley the oldest Yoke of Oxen . . .
. . . unto my Son Edward Colley the young Yoke of Oxen

. . . unto my Son Saunders Colley the House and Lott I
now possess joining on William Johnson's . . .
. . . my loving Son John Colley the whole & sole Ex^r
. . .

Witnesses: Jacob Lowery.
        her
    Frances + Lewery
      mark.
    John Cheshire   his
               Edward + Colley & Seal.
               mark.

MRS. ELIZABETH WARREN Deceased . . . (Nuncupative) . . .

Book I p. 256—(torn)—

(Abstract from the Original Will).

Dated 2 March 1752.

. . . the Bulk or Chiefest part of her Estate . . .to Mary Fishley her Sister's Daughter; and John Drury her Brother's Son . . .

. . . gave the two Houses down the Alley (meaning the alley called Yaxley Alley), to Mary Fishley; only the House that Mrs Higginbottom lived in she gave to Esther Thomas for Six Years to bring up the s^d Mary Fishley. The Land at Town Bridge . . . to Elizabeth Clark Daughter of her Sister Lydia Clark, and if either the s^d Mary Fishley or Elizabeth Clark should Die without Heir the part of her so dying should go the said John Drury.

. . . nine Gold Rings . . .

. . . her Eldest Brother's Son, John Drury . . .

. . . Elizabeth Warren said she had two Sisters (and more at York) . . .

. . . Spoken the 3 March, 1752 . . .

Test: Ashbury Sutton.
Katherine Browne.
    her
Ruth + McHenry.
    mark.

Summon: Thos. Drury.
Sarah McDuell.
& William Clark.
Next of Kin.

Also: Mr Asbury Sutton.
Mrs Kath: Brown.
Ruth McHenry.
Witnesses.

JOHN STEWART of Norfolk County and Parish of Eliz^a in Virginia.

Book I f. 271.

Dated 22 Oct. 1751.

Proved —— Aug. 1752.

. . . to my loving Son Thomas Stewart one half of the Land whereon I now dwell . . .the other half . . . to my Son John Stewart . . .

. . . to my loving wife Elizabeth Stewart one *Twelve* hh^d *flatt* and the *Hogs* that was called hers . . .

. . . the Remainder part of my Estate not before given . . . to be equally divided between my loving wife and three Children Tho⁸ John and Elizabeth . . . . . . wife Eliz⁸ Stewart my whole & sole Exʳ . . .

Witnesses: John Mercer, Junʳ
          Jnᵒ Hewitt.
          David Southerland.

his
John John Stewart & Seal.
mark

LEMᵗWILKINS of Norfolk County . . .

Book I f. 273.

Dated 23 Mch. 1752.

Proved 20 Aug. 1752.

. . . unto my Loving Son Willis Wilkins Fifty Acres of Land with Houses & Orchard that I now live upon with my Brandy Still and Hand Mill and Great Bible ⌄ . . .
. . . Unto my Loving Son Charles Wilkins Fifty Acres of Land bought of Thomas Hodges Joining to the Plantation I now live upon and fifty acres more bought of Thomas Winfield Joining upon John Williams . . .
. . . to my Loving Son Lemᵗ Wilkins a Feather bed . . . boat and Chest and Ten Pounds in Money . . .
. . . unto my Loving Son William Wilkins a feather Bed . . . Ten Pounds in Money . . .
. . . to my Loving Son Robᵗ Wilkins a Feather Bed . . . Ten Pounds in Money . . .
. . . to my Daughter Lydia Ann Wilkins a Feather Bed . . . Ten Pounds in Money . . .
. . . to my Loving Wife Sary Wilkins all the Rest of my Estate within and Without During her Widowhood . . .
. . . Appoint my Wife Sarah Wilkins and Willis Wilkins and Charles Wilkins my Hole and Sole Executors . . .

Witnesses: Lemuel Wilkins Junʳ
          William Wilkins.
             his
        Nazrath + Heulet.
           mark.

Lemuel Wilkins & Seal.

PATRICK KEETON of the County of Norfolk . . .

Book I f. 290.

Dated 4 Aug. 1752.

Proved 15 Nov. 1752.

   . . . to my Daughter Mary One Negro man Called Dumfie Mortgaged to me by Lem¹ Wilson . . .

   . . . unto my Daughter Sarah One Negro . . .

   . . . Mary my Beloved Wife . . .

   . . . Joseph Hodges Senᵣ & Benjam. Hodges Senᵣ . . . Ordain the sole Executors . . .

Witnesses: Shadrack Newhook.
         Christᵣ Cavanaugh.
         Robert Williams.

                              Patᵣ Keeton & Seal.

WILLIAM WILSON of Norfolk County in the Colony of Virginia . . .

Book I f. 294.

Dated 14 Oct. 1752.

Proved 21 Dec. 1752.

   . . . unto my Son Willis Wilson One Piece of Land I bought of John Armstrong allso allso a Certain Piece of Land Adjoining to it that was Given to me by my Father and also another Piece thats Joining thereunto which I pattented and also another Piece in the Back Woods that my Father Gave me Joining to Caleb Butts . . . But if my Son Willis should Die before he Comes of age Then the said Lands to return to my Wife Sarah Wilson . . .

   . . . if my Wife should die before my Son Willis, my Will and desire is that my Brother Josiah Wilson take my said Son and his Estate into his Care . . .

   . . . my Wife Sarah Wilson my Whole & Sole Execᵗ . . .

Witnesses: Joseph Stewart.
         James Butt.
         James Halstead.

                              William Wilson & Seal.

PETER TAYLOR of the Western Branch of Eliz* River, Norfolk County . . .

Book I f. 296.

Dated 1 Nev. 1752.

Proved "Jany Court 1753."

. . . unto my Loving Son Arthur Taylor all my Land and Plantation which I now live upon . . .

. . . unto my Son Paul Taylor all that Plantation I bought of Widow Elizabeth Ives . . .

. . . unto my Loving Wife Dorcas Taylor . . . the rest and Residue of my Estate of what kind & nature soever for and during her natural Life . . .after . . . to be Equally divided among all my Children . . . .

. . . Appoint my Loving Wife aforesaid and William Tart Senr Exec^r and Executrix . . .

Witnesses: Richard Harris.

Peter Taylor & Seal.

WILLIAM MOSELEY of Norfolk Borough . . .

Book I f. 296.

Dated 28 Oct. 1748.

Proved "Jany Court 1753."

. . . unto my Beloved Wife Edeth Mosely, a Negro Wench Named Sue . . .

. . . unto my beloved Son John Mosely One Negro boy named Dick and my House and Lands . . . One large Looking Glass, one large Seal Gold Ring Marked W: M and a large Cedar Chest, One Desk and One Oval table . . .

. . . to my Beloved Daughter Elizabeth Moseley one Negro Girle Named Ruth . . .

. . . my three Children, except the Negro Woman Sue . . . I give to my Son Willm Moseley . . . .

. . . Friends Mr John Osheal and Mr John Tucker to be my whole and sole Executors.

Witnesses: Joseph Hodges.
            Solomon Edey.
            Anth^y Lawson.

William Moseley & Seal.

JOHN GODFREY . . . Norfolk County . . .

Book I f. 298.

Dated 30 Jan. 1753.

Proved Feb. Court 1753.

   . . . unto my Brother Matthew Godfrey the Plantation I now Dwell on , . . .

   . . . unto my Brother William Godfrey the Plantation in Pasquotank County and all the Land belonging to it . . .

   . . . my Well beloved Wife . . .

   . . . my Sister Amey *Eusfen* . . .

   . . . m^r James Webb my hole and Sole Executor . . .

Witnesses: Richard Ballance.
         Aaron Prescott.
         Benj^a Miller.

                       John Godfrey & Seal.

WILLIAM DENBY of the County of Norfolk in the Colony of Virginia . . .

Book I f. 300.

Dated 2 Sep. 1749.

Proved Feby Court 1753.

   . . . unto two of my Sons (thats to say) my Son Arthur Denby and Dyer Denby all my Wearing Apparrell.

   . . . unto my Daughter Abigail, my Trundall bed and furniture the same which now Runs Under my Bed.

   . . . unto my youngest Daughter Margaret five pounds in Cash . . .

   . . . all my Worldly Estate, both within Doors & without to be Sold at Publick Sale for Ready Money . . . then . . . to be Equally Divided Between my Son William Denby, my Son Arthur Denby, and my Son Dyer and my Son Mattithias Denby and my Son Samuel Denby, and my Daughter Joice Marley & my Daugh^r Abigail Denby. and my Daughter Mary Marley & my Daughter Margaret Denby. I Desire that Abraham *Page* Called the Free Negro shall be Sold to the best advantage for the time he has to stay with me by Indenture.

. . . my well beloved Son Wm Denby and my Beloved
Friend Francis Wishart, to be my only and Sole Executors . . .

Witnesses: Lewis Connor.
　　　　　Joel Dunn.
　　　　　James Timberlake.

William Denby & Seal.

JAMES IVY of the County of Norfolk in the Colony and
Dominion of Virginia . . .

Book I f. 300.

Dated 4 Nov. 1752.

Proved 16 Nov. 1752, by all Witnesses.

. . . unto my Loving Son James Ivy the Plantation whereon
I now Live . . .

. . . unto my Loving Daughter Mary Robinson my Lott of
Land in Norfolk Borraugh lying between Samuel Smith
and Archibald Williamson . . .

. . . Negro boy *Tommay* I bought of Purdy . . .

. . . unto my Loving Daughter Ann Ivy my Negro . . .

. . . unto my Loving Daughter Marg^t Ivy my Negro Called
Papousa alias Judy . . .

. . . unto my Loving Daughter Betty Ivy my Negro Girle
Called Kate . . .

. . . I do hereby Give full Power to my Executors to Sell
and Dispose of the Tract of Land I purchased of M^r
William Langley lying in Princess Ann County . . .

. . . unto my Loving Wife one Fifth Part of my Personal
Estate . . . but if it should Exceed One thousand
Pounds I then Give her two Hundred Pounds and no more
. . .

. . . my Loving Brother Joseph Ivy . . .

. . . Appoint my Loving Wife and Samuel Boush the Elder
my Executors . . .

. . . unto my Loving Wife during her Widdowhood Liberty
to Cutt Timber of the Land I bought of Mr John Taylor.

Witnesses: Pat Murphy.
　　　　　　　his
　　　　　W^m W *Tuile*.
　　　　　　mark.

James Ivy & Seal.

JEREMIAH ETHERIDGE

Book I f. 302.

Dated 14 Jan. 1753.

Proved March Court 1753.

. . . unto my Son Matthias Etheredge my Manner Plantation and all the Land belonging to it to the Middle Branch on the South Side of my Plantation & to Run up the Branch to Doct^r Happers Land . . .

. . . unto my Son Jeremiah Etheredge all the Remainder Part of my Land from that Branch Joinin to William Porters and Doct^r Happers Land . . .

. . . unto my Son Thomas Etheredge two two year old yearlings . . .

. . . unto my Loving Wife all the Remaining Part of my Estate that I have not Mentioned.

. . . my Loving Wife my Executor of all my Estate . . .

Witnesses: James Wilkins.
        Edmun Creekmur.
            her
      Christian + Creekmur
         mark.
                Jeremiah Etheredge & Seal.

BENJAMIN BUTT . . . of Norfolk County . . .

Book I f. 302.

Dated 23 Jan. 1753.

Proved 15 Mch. 1753.

. . . unto my Mother Amsey Butt the Use of my Plantation and Land during her Natural Life that I now live On After . . . to my Brother Henrys Son Henry Butt . . .

. . . Negro . . . to Frances Butt, the Daughter of my Deceased Brother Ranford Butt . . .

. . . a New Case of Knives and Forks . . .

. . . all the Remainder Part of my Estate to be Sold and . . . Then . . . to be Divided between my Brother Henry Butt and my Sister Mary Etheredge I also Appoint

my Brother Henry Butt my whole and Sole Executor
. . .

witnesses: John Wilkins.
     Josiah Wilson.
       her
     Sarah S Butt
      mark.

          Benjamin Butt & Seal.

AMY WYATT of the Western Branch of Elizabeth River
  Norfolk County . . .

Book I f. 303.

Dated 22 Apr. 1746.

Proved 15 Mch. 1753.

. . . unto my Son Shadrack Wyatt One Feather Bed . . .

. . . unto my Son John Wyatt One Feather Bed . . .

. . . unto my Daughter Edith Bruce One Brass SKillit
. . .

. . . unto my Grandaughter Amy Harris One Peuter Dish
. . .

. . . unto my Son Shadrack Wyatt and my Land . . .

. . . unto my Children whose Names follow to Each of them
One Shilling Sterling with Intent to Cutt them off from
Claiming any Part of my Estate Viz^t my Daughter Jane
Harris, Amy Jenkins, Mary Collins, my Son John Bauns,
Ann Ward, Margaret Miars, Sarah Bishop and Alice Nor-
cott . . .

. . . Appoint my Son Shadrack Wyatt full and Sole Executor
. . .

witnesses: Richard Harris.
     Henry Norcott.

          Ame Wyatt & Seal.

THOMAS ETHERIDGE of the said County of Norfolk
. . .

Book I f. 303.

Dated 8 May 1752.

Proved 15 Mch. 1753.

. . . unto my Brother Lem¹ Etheredge my Land and Plantation I now live on Only Reserving that my Sister Charity who lives with me to have the Use of the said Land and Houses during her Natural life . . .

. . . unto Abiah Etheredge Daughter of my Sister Charity . . . Six pounds in Money . . .

. . . unto my half Brothers & Sisters That is to say to Jeremiah Etheredge Paul Etheredge, Dorcas Ballentine and Christian Creekmur to Each of them Twenty Shillings in Money . . .

. . . unto the four Children my Brother Moses left after his Death to say Moses & Thomas boys and Mary and Marg¹ Girles to Each of the Twenty-five Shillings in Money . . .

. . . my Brother Lem¹ Etheredge to my Executor . . .

witnesses: William Portlock.
Simon Portlock.
Seth Portlock.

his
Thomas + Etheredge.
mark.

JOHN COLLEY of Norfolk County in the Colony of Virginia . . .

Book I f. 304.

Dated 28 Oct. 1752.

Proved 15 Mch. 1753.

. . . unto my Son James Colley one Young Cow . . .

. . . unto my Son William Colley one Young Cow . . .

. . . unto my Son Lem¹ Colley one Young Cow . . .

. . . unto my Son Nath¹ Colley One Young Cow . . .

. . . unto my Son John Colley One Negro Fellow Peter . . .

. . . one young Heifer to my Grand Daughter Abigail Simmons at the day of her Marriage . . .

. . . the Rest . . . unto all my Sons, to be Equal to be Divided Amongst them . . .

. . . my Son Colley to be my whole and Sole Executor
. . .

witnesses: John Godfrey.

her

Persiller + Godfrey.

marke.

his

John + Colley & Seal.

mark.

JOSEPH STEWART . . . Virg⁴ Norfolk County . . .

Book I f. 305.

Dated 26 Feb. 1753.

Proved 15 Mch. 1753.

. . . I leave that tract of Land that my Store House is upon lying on the North West River also the Tract of Land lying Adjoining on Nicholas Slacks and William Edirge Land to be sold to pay my Lawful Debts . . .

. . . to my Well beloved Daughter Elizabeth Stewart all the Tract of Land I now live upon . . . and if my Daughter Elizabeth Stewart Die without heir . . . then I Give . . . unto Nicholas Slack . . .

. . . Appoint my Brother Nicholas Slack my whole and Sole Executor . . .

witnesses: William Taylor.

Silas Bright.

her

Jenat + Taylor.

mark.

Joseph Stewart & Seal.

EDWARD CARR of the said County . . .

Book I f. 305.

Dated 29 Jan. 1752.

Proved Feby Court by John Lambert and Lodged March Court Proved & Ordᵈ to be Recorded.

. . . to my Son Willis the Land and plantation I now live
On . . .

. . . to my Daughter Eliz^a Ann Carr One Heffer.

. . . to my Daughter Mary One Heifer.

. . . to my Daughter Frances One Heiffer.

. . . my wife Executrix . . .

. . . three Daughters Elizabeth, Mary & Frances . . .

witnesses :

        his

John + Lambert

    mark.

        his

Willis W. Carr

    mark.

                            Edward Carr & Seal.

LEMUEL BUTT Senr of Norfolk County . . .

Book I f. 305.

Dated 12 Apr. 1750.

Proved 15 Mch. 1753.

. . . unto my Cousin Penellopy Webb one Negro boy
. . .

. . . unto my Sister Mary Butt One feather Bed . . .

. . . unto Solomon Butt One gun and one Sword . . .

. . . appoint James Webb to be my whole Executor . . .

witnesses : Thos Jones.

        his

James J Stewart

    mark

John Coats.

                      Lem^l Butt & Seal.

CONSTANT GRIFFIN of the County of Norfolk and Colony of Virginia . . .

Book I f. 306.

Dated 15 Aug. 1751.

Proved Feby. Court 1753, by Langley & Purdy.

Mch. 16 1753 Administration with the Will Annexed
granted Hugh Purdy . . .

. . . unto William Purdy Son of my Brother William Purdy the Remainder Part of my Plantation where I now Dwell and the Remainder Part of the Woodland on the side of the Branch Called the *Reedy* Branch as I have not Given by Deed of Gift in Norfolk County . . .

. . . unto George Griffin Son of John Griffin the Remainder Part of my Land on the East side of the *Ready* Branch having a Small House and Cornfield on it and lies in Princess Ann County. . .

. . . to William Silvester and Francis *Gamewell* Daughter of James Partr*ee* One Negro . . .

. . . all the rest of my Estate Excepting the Negroes to be Equally Divided between my four Kinswomen, Frances *Paretree* & Abigail Brooks & Dinah Wand and Elizabeth Iives . . .

. . . Appointing Richard William Silvester my Hole and Sole Executor . . .

witnesses: Richard Willm Silvester.
          Jonathan Langley.
          Hugh Purdy.

her
Constant C. Griffen & Seal:
mark.

DAVID BALLENTINE of the County of Norfolk . . .

Book I f. 307.

Dated 11 March 1749/50.

Proved 16 March 1753.

. . . unto my Son Saml Ballentine yt Piece of Land whereon his House now stands Beginning at a Possimon tree standing at the head of a Cove or Branch so runing a Straight Line to a White Gum standing in the same Line of my Land . . . also . . . the sole Use of a Worke House on the Other side of the said Cove which he built for his Own Use . . .

. . . bequeath the Sole and Intire Use of my Houses and Land and Plantation not before Given away unto my Son David Ballentine during his Natural life . . . if he my said Son David should depart this Life without Iissue of his Body . . . Then . . . to my Son Peter Ballentine . . . But if he my said Son David should have Issue Male or Female then . . . to Such his Issue . . . But and if these my two Sons David and Peter should Depart this life without Issue then . . . to my Son Sam¹ Ballentine . . .

. . . One Spade Mare . . .

. . . to my Daughter Mary Deford my next best Bed . . .

. . . unto my Son Paul Ballentine Twenty Shillings Cash . . .

. . . The Remainder of my Estate not before Given away . . . be Equally Divided Between my Son Peter Ballintine & my Daughter Mary Deford . . .

. . . Appoint my Son David Ballentine and my Son Samuel Ballentine to be Execʳˢ . . .

witnesses: William Portlock.
John Herbert.
Sam¹ Folk.

David Ballentine & Seal.

WILLIAM WALLIS . . . Norfolk County . . .

Book I f. 313.

Dated 24 March 1753.

Proved May Court 1753, by Solomon Cherry & Thomas Culpeper.

. . . to my Son William Wallis the Plantation that I now live on and all the Land belonging to it being One Hundred and Twenty Nine Acres more or Less . . .

. . . Appoint my Dearly beloved Wife to be my whole and Sole Executor . . .

witneses: Solomon Cherry.

her
Ann + Maning.
mark
Thomas T. Culpeper
mark

his
William W. Wallis & Seal.
mark.

THOMAS PRESCOTT of Norfolk County Precinct in the County and Colony Aforesaid . . . Virginia . . .

Book I f. 313.

Dated 24 Mch. 1753.

Proved May Court 1753.

. . . to my Brother Willis Prescott my Bed & Furniture . . .

. . . to my Brother Moses Prescott my Cross saw . . .

. . . to my Sister Dinah *Fer*bush two Pails . . .

. . . the rest of my Estate . . . to be Equally Devided betwixt my two Brothers Willis and Moses . . .

. . . Appoint Joseph Corbell to be my hole and Sole Exec^r . . .

        his
   Thomas T. Gisborn
        mark
        her
  Providence + Simmons
        mark

                 his
          Thomas + Prescott & Seal.
           mark.

SUDDEN OAST of the County of Norfolk and Colony of Virginia . . .

Book I f. 314.

Dated 12 Feb. 1753.

Proved May Court 1753.

. . . to my Son George Oast my Gun . . .

. . . to my Son William Oast a Good Gun to be provided for him by my Executor fitting for the field Eair sise . . .

. . . to my Loving Wife Rachael Oast my best Bed & Furniture . . .

. . . three Daughters Mary Oast, Blandinah Guy my wife's Daughter, and Betty Oast my youngest Daughter . . .

. . . . five Children . . . .

. . . . wife Rachael Oast my Sole Executrix . . .

witnesses: his

       Samuel + Piper

          mark.

         his

       Thomas + Wackfields

          mark.

       Bonner.

                      Sudden Oast & Seal.

MARY BURGESS of Norfolk County in Virginia . . .

Book I f. 316—(Checked by Original).

Dated 17 Apr. 1751.

Proved May Court 1753, by Matt^w Godfrey & Robt Hodges.

. . . to my Son Amanuall Burgess a Horse . . . **five** leather Chairs . . . three Guns . . . also the Great Bible and Hole Duty of Man . . .

. . . to my Daughter Mary and my Daughter Lucy . . . two two Year Old Barrows Uses in the the Back Swamp . . .

. . . one Small Gilt Trunk . . .

. . . two turned Chairs 1 High 1 low . . .

. . . One Common Bible & Prayer Book . . .

. . . Eight Plantation Hogs . . .

. . . Set of Heaters . . .

. . . unto my Daughter Elizabeth Thorenton One Cow . . .

. . . my Grandson William Thorinton . . . at the Age of Sixteen . . .

. . . my Grandaughter Mary Thorintun . . .

. . . my Grandaughter Sarah Thorntun . . .

. . . all the rest of my Estate . . . Divided between my Son Amaniel Burgess my Daughter Mary Burgess & Lucy Burgess.

. . . my Son Amanuell Burgess to be my whole and Sole Executor & Adm^r . . .

witnesses: Matthew Godfrey.

        his

    Henry + Hart

       mark

    Robt Hodges.   her

                            Mary M Burgess & Seal.

                            mark.

KESSIA LANGLEY of the County of Norfolk . . .

Book I f. 317.

Dated 2 Jan. 1753.

Proved May Court 1753.

. . . to my two Youngest Brothers my two Negroes . . .
. . . the Remainder of my Estate to my Eldest Brother Excepting One Ring and a Pair of Studs which I give to my Brother Moses I Constitute and Appoint Mr Thomas Langley Executor . . .

Witnesses: Archib^d Campbell.
    Joel Simmons.

                                    +

                                 only

ANTHONY CURLING of the County of Norfolk . . .

Book I. f. 317.

Dated 16 June 1752.

Proved May Court 1753.

. . . to Frances my beloved Wife One Feather Bed . . . the Gang of Hogs . . . the Use of the House and Plantation I live upon | that Part my Son Anthony lives Upon Excepted | During her Natural life . . .
. . . unto my Son Joseph Curling One Negro . . .

. . . to my Son John the Plantation I bought of William Wallace Containing One Hundred & fifty Acres more or Less . . .
. . . to my Son Daniel One Negro . . .

. . . unto my Daughter Ede Smith . . . One Negro
. . .
. . . unto my Daughter Betty Ann Lockhart One Negro
. . . to my Daughter Martha Ten Pounds . . .
. . . unto my Son Anthony . . . after the Decease of
Frances my Wife . . . the House and Plantation I
now Live upon . . .
. . . My Son Anthony . . . my Sole Executor . . .

Witnesses:

James Holgis.
Rob. Tucker, Junr.
Robt Williams, Joiner.

The mark of
Anthony A Curling & Seal.

RICHARD INKSON of the Borough of Norfolk Tavern
Keeper . . .

Book I f. 323.

Dated 19 May 1753.

Proved June Court 1753.

. . . to my Loving Wife Dinah During her Natural life all
that Dwelling House Out Houses &c°. On One half of
that Lott of Land which I bought of Col° Anthony Walke
and at her Decease to my Son Richard Jackson . . .
. . . unto my Daughter Elizabeth Jackson the Other half
of the Said Lott of Land Adjoining to the said Dwelling
House not Built on . . .
. . . bequeath in Trust to my Exec^x all my Land with the
Buildings thereon on the Western Branch in Eliz^a River
to be Sold . . .
. . . Appoint my Loving Wife Dinah Inkson to be my whole
and Sole Executrix . . .

Witnesses: Josiah Smith.
Richd Frazier.
John Terry.
Patience Hamilton.

his
Rich^d J Inkson & Seal
mark.

ALEXANDER COLLICK now Resident in the Borough of Norfolk and Blessed be Almighty God for it . . .

Book I. f. 323.

Dated 15 May 1753.

Proved June Court 1753.

> . . . unto my Loving Wife Mary Collick the House and Lott that I now live on . . .
>
> . . . unto Eliz^a Portlock ye Daughter of Samuel Portlock One Lott of Land joining on Mr Samuel Boushes Line . . .
>
> . . . unto John Portlock the Son of Saml Portlock One Lott of Land joining to the Lott given to Elizabeth Portlock . . .
>
> . . . unto Thomas Williamson One pair of Silver Shoe Buckles.
>
> . . . unto Ann Williamson One Gold Ring.
>
> . . . unto Margaret Williamson One Pair of Gold Buttons . . .
>
> . . . Appoint . . . my Loving Wife Mary Collick to be whole and Sole Executor . . .

Witnesses:
              his
      Robt + Cupper.
            mark
            his
      Nicholas N *Weldon*
            mark.
      John Cheshire.
            her
      Alice O. Lewelling
            mark.

                        his
           Alexander A. O. Collick & Seal.
                mark.

WILLIAM ASHLEY SHIPWRIGHT now Resident in the County of Norfolk . . .

Book I. f. 324.

Dated 6 May 1753.

Proved June Court 1753.

. . . unto my Beloved Wife Lidia Ashley One Negro man Named Dick . . .

. . . unto my Beloved Daughter Frances One Negro Girl Named Pegg . . .

. . . unto my Beloved Daughter Mary One Negro Girl Named Nancy . . .

. . . unto my Beloved Daught^r Elizabeth One Negro boy Names Charles . . .

. . . unto my Beloved Daughter Nancy One Negro boy Named Quash . . .

. . . Ordain my beloved Friends Joshua Nicholson and Mr Matthew Godfrey Junr of Norfolk County to be my whole and Sole Executors . . .

Witnesses :   her

       Elizabeth + Miller.

          mark.

       Thomas Lovall.

       John Cheshire.

                Wm. Ashley & Seal.

EDMUND ASHLEY of the Borough and County of Norfolk . .

Book I f. 325.

Dated 16 March 1753.

Proved June Court 1753.

. . . to my Loving Wife Ruth my Negroes Horses and all Movables . . . during her natural Life and after her Decease to return to my Sisters Children, *if she* not *being with Child at this Present & if she is To pass to that,* Mary Dison and James Dison and to my Brother James Ashleys Son James my Estate to be one half to my Sister Daughter Mary Dison and the Other half to be Equally Divided between the two boys James Dison and James Ashley Son of my Brother James . . .

. . . Leave for Executors Phillip Dison and John Goyles
. . .

Witnesses: James Ashley.
          William Guy.
          Elizabeth Ashley.

                        Edmund Ashley & Seal.

"N. B. The Interlined is Just as it is in the Will as I did not understand it.

                        Sam¹ Boush C¹ C⁰"

(Interlined is in Italics).

LEWIS CONNER of Norfolk County in the Colony of Virginia . . .
Book I f. 326.
Dated 25 Oct. 1752.
Proved June Court 1753.

. . . I do hereby Impower my Executors or the Survivors or Survivor of them to Sell to the best advantage they Can all my Lands or Such Part as they shall think Proper in North Carolina . . . and to Convey the same to the Purchaser or Purchasers by Good and Sufficient Deeds in Law . . . and I do further Impower my said Executors or the Surviv⁰ or Survivor of them to sell my Land at Cape Henry & my Land at Matchapungo in Princess Ann County and my Land at or near the Cross Roads in Tanners Creek in Norfolk County & Convey the Same by Good and Lawfull Deeds to the Purchasers . . .

. . . My Will and I do hereby Impower my Exec⁰ the Surviv⁰ or Survivor of them as Soon as Conveniently Can be to purchase out of the Money Arising by the Sale of my Lands that they or the Surviv⁰ or Survivor of them Purchase a Tract of Land in the County or Princess Ann as Convenient as Possible of about the Value of two Hundred Pounds Cur¹ Money of Virginia and the Overplus of the Sale of my Said Lands to lay out in young Negroes which said Land and Negroes I Give the Use of to my Loving Wife during her natural Life or Widowhood which shall happen first to be Ended and after her Death or Marriage I Give the said Land (Ordered to be Purchased) to my Son Joseph Conner and his Heirs forever.

. . . unto my Son Joseph Conner All my Trooping furniture with my Small Gun . . .

. . . unto my Son Joseph Conner my Clock now lying in the Hands of Mr Jones in Norfolk Town . . .

. . . unto my four Sons Lewis, Charles, Samuel and Lawson Conner Each One Silver hilted Sword to be sent for by my Executors or the Surviv^rs or Survivor of them or my Loving Wife Margaret Conner.

. . . unto my Loving Daughter Mary Conner . . . One Cow . . .

. . . all the Rest of my Estate (not here Disposed off) both Real and Personal to my Loving Wife Margaret Conner During her natural Life or Widowhood which Shall first Happen and after . . . Save the Land Given to my Son Joseph . . . to be Equally Divided between my Six Children Mary Conner, Joseph Conner, Lewis Conner, Charles Conner, Samuel Conner & Lawson Conner Each an Equal Part . . .

. . . Appoint my Wel beloved Friends Col° William Craford Saml Boush the Elder Capt James Ivy and Mr John Swan Attorney at Law in North Carolina to be Executors . . .

Witnesses: James Thedaball.

James Thedaball.

Wm Langley.

George Collins.

Lewis Conner & Seal.

(Codicil):

As it hath Pleased Almighty God to take from us my Friend Capt. James Ivey I do hereby Appoint my Good Friends Mr Thos Wishart of Princess Ann County and Mr Samuel Boush Junr of Norf° Borough Exec^rs . . . Give them full power to Act . . . set again my hand & Seal this 11th day of November 1752.

Witnesses: William Ivy.

Edward Portlock.

Lewis Conner & Seal.

SAMUEL SWENY of the County of Norfolk Planter   .   .   .

Book I f. 327.

Dated 14 March 1753.

Proved June Court 1753.

.   .   .   unto my Welbeloved Wife Ann Sweny two Hundred
and fifty acres of Land Adjoining to Foulchers House
with the Houses of said Fulchers Included   .   .   .

.   .   .   unto my Son Charles Sweny all my Other Lands
.   .   .

.   .   .   unto Lem¹ Willoughby   .   .   .   Negroes   .   .   .

.   .   .   unto John Willoughby the other One half of my Stock
.   .   .

.   .   .   my Welbeloved Wife to be my Executrix   .   .

Witnesses: Thomas Willoughby.

   Ann Willoughby Sen'

   Wᵐ Person.

          Sam¹ Sweny & Seal.

THOMAS WILLOUGHBY of Norfolk County Gent   .   .   .

Book I f. 328.

Dated 5 Sept. 1752.

Proved June Court 1753.

.   .   .   to my Eldest Son John Willoughby Seven Negroes
.   .   .   and my Maner Plantation & all the Land belonging to it   .   .   .

.   .   .   to my Son Lem¹ Willoughby Eight Negroes   .   .   .

.   .   .   to my Son Thomas Willoughby Seven Negroes   .   .   .
also   .   .   .   One Lott of Land in Norfolk Town in Cumberland Street & One Bed   .   .   .

.   .   .   unto my Son Willᵐ Willoughby Six Negroes   .   .   .
also   .   .   .   my Plantation wᵗʰ The Land belonging to
it up the Head of Mason's Creek   .   .   .

.   .   .   to my Daughter Elizabeth Willoughby one Lott of Land
in Norfᵒ Town in Cumberland Street Joining to a Lott
that I Gave to my Son Thomas Willoughby he taking his
Choice   .   .   .

.   .   .   to my Welbeloved Wife Ann Willoughby   ,   .   .   One
Hundred Acres of Land lying in the North West Woods
that Abraham Beasley Now lives On to Sell, and Make Use
of the Money   .   .   .

. . . when my two Youngest Children Comes of Age . . .
. . . Appoint my Loving Wife Ann Willoughby & my Son
John Willoughby my Whole & Sole Exec^{rs} . . .

Witnesses: Wm Person.

his

John + Banks

mark.

her

Kassiah + Wakefield

mark.

Sudden Oast.

Aaron H*ues*.

Thomas Willoughby & Seal.

DUGALD McINTYRE . . .

Book I f. 329.

Dated 4 May 1753.

Proved June Court 1753.

. . . all my Estate of what kind soever unto my Loving
Brother Malcom McIntyre . . .
. . . Appoint my Good Friends Archibald Campbell and
George Logan Executors . . .

Witnesses: Duncan McC*a*ll.
Willm Gray.

Dugald McIntyr & Seal.

JAMES FEREBEE of the County of Norfolk . . .

Book I f. 329.

Dated 2 May 1753.

Proved June Court 1753.

. . . unto my Son John Ferebee the Plantation and Land he
now lives on Containing about ninety acres Beginning at a
Live Oak Corner tree Standing in Timothy Ives' Line so
Running up a Branch to a Sweet Gum then a South and
by West Course up the Swamp, be the same more or Less
during his Life and after his Decease . . . to my

Grandson John Ferebee and his Heirs & in Case he fails of an Heir the Said Plantation to be Invested in my Grandson Willis Ferebee . . .

. . . unto my Son James Ferebee One Tract or Parcell of Land lying in Deep Creek Containing fifty acres be the same More or Less Joining on Timothy Ives's Land and also the Mill Run Beginning at a Branch at the Old Mill Landing and Runing up the said Branch to the said Timothy Ives's Line, Giving to him the said James all my Land on the Westward side of the Mill Run . . .

. . . unto my Son Peter Ferebee One Tract or Parcel of Land Containing About Seventy five Acres be the Same More or Less Joining to my Son James's Land Begining at his Line and Running by a Line of Marked trees, through the Plantation and up the Swamp to a Marked Pine Then Runing a South and by West Course to the Head of my Land the Said Land Joining to my Son John's Land, and Timothy Ives's Land . . .

. . . unto my Son Thomas Ferebee the Remaining Part of my Land, being that part I now Live on being about Seventy five acres be the Same more or Less and is Bounded by the Mill Run On One side and by my Son Peter's Land on the Other side . . .

. . . unto my Daughter Mary Cherry One feather Bed . . .

. . . unto my Daughter Dinah Ferebee a Parcell of New Feathers which are now in the House . . .

. . . unto my Daughter Lydia One Feather Bed . . .

. . . unto my Grandson John Ballentine five shillings in full of his Portion . . .

. . . unto my Grand Daughter Frankey Ferebee One Heifer . . .

. . . Appoint my Sons John and James Ferebee Sole Executors . . .

Witnesses:

    his
John + Brown
    mark
    his
James + Brown
    mark
John Gibson.

                              James Ferebee & Seal.

JOHN MOREY now Resident in the County of Norfolk and blessed be Almighty God for it . . .

Book I f. 333.

Dated 12 May 1753.

Proved July Court 1753.

. . . to my Son James Morey my Land that I now Live on
. . .

. . . to my Son John Morey my House & Lands in Norfolk Borough.

. . . unto my Daughter Betty Morey One Cow . . . at the day of marriage . . .

. . . unto my Daughter Jane Morey One Cow . . . at the day of marriage . . .

. . . unto my Daughter Ann Morey One Cow . . . at the day of marriage . . .

. . . to my Child that is now Unborn One pair of Silver Shoe Buckles One pair of Silver Knee buckles One Stock buckle One pair of Silver Buttons One Desk.

. . . my Silver Watch & two Cotts, and my *Halter* Furnis and Tools, Fur One Gun and One Sword & Cartou*ch* box & One Cain be Sold . . .

. . . my Loving Wife Elizabeth Morey . . .

. . . Ordain my Wel beloved Friends Mr John Simmons & Mr Solomon Lambert Executors . . .

Witnesses:

his
John + Simmons
mark.
Solomon Lambert.
Isaac Talbutt.

John Morey & Seal.

LIST OF WILLS

1710 - 1753

Note—When the name of the testator, in the caption of the will, differs in spelling from the signature, the index follows the signature.

INDEX OF NAMES

Though it is proper that, in the text, the variations in spelling in the recorded wills should be followed, it is felt that in an index this is not necessary except when required for identification.

It should be borne in mind that though a name may appear several times on a page, only one reference is given in the index.

In the "Miscellaneous Index" all place-names are given except "Norfolk County" as this appears in practically every will.

Natha, 9; William, 210; Wilson, 155.

Nichless, Matthew, 285.

Nichalson, Abigall, 118; Alice, 118, 127, 219; Ann, 220, 221; Anne Butt, 118; Dinah Wilson, 119; Dinah, 220, 233; Elizabeth, 118; George, 118, 219, 220; John, 118, 220; Joshua, 118, 127, 220, 314; Lemuel, 118, 127, 219, 229; Malachi, 127, 219, 220; Mary Langley, 118; Prudence, 127; Sarah, 119; Thomas, 118, 127; William, 118, 127, 220, 248; William (Jr.), 118; Wilson, 220.

Nicholas, Nicholes, Henry, 31; John, 84.

Nicholls, Nichols, Alice, 257, 258; Elizabeth, 139, 257, 258; Henry, 138; Henry (Jr.), 139; John, 139, 240, 257, 258; Juderth, 94; Judith, 78; Mary, 257, 258; Mathew Spivey, 94; Nicholas, 139; Sarah, 257, 258; William, 257, 258.

Nimmo, James, 170, 219, 278; William, 143, 187, 186, 199, 271, 278, 295; William (Jr.), 142, 144, 264.

Noas, Anne, 203.

Norcutt, Norcott, Norkott, Alice, 303; Anne, 7; Elizabeth, 7; Henry, 178, 200, 303; James, 7; John, 7, 56; Katherine, 7; Mary, 7; Thomas, 7, 200; William, 7, 200.

Norris, Mr., 60.

Nosay, Mary, 186; Nathaniel, 137; Thomas, 229, 230.

Oast, Betty, 309; Elizabeth, 31; George, 309; Godwin, 68; Golwin (Jr.), 66; Mary, 309; Rachael, 309, 310; Sudden, 309, 318; William, 309.

O'Deon, William, 29, 30.

Odeon, Odean, Aan, 183; Elizabeth, 183; Mary, 183; Patience, 183; Patient, 10; William, 10, 183.

Oerngs, John, 97.

Oliver, Aron, 63.

Osheal, John, 299.

Outlaw, Edward, 20, 39; Edward (Jr.), 39; Elia, 39; Elizabeth, 39; Ralph, 20, 39; Sarah, 39.

Owens, Ann, 13; Edward, 12; Elizabeth, 13; John, 12, 120, 276, 283; Margaret, 276; Mary, 12,

13; Thomas, 12, 13, 120; Willa, 120; William, 12, 120; William (Jr.), 12.

Paderick, John, 287.

Paine, Samuel, 45.

Partree, Francis, 307; James, 307.

Pasteur, James, 250, 264.

Pead, Ann, 245.

Pearce, John, .109.

Peaton, Abigail, 209; Dinah, 202; James, 202; Lemuel, 202, 203; Samuel, 203; Sarah, 202; Timothy, 202; William, 202.

Penney, Pinne, Penny, Brian, 234; Bryan, 180; Edward, 180; Elizabeth, 180, 214; Thomas, 180.

Perkins, Christopher, 260, 263; Elizabeth, 99; John, 99; Sarah, 99; William, 99.

Perry, Jackson, 58; Joseph, 57, 58.

Person, William, 317, 318.

Petters, Jno., 13.

Phillips, Daniell, 90; John, 53, 55, 90, 91; Susannah, 91; William, 42.

Phripp, John, 106, 133, 136, 193, 194, 199, 209, 210, 237.

Pilkington, James, 259; John, 94, 159, 240; Mary, 159.

Piper, Samuel, 310.

Pitt, William, 179.

Plunkitt, Garratt, 184.

Poole, Pool, William, 225, 261, 275, 292.

Porter, Ann, 68; Amy, 68; Elizabeth, 68; Joshua, 83; John, 22; Margaret, 21; Mary, 68; Samuel, 51, 66, 68; Samuel (Jr.), 68; William, 68.

Porteen, Ann, 38; Crodick, 38; Daniel, 38; Elizabeth, 38.

Porter, John, 68, 158; Patience, 191; Wiliam, 60, 191, 302.

Portlock, Ann, 54; Anne, 150; Courtney, 285, 286; Charles, 43, 181; Edward, 43, 181, 287, 316; Elizabeth, 42, 43, 83, 146, 291, 313; John, 42, 55, 56, 83, 179, 180, 287, 313; John (Jr.), 42, 181; Lemuel, 43; Lidia, 43; Margaret, 287; Mary, 114, 146, 180; Matthew, 180, 286; Paul, 42, 53, 136, 181, 238, 291; Nathaniel, 181, 291; Peter, 43, 227; Phebe, 291; Rebecca, 291; Samuel, 313; Sarah, 180; Seth, 286, 304; Simon, 228, 286, 304; Thomas, 286;

MISCELLANEOUS INDEX